Guide to America's Outdoors

Northern Rockies

Guide to America's Outdoors
Northern Rockies

Jeremy Schmidt and Thomas Schmidt

NATIONAL
GEOGRAPHIC
WASHINGTON, D.C.

Contents

*Page 1: Pika, Absaroka Range, western Wyoming   Pages 2-3: Wind River Range, Wyoming
Opposite: Field of lupine, Bighorn National Forest, Wyoming*

Treading Lightly in the Wild

Gray wolf

NATIONAL GEOGRAPHIC GUIDE TO AMERICA'S OUTDOORS: NORTHERN ROCKIES takes you to some of the wildest and most beautiful natural areas in a region remarkable for its spired peaks and grassy plains, tundra meadows and geothermal bubblers, glacial lakes and racing rivers.

Visitors who care about this spectacular region know they must tread lightly on the land. Ecosystems can be damaged, even destroyed, by careless misuse. Many have already suffered from the impact of tourism. The marks are clear: litter-strewn acres, polluted waters, trampled vegetation, and disturbed wildlife. You can do your part to preserve these places for yourself, your children, and all other nature travelers. Before embarking on a backcountry visit or a camping adventure, learn some basic conservation do's and don'ts. Leave No Trace, a national educational program, recommends the following:

Plan ahead and prepare for your trip. If you know what to expect in terms of climate, conditions, and special hazards, you can pack for general needs, extreme weather, and emergencies. Do yourself and the land a favor by visiting if possible during off-peak months and limiting your group to no more than four to six people. To keep trash or litter to a minimum, repackage food into reusable containers or bags. And rather than using cairns, flags, or paint cues that mar the environment to mark your way, bring a map and compass.

Travel and camp on solid surfaces. In popular areas, stay within established trails and campsites. Be sure to choose the right path, whether you are hiking, biking, riding, skiing, or four-wheel-driving, and travel single-file in the middle of the trail, even when it's wet or muddy, to avoid trampling vegetation. When exploring off the trail in pristine, lightly traveled areas, have your group spread out to lessen impact. Good campsites are found, not made. Travel and camp on sand, gravel, or rock, or on dry grasses, pine needles, leaf litter, or snow. Remember to stay at least 200 feet from waterways. After you've broken camp, leave the site as you found it.

Pack out what you pack in—and that means *everything* except human waste, which should be deposited in a cathole dug away from water, camp, and trail, and then covered and concealed. When washing dishes, clothes, or yourself, use small amounts of biodegradable soap and scatter the water away from lakes and streams.

Be sure to leave all items—plants, rocks, artifacts—as you find them. Avoid potential disaster by neither introducing nor transporting non-native species. Also, don't build or carve out structures that will alter the environment. A don't-touch policy not only preserves resources for future generations; it also gives the next guy a crack at the discovery experience.

Keep fires to a minimum. It may be unthinkable to camp without a campfire, but depletion of firewood does harm the backcountry. When you can, try a gas-fueled camp stove and a candle lantern. If you choose to build a fire, first consider regulations, conditions, weather, skill, use, and firewood availability. Where possible, employ existing fire rings; elsewhere, use fire pans or mound fires. Keep your fire small, use only sticks from the ground, burn the fire down to ash, and don't leave the site until it's cold.

Respect wildlife. Watch animals from a distance (bring binoculars or a telephoto lens for close-ups), but never approach, feed, or follow them. Feeding weakens an animal's ability to fend for itself in the wild. If you can't keep your pets under control, leave them at home.

Finally, be mindful of other visitors. Yield to fellow travelers on the trail, and if you encounter pack stock, step quietly toward the downslope to let them pass. Above all, keep voices and noise levels low so that the sounds of nature can be heard.

With these points in mind, you have only to chart your course. Enjoy your explorations. Let natural places quiet your mind, refresh your spirit, and remain as you found them. Just remember, leave behind no trace.

MAP KEY and ABBREVIATIONS

National Battlefield	Interstate
National Historical Park .... N.H.P.	(90)
National Historic Site .... N.H.S.	
National Memorial Parkway	
National Monument .... NAT. MON.	U.S. Federal or State Highway
National Park .... N.P.	(20)(47)
National Recreation Area .... N.R.A.	
National Reserve	
	Other Road
National Forest .... N.F.	261
National Grassland	Canadian Provincial Highway
	14
National Conservation Area	
National Wildlife Refuge .... N.W.R.	Trail
Wild Horse Range	
Wildlife Area	
Wildlife Management Area	State or National Boundary
Wildlife Refuge	
State Archaeological Site .... S.A.S.	Continental Divide
State Historical Park .... S.H.P.	
State Park .... S.P.	
State Recreation Area .... S.R.A.	Boundaries
Indian Reservation .... I.R.	FOREST I.R. N.P. WILDERNESS
National Wild & Scenic River N.W.& S.R.	

ADDITIONAL ABBREVIATIONS

Cr.	Creek
Fk.	Fork
Ft.	Fort
HWY	Highway
Jct.	Junction
Mem.	Memorial
Mt.-s.	Mount-ain-s
NAT.	National
PKWY.	Parkway
Ra.	Range
Res.	Reservoir

□	Point of Interest	⤨	Pass
⊛	State capital	=	Falls
I	Dam	○	Geyser
+	Elevation	◬	Glacier
P	Parking		

POPULATION

• **Pocatello**	50,000 to under 500,000
• Sheridan	10,000 to under 50,000
• Jackson	below 10,000

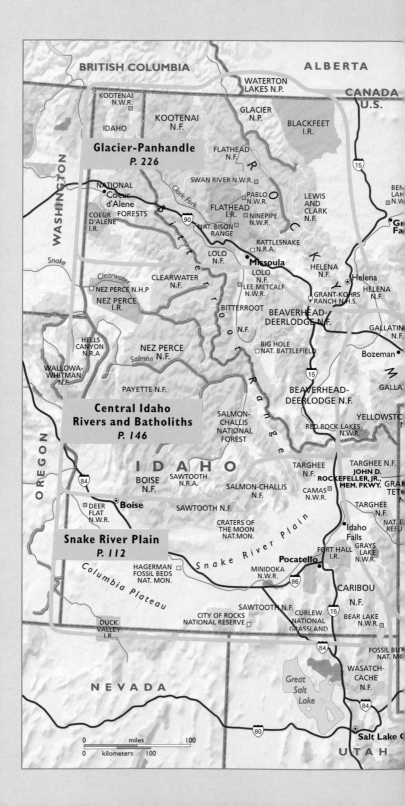

BRITISH COLUMBIA

ALBERTA

WATERTON
LAKES N.P.

CANADA
U.S.

KOOTENAI
N.W.R.

KOOTENAI
N.F.

GLACIER
N.P.

BLACKFEET
I.R.

IDAHO

15

FLATHEAD
N.F.

Glacier-Panhandle
P. 226

SWAN RIVER N.W.R.

BEN
LAK
N.W

Clark Fork

PABLO
N.W.R.

LEWIS
AND
CLARK
N.F.

Gr
Fa

NATIONAL
Coeur
d'Alene
FORESTS

COEUR
D'ALENE
I.R.

90

FLATHEAD
I.R.

NINEPIPE
N.W.R.

NAT. BISON
RANGE

WASHINGTON

Snake

Clearwater

RATTLESNAKE
N.R.A.

LOLO
N.F.

Missoula

HELENA
N.F.

Helena

HELENA
N.F.

CLEARWATER
N.F.

NEZ PERCE N.H.P

LOLO
N.F.

LEE METCALF
N.W.R.

GRANT-KOHRS
RANCH N.H.S.

NEZ PERCE
I.R.

BITTERROOT
N.F.

BEAVERHEAD-
DEERLODGE N.F.

HELLS
CANYON
N.R.A

NEZ PERCE
N.F.

Salmon

BIG HOLE
NAT. BATTLEFIELD

GALLATIN
N.F.

WALLOWA-
WHITMAN
N.F.

Bozeman

PAYETTE N.F.

15

**Central Idaho
Rivers and Batholiths**
P. 146

SALMON-
CHALLIS
NATIONAL
FOREST

BEAVERHEAD-
DEERLODGE N.F.

GALLA

YELLOWSTO

RED ROCK LAKES
N.W.R.

OREGON

I D A H O

BOISE
N.F.

SAWTOOTH
N.R.A.

SALMON-CHALLIS
N.F.

TARGHEE
N.F.

TARGHEE N.F.
JOHN D.
ROCKEFELLER, JR.,
MEM. PKWY.

GRAN
TET
N

84

DEER
FLAT
N.W.R.

Boise

SAWTOOTH N.F.

CAMAS
N.W.R.

TARGHEE
N.F.

NAT. E
REFU

CRATERS OF
THE MOON
NAT. MON.

Snake River Plain

Idaho
Falls

Snake River Plain
P. 112

HAGERMAN
FOSSIL BEDS
NAT. MON.

Columbia Plateau

FORT HALL
I.R.

GRAYS
LAKE
N.W.R.

Pocatello

MINIDOKA
N.W.R.

86

CARIBOU

N.F.

DUCK
VALLEY
I.R.

SAWTOOTH N.F.
CITY OF ROCKS
NATIONAL RESERVE

CURLEW
NATIONAL
GRASSLAND

15

BEAR LAKE
N.W.R.

84

FOSSIL BUT
NAT. MO

WASATCH-
CACHE
N.F.

NEVADA

Great
Salt
Lake

0   miles   100
0   kilometers   100

80

Salt Lake C

UTAH

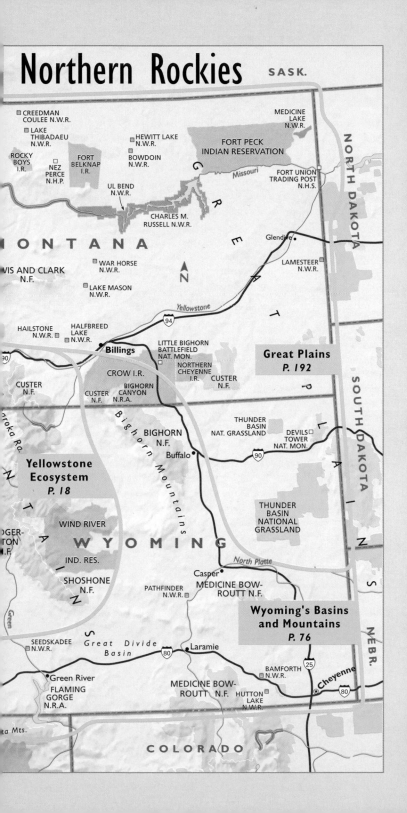

Northern Rockies

SASK.

□ CREEDMAN
COULEE N.W.R.

MEDICINE
LAKE
N.W.R.

□ LAKE
THIBADAEU
N.W.R.

□ HEWITT LAKE
N.W.R.

FORT PECK
INDIAN RESERVATION

ROCKY
BOYS
I.R.

□ NEZ
PERCE
N.H.P.

FORT
BELKNAP
I.R.

□ BOWDOIN
N.W.R.

G
R
E
A
T

Missouri

FORT UNION
TRADING POST
N.H.S.

UL BEND
N.W.R.

CHARLES M.
RUSSELL N.W.R.

Glendive

NORTH DAKOTA

M O N T A N A

□ WAR HORSE
N.W.R.

N

LAMESTEER
N.W.R.

WIS AND CLARK
N.F.

□ LAKE MASON
N.W.R.

Yellowstone

E

HAILSTONE
N.W.R.

HALFBREED
LAKE
N.W.R.

94

T

Billings

LITTLE BIGHORN
BATTLEFIELD
NAT. MON.

**Great Plains
P. 192**

90

CUSTER
N.F.

CROW I.R.

NORTHERN
CHEYENNE
I.R.

CUSTER
N.F.

CUSTER
N.F.

BIGHORN
CANYON
N.R.A.

oka Ra.

P
L
A

SOUTH DAKOTA

THUNDER
BASIN
NAT. GRASSLAND

BIGHORN
N.F.

DEVILS
TOWER
NAT. MON.

**Yellowstone
Ecosystem
P. 18**

Buffalo

90

N

Bighorn Mountains

THUNDER
BASIN
NATIONAL
GRASSLAND

WIND RIVER

W Y O M I N G

I
N

IND. RES.

OGER-
TON
N.F.

North Platte

SHOSHONE
N.F.

Casper

PATHFINDER
N.W.R.

MEDICINE BOW-
ROUTT N.F.

**Wyoming's Basins
and Mountains
P. 76**

N

SEEDSKADEE
N.W.R.

Great Divide
Basin

80

Laramie

N
E
B
R.

Green

Green River

FLAMING
GORGE
N.R.A.

MEDICINE BOW-
ROUTT N.F.

BAMFORTH
N.W.R.

25

Cheyenne

80

HUTTON
LAKE
N.W.R.

ta Mts.

C O L O R A D O

Call of the West

THE TWO OF US BROTHERS GREW UP IN THE MIDWEST and moved to the northern Rockies independently. Still, each of us made the move for many of the same reasons, almost all of them related to outdoor activities—skiing, climbing, backpacking, and river running in a region blessed with large wilderness areas and unsurpassed scenery. We were drawn to the West, and could not ignore its call. Neither could we ignore the challenge of its geography.

"So you're headed to the Sawtooths?" one of our neighbors might ask. "Ever gone by way of the Lemhi Valley? You know there's a back road along Trail Creek that drops you right into Ketchum." Listening, you know that the speaker is picturing the landscape along the way. From memory, he imagines driving up broad sage-covered valleys beneath towering snowy peaks and through cool pine forests. Simply talking about the route conjures up a full and pleasant range of mental images.

For many of us, being able to do that—to piece the country together mentally, to understand drainage patterns, to know what lies over the next ridge, and which plants and animals live there—is an essential part of feeling at home in a landscape. If we find gaps in our knowledge, we feel a strong urge to run out and see for ourselves how the land lies. Of course you learn a landscape only by walking, driving, flying, and paddling through it, which in the Rockies is never a chore.

Rambling through Idaho, Montana, and Wyoming is what this guidebook is all about. We hope that we have provided useful information on both the great and the small, from the grand panorama to the fragile wildflower. Although much of the geography is dramatic on the large scale, it's more personal on the small scale. Forbidding canyons shelter quiet pools filled with trout. Jagged mountains hold sweet wildflower meadows. The seemingly vast and empty prairie hides thriving and complex biotic communities.

This book is not intended to be an encyclopedic listing of every outdoor site in the region. Rather, it represents our selection of the best and most rewarding places we know. In some cases, we've provided very specific advice about where to go and how to get there; in other cases, it seemed more useful to point readers in a likely direction, understanding that one of the biggest pleasures of outdoor travel is the unexpected discovery, the hidden secret found along the way. One thing is sure. In the northern Rockies you can go far, but you can't go wrong.

Jeremy Schmidt and Tom Schmidt

The Chinese Wall, Montana's Bob Marshall Wilderness

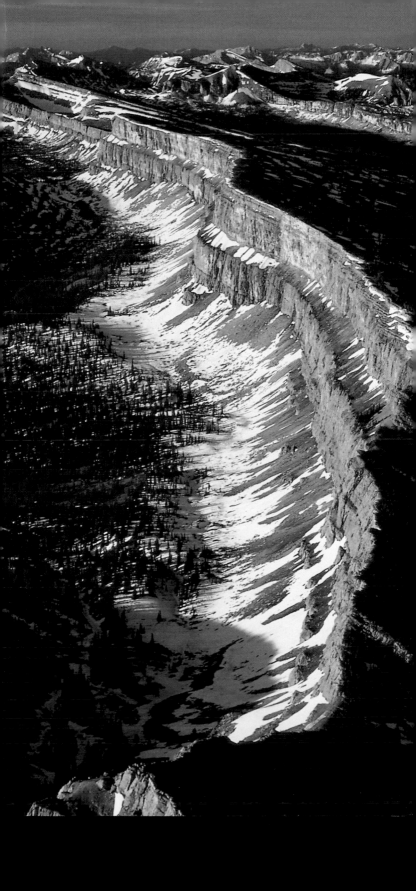

The Rockies Landscape

ACCORDING TO AN OLD STORY, the legendary mountain man Jim Bridger once boasted that he could be dropped blindfolded anywhere in the Rocky Mountains and within minutes of untying the scarf he'd know right where he was. He wouldn't need cultural landmarks. He could tell by the rocks, the shape of the land, the particular combination of plants and animals—in short, he could recognize the smell and feel of any place in the region.

It might not have been an idle boast. Bridger, among all his well-traveled peers, was famous for his knowledge of the territory, and by the time he retired to a farm in Missouri in 1855, he had explored vast sections of the northern Rockies. Whether he could really have done it or not, it's an appealing idea that a person could become that familiar with an area measuring some million square miles.

Of course, it would not be hard to tell the Great Plains of eastern Montana from the moist forests of western Montana; or the tangled

Steamboat Point, Bighorn National Forest, Wyoming

canyons of central Idaho from the massive sedimentary peaks of Glacier National Park. And once you've seen them both, you would never mistake the Missouri River for the Snake River. One flows east, the other west; one cuts through sedimentary badlands and limestone cliffs, while the other is rimmed by dark volcanic rocks.

But how would you distinguish the Upper Selway River from the Middle Fork Salmon? Both are in central Idaho. Both flow north, cold and clear, through deep forest in the bottoms of rugged canyons. Picking the actual river would be a puzzle for Jim Bridger or any knowledgeable person. Yet the interesting thing is, there'd be no doubt about it being central Idaho, and it wouldn't take a whole lot more experience to know that there are only a few north-flowing rivers of that size in the area. Some might say that narrowing things down to a few rivers would be shooting pretty close.

One of the great pleasures of traveling through country as varied and interesting as the northern Rockies is the chance to learn the

White-water rafting on the Flathead River's Middle Fork, Montana

landscape in the style of Jim Bridger—to understand what makes
one mountain range different from another, and in what ways they
are alike. In organizing this book, we've tried to pay attention to those
natural distinctions.

Accordingly, we've divided the three states covered by this guide into
six biogeographic regions defined not by political boundaries and survey
posts but by natural markers: moisture, rock type, microclimate, elevation, aspect, latitude, altitude, geologic history, and so forth. There's no
way to do this neatly. The region in question is far too diverse for easy
categorization. Yet broad themes do exist, as follows.

Central Idaho (Chapter 4) is mainly a story of granitic mountains and
the river canyons that separate them. Western Montana and northern
Idaho (Chapter 6), also mountainous, are generally wetter, their forests
more dense, the undergrowth greener. The Yellowstone Plateau (Chapter
1) is the volcanic heart of a large subalpine ecosystem surrounded by low
valleys. Southern and eastern Wyoming (Chapter 2) is a land of isolated
mountain ranges, broad expanses of desert and steppe terrain, and meandering river valleys.

Beyond the region's mountainous core, the high plains of eastern
Montana (Chapter 5) are filled with interesting sites: badlands, wooded
coulees, marshes, river breaks, and patches of native prairie. Southern
Idaho (Chapter 3) is a volcanic landscape marked by an arid climate,
sliced by the Snake River, adorned with geographic oddities including
lava plains, sand dunes, extravagant canyon springs, strange rock formations, narrow gullies, and scattered desert mountain ranges.

Mountains dominate the scene in all three states. The Continental
Divide runs down the approximate center of the region, with high crests

flanking it to the east and west. Almost all the mountains belong to the continent's greatest range, the Rocky Mountains. Only a few on the periphery do not. The Rockies are not a single unified range. They encompass many sub-ranges, all of them related somehow to the grand earth movements that built the Rockies, but also distinct enough in geology, profile, and habitat to warrant their own names. They include the Missions, the Beartooths, the Beaverheads, the Bitterroots, the Tobacco Roots, the Pintlers, the Tetons, the Bighorns, the Absarokas, the Winds, the Lemhis, the Sawtooths, and many more.

The Rockies are relatively young mountains, the result of an uplift that began some 100 million years ago with a collision between two plates of the earth's crust. In the simplest of terms, the North American plate, moving west, collided with the eastward moving floor of the Pacific Ocean. Something had to give; the denser oceanic plate slid under the continental plate, thickening the crust at that point, causing it to rise, buckling and folding the western part of North America.

A great deal of activity followed from that event. There were periods of additional uplift. Large bodies of molten granite rose to just below the surface, hardening to form massive batholiths. Huge volcanoes erupted. From great fissures, molten basalt inundated the land. Entire mountain ranges came loose and slid or were pushed tens of miles eastward. Erosional sediments piled up thousands of feet deep. Glaciers carved the heights. Enormous floods scoured valleys. Sections of the crust fractured along faults and into blocks that rose or sank or tilted, creating mountains on one hand and valleys on the other.

Mountain building hasn't ended. Wyoming's Teton Range is less than six million years old and still rising. Only 600,000 years ago, Yellowstone experienced a colossal volcanic eruption—the latest in a series that is probably not finished. Magma just below the surface superheats the groundwater, creating the region's famous geothermal features and reminding us that we live in a relatively—but temporarily—peaceful geologic time.

The Great Plains are a different matter. For several hundred million years, what is now eastern Montana lay beneath an inland sea that ebbed and flowed and finally retreated as the Rockies pushed skyward. As the Rockies began eroding, huge quantities of sediment were carried downhill by rivers and deposited in the shallow waters or along the retreating shoreline of a subtropical floodplain. Those eroded sediments now comprise the rugged badlands and rolling prairie hills the region is known for.

Over time, climactic conditions have changed, and have had their own effects on the landscape. Erosion accelerated during wet times. Deposition occurred during dry periods. Between 10 and 20 million years ago the northern Rockies experienced a tropical climate similar to today's Caribbean. In total contrast, the most recent ice age ended only about 10,000 years ago; it involved not only the continental ice sheet pushing down from Canada into northern Idaho and Montana, but also hundreds of separate alpine glaciers that built up over highlands like those in Yellowstone, Grand Teton, and Glacier National Parks.

Currently, the regional climate is temperate, with conditions tremendously variable depending on location. In general, winter conditions prevail from early November to late March. Spring is an unsettled time lasting well into June at higher elevations and latitudes. High in the mountains, summer is short and painfully sweet; it lasts a bare two months, from late June to late August. Autumn may arrive early, but in some years it's a beautiful time of clear warm days and frosty nights that gradually give way to the hard, gray cold of November. From an outdoor traveler's perspective, the season begins in April at lower elevations and southern locales and only gradually moves north and into the mountains as snow melts and the days lengthen. July 4 marks the traditional start of the high altitude alpine summer, and pleasant conditions continue into late October.

To understand the western climate and landscape, it's important to keep in mind the effects of topography. The northern Rockies topography is especially precipitous. Prevailing winds and their associated weather systems come generally from the west, which explains why the western slopes of the Rockies are wetter than eastern slopes. Also, the bulk of the year's moisture falls as snow during winter, and more abundantly at high elevations than low, which explains why valleys are often drier than nearby mountains. Additionally, shaded north-facing slopes stay moist and support forests while south-facing slopes, exposed to the full power of the high-altitude sun, dry out and remain treeless.

In essence, mountains create their own weather. Warm, moist air moving from the Pacific Ocean is forced to rise when it meets the Rockies. When it does, it expands and cools, forms clouds, and releases moisture as rain or snow on western slopes. But on the eastern (that is, downwind) side of a range, the air sinks and compresses, warms, and the clouds disappear; instead of dropping moisture, the air can actually become an evaporative force. The result is a rain shadow, a dry zone on the eastern, leeward side of a range. You can see this effect throughout the Rockies. On the east side of Yellowstone, for example, the Bighorn Basin is a dusty desert that receives, in places, only 6 inches of rain per year. Adjacent mountains receive upward of 30 to 40 inches.

On a larger scale, the Rockies as a whole throw a rain shadow across the high plains all the way to the central Dakotas, where the 100th Meridian of longitude marks the traditional boundary of unirrigated agriculture. West of the Meridian and east of the Cascades of Oregon and Washington, natural rainfall alone is generally insufficient to support crops. Fortunately for western farmers, the mountains store moisture well into the summer; the slow release of meltwater, coupled with artificial reservoirs and deep aquifers, makes agriculture possible in areas that would otherwise be too arid for anything but pastureland. For mountain travelers, the slow release of meltwater means that streams and rivers stay cool and alive through the dry days of midsummer.

The plains are not too dry for native vegetation, or for the wildlife it supports. When Lewis and Clark traveled across the Dakotas and eastern

Packing along the Continental Divide, Wyoming

Montana in 1805 and 1806, they saw astonishing numbers of elk, bison, and pronghorn on the plains. Wolves, coyotes, and grizzly bears were also common, and bighorn sheep lived in the cliffs along the Missouri River. Of these animals, only the coyotes and pronghorn roam the open lands today, but all of them survive, in some places abundantly, in the mountains. There's an old popular belief that elk did not live in the mountains back in the time of Lewis and Clark—that they were plains animals who were driven by hunting to seek shelter in the alpine forests. But anecdotal evidence from Native Americans and early explorers about the historic fossil record suggests that for thousands of years elk have been mountain animals comfortable even in dense forest. The elk of Yellowstone live on their ancestral homeland, as do the pronghorn, bison, and grizzlies.

That's not to say that the mountains and plains are pristine. On the contrary, many aspects of even the wildest areas in this region have suffered severe environmental impacts over the past century as a result of mining, logging, overgrazing, and development. Among the most serious is the loss and potential extermination of Pacific salmon over much of their historic range. In general, habitat loss connected with a booming human population of the region has accelerated despite strong conservation efforts. The need for careful, foresighted planning—and for coordination among the various public agencies and private owners who have responsibility for the land—has never been greater. On the other hand, there are some success stories. Peregrine falcons, bald eagles, gray wolves, bison, whooping cranes, trumpeter swans, and grizzlies have all benefited from efforts made on their behalf. They've also suffered from contrary efforts, and it would be rash to declare that any of them has a secure future.

Yet there they are, still surviving, often thriving in some of the finest parks and nature reserves on the continent. So far, so good. ∎

Yellowstone
Ecosystem

Great Fountain Geyser, Yellowstone National Park

THE YELLOWSTONE REGION is a clearly defined ecosystem centered on northwest Wyoming. You can pick it out on any large-scale topographic map or satellite photo: An alpine plateau rimmed by mountains and flanked on all sides by subsidiary ranges that stretch outward for many miles.

The world's first national park is just the starting point. All told, the region includes two national parks, seven national forests, more than ten wilderness areas,

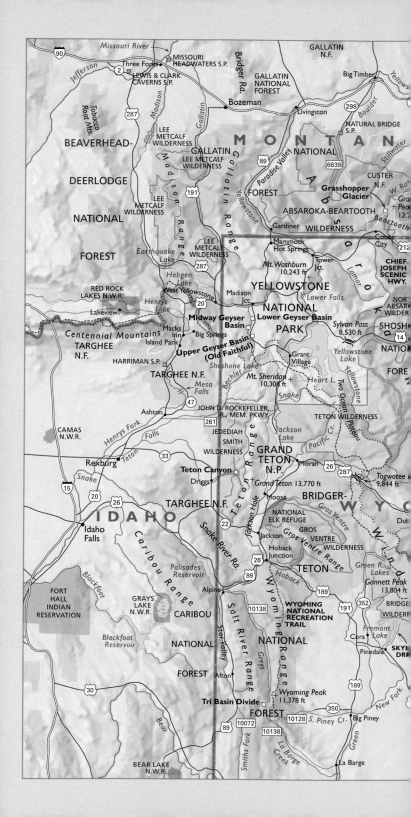

a dozen mountain ranges, and the highest points of both Wyoming and Montana (Gannett Peak reaches 13,804 feet in the Wind River Range; Granite Peak crowns the Beartooth Range at 12,799 feet). The Continental Divide wends its way from northwest to southeast through the region. From its heights spill the waters of important rivers including the Snake, the Green, the Yellowstone, the North Platte, and many others. This is true headwaters country. Only clouds lie upstream of Yellowstone.

The wildlife list is a virtual who's who of biotic charisma: Grizzly bears, black bears, gray wolves, coyotes, mountain lions, wolverines, bison, mule deer, white-tailed deer, elk, bighorn sheep, mountain goats, pronghorn, golden eagles, bald eagles, ospreys, peregrine falcons, trumpeter swans, whooping cranes, sandhill cranes, great gray owls, and so much more. Of these species, some have returned from the brink of extinction. Some are still threatened. Gray wolves were nearly exterminated by government hunters in the early part of the century. In 1995 they were reintroduced and have come back strongly. With their presence, the ecosystem once again includes every species known to have existed here when Yellowstone National Park was established in 1872.

The geologic story is complicated and fascinating, but one dominant force explains much of what we see here—volcanism. Beneath Yellowstone is an unusual upwelling of magma called the

Sunset at Shoshone Lake, Yellowstone National Park

Yellowstone hot spot, a plume-shaped body of hot molten rock that stretches outward from the earth's core to within several miles of the ground's surface. Pushing upward, it deforms the land and creates a network of cracks, or faults. Mountains rise and valleys fall around these faults; the Teton Range is a prime example and a good indication of how vigorous the activity is. Yet the most dramatic part of the story is harder to see. In the past 2.1 million years, Yellowstone has been rocked by three giant volcanic eruptions. They happened when the hot spot, having built up tremendous pressure, exploded through the surface with mind-boggling violence. In comparison, the eruption of Mount St. Helens in 1980 was trivial. Yellowstone's eruptions—the most recent of which occurred roughly 630,000 years ago—may have been thousands of times more powerful. They destroyed whole mountain ranges and sent debris around the globe. They didn't simply shape the landscape, they erased it and started over.

The Yellowstone area is not all a volcanic landscape. Faulting has pushed a number of hard old Precambrian blocks of so-called basement rock to the surface, where erosion has carved them into the region's most rugged and scenic mountains. These include the Wind River Range, which stretches toward central Wyoming; the Beartooths, on Yellowstone's northeast corner; the Tetons, which rank as the champion crags in all the northern Rockies; and the Bighorns, standing alone and proud on the other side of the Bighorn Basin. Two other mountain chains south of the Tetons deserve inclusion here—the little-known but lovely Salt River and Wyoming mountain ranges.

The region is dominated by mountains, but there's so much more to consider: The high basin of the upper Green River, where pronghorn and coyotes race through the sagebrush and golden eagles ride the

Teton peak known as The Grand

wind that seems to blow continually; the lower, drier Bighorn Basin, where oil pumps creak among the multicolored badlands; and the deep, red-and-white limestone gorge of Bighorn Canyon. To the west of Yellowstone, trout-filled Henrys Fork of the Snake River, fed by the abundant clear waters of Big Springs, winds through the placid meadows of Harriman State Park, a wildlife and fishing mecca. A few miles to the north, the Madison River flows from Yellowstone National Park to Earthquake Lake, a narrow body of water created in 1959 when a magnitude 7.5 earthquake initiated a landslide in the Madison River Canyon. From there, the river drops through some of the world's most beautiful ranch country on its way to Three Forks, where the Madison, the Gallatin, and the Jefferson Rivers come together to form the Missouri River. In an isolated valley along the Idaho-Montana border, the Red Rock Lakes National Wildlife Refuge is the scenic summer home of trumpeter swans, sandhill cranes, and many other creatures.

And still, there are other mountain ranges to consider. Within Yellowstone are the Red Mountains. Off the park's northwest corner are the Gallatin and Madison Ranges and the Centennial Mountains. The 50-million-year-old volcanic Absarokas rise near Livingston, Montana, march south to Yellowstone, wrap themselves around its eastern side, and continue southward to hook up with the little-known Owl Creek Mountains and with the Gros Ventre Range that forms the eastern wall of Jackson Hole. The Gros Ventres, in turn, carry the high country south and mix it up with the Wind River Range.

If this all sounds confusing, it's only natural. You can spend a lifetime trying to sort out the geography of this remarkably rich and diverse landscape. Many have tried; it's doubtful that anyone has ever fully succeeded. But everyone enjoys the process. ■

The Yellowstone River plunging over Lower Falls

Yellowstone National Park

■ 2.2 million acres ■ Northwest Wyoming ■ Season is year-round,
primarily summer, when the park is crowded. In summer campgrounds
fill early in the day; advance reservations are necessary for lodging. Spring
and fall are rewarding times to visit. Be prepared for cold in winter. Most
park roads are open early May–late Oct., sometimes longer depending on
weather. The northern road from Gardiner to Cooke City is open year-
round. In winter, snowcoaches and snowmobiles provide transport to interior,
particularly to Old Faithful, where the Snowlodge (307-344-7311) offers winter
lodging ■ Camping, hiking, boating, fishing, wildlife viewing, geothermal areas
■ Adm. fee and user fees; permits required for backcountry camping, boating,
and fishing ■ Bison, moose, and bears can be dangerous when encountered
at close range; pay attention to warnings issued by park rangers ■ Contact
the park, P.O. Box 168, Yellowstone National Park, WY 82190; phone
307-344-7381. www.nps.gov/yell

THERE IS NOWHERE like Yellowstone. The first national park in the
world and still the most famous, it calls to mind a wealth of images.
Geysers and hot springs, of course; wildlife, including recently reintroduced gray wolves and threatened grizzly bears, thousands of elk, bison
reminiscent of the great herds that once darkened the plains, superb
trout fishing; summer crowds and winter snowmobiles; mountains,
forests, and forest fires. The park is a continually renewing inspiration

for environmental philosophy and a perennial flashpoint for environmental controversy. Called Wonderland in the early years, it has filled untold numbers of photo albums, providing vacation memories for millions of families, and for generations within those families. For these reasons and more, Yellowstone is one of the world's most important natural areas.

Its importance increases with each passing year. Originally set aside for the geologic oddities that are still a prime draw, the park has come to represent deeper values than its founders could scarcely have predicted. When established in 1872, Yellowstone was little more than a distant curiosity far from the centers of population. The transcontinental railroad had been completed only three years earlier. Custer was still four years away from his disaster at the Little Bighorn. The great bison slaughter had not yet begun. For a country vigorously subduing its frontier, the setting aside of a large chunk of land was an unusual and perhaps visionary act.

Yellowstone divides roughly into three zones: west, east, and north. The **western zone** claims the most important geothermal areas, beginning with the Upper Geyser Basin, home of Old Faithful. There are also many other geysers and hot springs scattered along the Firehole River and extending northward for about 30 miles. Of course, hot springs and geysers are found throughout the park, as are mountains and lakes and wildlife.

The **eastern zone** includes the huge and glittering Yellowstone Lake backed up by the snowy summits of the Absaroka Range. The Yellowstone River, the other dominant feature on this side of the park, forms a wilderness wetland where it enters the lake's south end; after flowing out at the north end, it winds through the magnificent wildlife habitat of Hayden Valley before crashing over its two famous waterfalls into the Grand Canyon of the Yellowstone.

The **northern zone** is lower in elevation, drier, and more open. Its character is defined by the Lamar Valley, a broad open area beneath the Absaroka Range; and by the Yellowstone Valley below its junction with the Lamar. In contrast to the pine-covered interior of the park, the northern range has abundant sagebrush, aspens, cottonwoods, willows, and grasses. With less snow cover and good grazing, it provides important wintering ground for bison and elk.

There's a good bit of overlap in these three zones, but nonetheless they make for practical divisions from a visitor's perspective. The park road system forms a figure eight with branches extending to the five entrances—north, west, south, east, and northeast. The layout was developed in the early days of tourism, when visitors booked the Grand Tour, usually starting at Mammoth Hot Springs and taking a week or more to loop through the major locations: Mammoth, Old Faithful, Yellowstone Lake, and the Grand Canyon of the Yellowstone, with perhaps a few side excursions. That general pattern still prevails, with Old Faithful ranking as the paramount sight.

What to See and Do
Western Yellowstone: The Geyser Basins

As they described it, the pioneering members of the 1870 Hayden Expedition walked out of the woods just as **Old Faithful** erupted. It surprised them with a display of wilderness power and they responded with hat-tossing enthusiasm. Now, enshrined as a national icon, the geyser erupts in the close embrace of parking lots, hotels, curio shops, gas stations, and restaurants. In summer, mid-day eruptions attract thousands of visitors at a time. The development obscures the mystery somewhat, but a sense of wonder can still be had, particularly in early morning or at dusk when few visitors are about. If the air is cool, geyser mist builds more densely, shifting and swirling like curtains on a fantasy stage. Through the fog, elk and bison appear and disappear; coyotes howl and ravens croak.

Morning and evening are the best times to walk through the geyser basin to the other large geysers. About 3 miles of easy walking takes in the main features on both sides of the Firehole River. Check with the visitor center at Old Faithful for a trail map and estimated times of eruption; this will help you plan a route with the best chance of seeing geysers in action. Among predictable ones, **Castle** begins with a water phase, then shifts to thundering steam. **Daisy** is a frequent performer, with an interval of about 100 minutes. On occasion, it is joined by **Splendid Geyser** in a dual eruption. **River-side** shoots a graceful arc over the Firehole River. **Grand** is the park's tallest predictable geyser. Because it erupts in explosive bursts from a hot pool, it is called a fountain-type geyser, different from the concentrated jets of water shot out by cone-type geysers including Old Faithful. There are many other small geysers and hundreds of hot springs. **Morning Glory Pool** is famous for its pale blue water, but others are equally lovely and some are more colorful.

Five miles north of Old Faithful, **Midway Geyser Basin** offers two enormous thermal features. **Excelsior Geyser,** a lake-size pool of blue boiling water, throws off a thick cloud of steam that keeps it partly obscured. Having been inactive for about a century, it has erupted several times in recent years, producing huge fountainlike bursts. These events are rare and unpredictable. Directly beside it, the equally large but placid **Grand Prismatic Hot Spring** sports a bright bed of multicolored algae. The colors are related to water temperature, darker colors indicating cooler water.

A few miles downriver, the **Lower Geyser Basin** occupies a broad plain with sparse forest and many thermal areas. To see the basin, start with the Firehole Lake Drive. First stop is **Great Fountain Geyser,** whose large fountain-type eruptions occur about twice a day. Nearby **Pink Cone Geyser** sports an impressive cone but puts out only a weak spray. **Firehole Lake** covers several acres with water of varying temperature.

Bison basking in heated springs, Yellowstone National Park

Rejoin the main road at the **Fountain Paint Pot** area, named for its bubbling mud pots. Clay the consistency of thin pudding blurps and spits, forming miniature volcanoes and delighting observers—particularly children. There are also several geysers and hot springs nearby; **Clepsydra** erupts constantly. Several miles north a dead-end road called **Fountain Flat Drive** leads to pleasant picnic areas, lakes, and thermal areas. **Ojo Caliente Hot Spring** is worth a stop; as with other hot springs, you might see whitened bones on the bottom, the remains of unfortunate wild animals that fell in. There are numerous fishing access points along the river, and **Goose Lake** is a peaceful shady retreat. Near Midway Geyser Basin, the road passes the trail to lovely **Fairy Falls** and **Imperial Geyser.**

One other side road is worth exploring. Near Madison Junction, **Firehole Canyon Drive** climbs through a narrow gorge of rhyolite past **Firehole Cascades** and some deep river pools just above. Below the canyon, the Firehole River joins the Gibbon River to form the Madison, smooth and clear, a favorite haunt of elk, bison, and trumpeter swans and filled with big, hard-to-catch trout. The Madison flows 16 miles to the park boundary north of West Yellowstone on its way to Three Forks, where it joins the Gallatin and the Jefferson to form the great Missouri.

If you follow the Gibbon River up through its canyon, you'll pass **Gibbon Falls,** where ravens panhandle for treats. A short distance farther, the large open plain called **Gibbon Meadows** is a prime spot for seeing elk in early morning and evening. A half-mile hike through lodgepole forest leads to **Artist Paint Pots,** a collection of small hot springs known for their mineral-tinted waters. Another extensive clearing, **Elk Park** opens up a mile to the north and offers another good chance to see large animals.

Walking among elk near Yellowstone National Park

Norris Geyser Basin should not be overlooked. This is the hottest ground in the park and home of the world's tallest active geyser, **Steamboat,** whose prodigious but uncommon eruptions reach heights of more than 300 feet. Chances of seeing its display are slim, but numerous smaller geysers and boiling pools are in near constant activity. Start at the museum at Norris for a rundown on geyser geology, then head out on the **Back Basin Trail** past Steamboat and a number of smaller geysers and springs. The trail loops back to the museum.

On the road north to Mammoth, keep an eye out for elk and moose in the numerous meadows. Among noteworthy stops are **Roaring Mountain,** a big steaming patch of bare hillside—very impressive on a cold morning. **Obsidian Cliff** is a hill of a different color. Created by the rapid cooling of hot lava, it contains large chunks of black volcanic glass. Long before Europeans arrived on the scene, Native Americans came here to quarry this valuable material for stone tools.

Hikes to Geyser Hill and Observation Point

To see a diversity of thermal features up close, follow the circular walkway to the back side of Old

Gray Wolves

Intentionally pushed to near extinction by early park managers who did not understand the importance of predators to the environment's natural function, gray wolves have been successfully reintroduced to the park. Fourteen were released in 1995, another 17 in 1996. By late 1998, the population had grown to about 120 ranging throughout Yellowstone and the Tetons. The best chance to spot wolves is in winter and spring, with top spots being Lamar Valley in Yellowstone and the National Elk Refuge (see pp. 64-65).

Faithful Geyser, where an easy, 1-mile paved trail drops gently to the Firehole River, crosses it on a footbridge, and angles up to **Geyser Hill.** The hill is a white mound of sinter (silicon dioxide), deposited by thermal waters and now pierced by numerous hot springs and geysers. The board-walk loops past geysers such as **Giantess,** an infrequent but impressive erupter, and **Plume,** whose short small eruptions occur frequently. **Beehive,** named for its rounded cone, shoots a concen-trated blast more than 100 feet high two or three times a day. Nearby is the **Lion Complex;** of four clustered geysers only one, **Little Cub,** is consistently active. The hot springs are as various as the geysers. Note their different shapes, their delicate overhanging edges, and their colorful runoff channels. The colors are caused by heat-loving algae. Yellow marks the hotter water; as temperatures cool, algae colors darken.

Back near the Firehole River, a signpost marks the **Observation Point trail,** another excellent hike. It climbs about 250 feet through lodgepole-pine forest to a fine overview of the geyser basin.

Eastern Yellowstone: Lakes and Canyon

If you could fly over Yellowstone Lake and look south, you would see a vast rolling forest of lodge-pole pine broken somewhat by the great fires of 1988, which burned extensively in this part of the park. A few landmarks stand out from the trees. There are three medium-size lakes (Shoshone, Lewis, and Heart), a bald-topped plateau called the Pitchstone, several high ridges, and a network of narrow meadows stitched along the Snake, the upper Yellowstone, and the Bechler Rivers. Steam rises from a

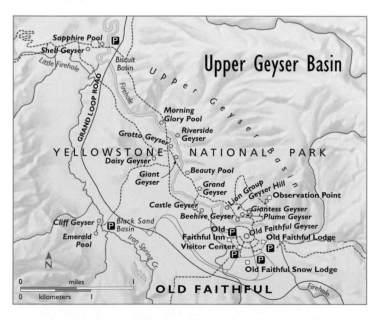

Life on the Algae Mats

A self-contained life system exists in the steamy warmth of hot spring outflow channels. Filamentous bacteria, growing in long, hairlike strands, join with mats of colored algae to provide food for brine flies. If you look close, you'll see little orange spots on some of the flies; these are parasitic mites. The flies are also preyed upon by fast-moving spiders and avian invaders such as killdeer. Even in winter, temperatures near the ground stay warm enough to support what is in effect a natural terrarium. Nearby, in steam-heated hollows, leafy plants stay green, sometimes blooming even in January. Look for yellow monkey flowers that hug the edges of hot streams.

number of points, notably the geyser basins at Shoshone and Heart Lakes, but also from dozens of smaller sources scattered through the forest. Not far to the south rise the steep crags of the Teton Range in Grand Teton NP.

The area is largely wilderness. To reach the park's extreme southwest corner, take little-used Cave Falls Road via Idaho 47 and Marysville Road. Otherwise, the only road access is through the south entrance. That route climbs onto the plateau past several worthwhile stops. The 1988 fires cleared the forest around **Lewis River Canyon,** affording great views to the east. **Lewis Falls** is

a family-pleaser (a short walk along the south side of the river takes you to an overlook). The river itself offers moderately good fishing, and **Lewis Lake** is a fine place for a canoe.

The best ideas along the south entrance road, however, are backcountry trips. They include canoeing from Lewis Lake to **Shoshone Lake,** which should be done as an overnight. The trail to **Heart Lake** is a classic, 7 miles each way; backpackers might wish to hike to the fire lookout on the summit of **Mount Sheridan.** Distance hikers can follow trails into the park's far corners: the **Thorofare region** in the east and the **Bechler region** in the west. For an excellent short day hike through the forest, suitable for a family, visit **Riddle Lake.**

Yellowstone Lake is the dominant feature on this side of the park. It occupies a part of the caldera created by the last great volcanic eruption 600,000 years ago and ranks as the biggest alpine lake in America: roughly 14 by 20 miles, with a depth of 339 feet and 110 miles of shoreline. For about half the year, its surface is frozen, and even in summer it remains cold—ideal habitat for native cutthroat trout. The Yellowstone River flows into the lake at **Southeast Arm,** one of several fingerlike inlets, and flows out beneath Fishing Bridge on the north shore. In addition to the Absarokas, which rise to the east, the Red Mountains stand a few miles south with their toes in Heart Lake.

From the west the south entrance road meets the lake at Grant Village, which offers a campground and other facilities including a visitor center. Nearby, the **West Thumb Geyser Basin** is perched on the shore of the lake. Some of its hot springs are actually in the lake. West Thumb is a large round bay created 150,000 years ago by a volcanic explosion. The road continues along the lakeshore past stony beaches and small wetlands, with many attractive stopping places for anglers and picnickers. To get away from traffic noise, take side roads to Sand Point or Gull Point. Near **Bridge Bay,** site of a campground and marina, a 1-mile road leads to a 150-foot-high natural bridge.

At **Fishing Bridge,** one road heads over the Absarokas toward Cody. Even if you're not headed that way, consider driving 9 miles to **Lake Butte Overlook** for a sweeping panoramic view. Along the way you'll pass **Pelican Creek,** where moose are common in summer, and **Indian Pond,** a crater formed by a steam explosion. A mile-long trail goes past the pond to Storm Point. Fishing Bridge itself was once crowded with anglers trying to catch native cutthroat trout. Fishing is prohibited now, and the bridge a place to see giant trout finning in the current.

Heading north from Fishing Bridge, the road parallels the Yellowstone River. Look for trout at **Le Hardy Rapids;** in early summer the trout head for spawning streams around the lake, and you can see them jumping like salmon. At **Mud Volcano,** boardwalks lead up the hillside past some delightfully nasty hot springs, their dark, muddy waters exploding and making deep thumping sounds. There's often a small herd of bison in this area, but

if you don't see them, there are more ahead, in the big open spaces of **Hayden Valley.** Hayden is a place for slow driving, frequent stops, and binoculars—this is one of Yellowstone's richest wildlife areas.

The Yellowstone River that meanders peacefully through Hayden Valley changes dramatically when it pours over two great waterfalls into the **Grand Canyon of the Yellowstone.** Allow plenty of time to walk the rims, and then get close to the Lower Falls. **Uncle Tom's Trail** on the south rim puts you near the thundering face of the 308-foot curtain of water; from the north rim the **Brink of the Falls Trail** descends to the head-spinning edge of the falls. Both trails are worth the moderate effort.

From Canyon Junction, Grand Loop Road heads north over **Mount Washburn** (see hike p. 36). It's a winding route up the side of the **Yellowstone Caldera,** offering good views to the east and south. From high points, you can see 37 miles south to Mount Sheridan, the other end of a range that once stretched that whole distance, but disappeared when the great volcano exploded.

Northern Yellowstone: Mountains and Valleys

The park's north entrance at Gardiner, Montana, is marked by a grand stone arch dedicated by Theodore Roosevelt in 1903. In the early years, most visitors began their tours here, transferring from steam train to horse-drawn stagecoach. You can still drive the old stage road (one-way only, from Mammoth north, downhill to Gardiner), but the modern road follows the **Gardner Canyon** for

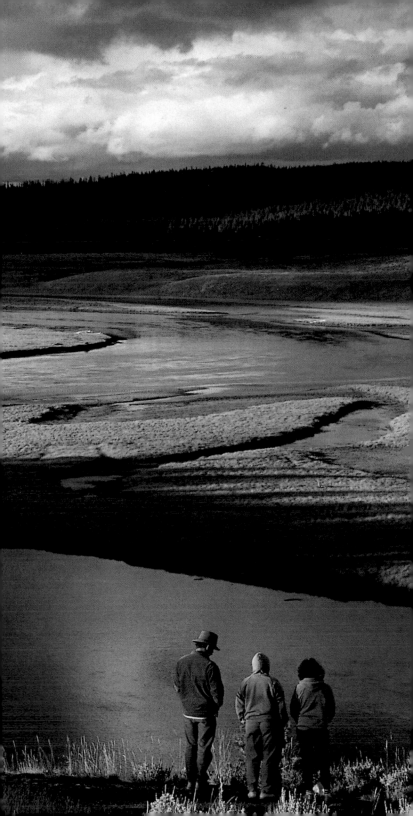

Preceding pages: Overlooking   Moonrise over Lamar Valley, Yellowstone National Park
Hayden Valley

5 miles to park headquarters at **Mammoth Hot Springs.** The wildlife show begins right away. There might be pronghorn grazing on the flats near the arch; look also for bighorn sheep on the cliffs of the canyon. Elk and mule deer on sage-covered hills calmly watch traffic pass.

Thousands of steaming gallons gush to the surface to form the brilliant white terraces that rise beyond the headquarters buildings. In fact, hot springs created the flat space around which cluster the hotel, shops, and administrative buildings. The U.S. Army put up the red-roofed structures during the time it ran the park, from 1886 to 1916.

Stop at the museum and visitor

center for a general orientation and a glimpse of the park's history. Then head straight for the terraces. Walk up from below, or drive around to the upper side, where a one-way loop drive winds through the ever changing landscape of hot-spring deposition. Either way, be sure to stroll the boardwalks past the big springs: **Jupiter, Minerva,** and **Canary.**

There are more hot springs across the park's north end, but in general this is a region of open valleys and high mountains. Lower in elevation than the rest of Yellowstone, it is warmer in winter. Grazing is good, making it a preferred place for bison and elk. The road from Mammoth to the northeast entrance, near Cooke City, is 47 miles of broad views. The first section winds through mixed meadows and forest above the Black Canyon of the Yellowstone River. Seasonal small wetlands are home to waterfowl including trumpeter swans. The **Blacktail Plateau Drive** is a worthwhile one-way side trip. Stop often to scan the hills; in spring you might see grizzly bears hunting elk calves in the distant meadows. Near the Lost Lake Trailhead at the road's end, a petrified tree stump stands inside a protective fence. The stump was buried and petrified by ash from the long sequence of volcanic eruptions that built the Absaroka Range. **Specimen Ridge,** south of Tower Junction and east of Lamar Valley, holds the remains of at least 27 forest layers, each representing a forest that grew up during a quiet period and was buried in the next round of eruptions.

At Tower Junction, the loop road heads south over Mount Washburn. Even if you're not going that way, it's worth the short side trip to see **Tower Fall,** a graceful chute set among pinnacles of volcanic ash. Stop also at **Calcite Springs Overlook** for a good look at the Yellowstone River where it cuts through some dramatic examples of columnar basalt.

East of Tower Junction, the road continues to the **Lamar Valley.** With the Absarokas on one side and Specimen Ridge on the other, it is a rich field of grass and sedge punctuated by stands of cottonwood and aspen. It was here where some of the country's last bison were ranched like cattle in the hopes of saving a remnant of the once great herds that roamed the plains. Once success was assured, the Buffalo Ranch ceased operating. It's now a ranger station and classrooms for the Yellowstone Institute, a public educational program.

Lamar Valley has become a good spot to see gray wolves (see sidebar p. 28). Nearly extinct by the 1930s, wolves, like the recovered bison, now range throughout the park—and outside the park, generating controversy over the management of both species.

Lamar Valley pinches out beneath the steep crags of the Absaroka Range. This is Yellowstone's most mountainous corner, a mix of towering summits and deep valleys. Beyond the park boundary, the landscape only becomes more spectacular. East lies the Beartooth Highway (see p. 42), the Clarks Fork Yellowstone River, and the Chief Joseph Scenic Highway (see p. 41), but surprisingly few visitors follow that route. If they only knew.

The trails climb through alpine meadows and conifer groves, with wildflowers abundant in July and early August. Bighorn sheep are often seen grazing or resting among the flowers. The view is fine from the beginning, and opens up at the summit to include distant landmarks: the Teton Range to the south, **Electric Peak** near the north entrance, the **Absarokas** on the eastern horizon, and even a few puffs of steam from the Old Faithful area. From this vantage point, the rim of the Grand Canyon of the Yellowstone appears as a dark gash in the pine-clad surface. If the air is cool, the two waterfalls send up columns of mist that rise well above the canyon rims. Other steam plumes rising through the forest mark small backcountry thermal areas which are themselves interesting hiking destinations. To the west, the low peaks of the Washburn Range show the scars of the North Fork Fire, the largest of the 1988 blazes. In this steep, rugged terrain the fire burned with particular intensity, sometimes rushing up the slopes drawn by chimney-effect winds, at other times pushed the other way by powerful downdrafts.

Mount Washburn marks the northern edge of the Yellowstone caldera. Notice the small isolated range—the Red Mountains—that stands about 40 miles to the south across Yellowstone Lake. Evidently, a line of mountains once connected Mount Washburn with the Red Mountains, but the great eruptions destroyed them—giving us an impressive measure of the size and power of the volcano. ■

Hike to Mount Washburn

The best single overview of Yellowstone awaits atop Mount Washburn, an old volcano created during the Absaroka eruptions. Two moderate trails, each about 3 miles long, reach the summit via abandoned roads. One starts at Dunraven Pass, north of Canyon Junction. The other starts at the end of Old Chittenden Road *(5 miles N of Dunraven Pass)*. It's feasible to walk up one trail and down the other; they require equivalent effort.

Yellowstone's Mammoth Hot Springs

Granite Peak, Gallatin National Forest

Absaroka and Beartooth Ranges

■ Southwest Montana and northwest Wyoming, north and east of Yellowstone NP ■ Beartooth Hwy. and Chief Joseph Scenic Hwy. closed in winter and during occasional summer storms. US 14/16/20 from Cody open year-round as far as Yellowstone's east entrance, where it is closed by snow in winter ■ Camping, hiking, fishing, wildlife viewing, auto tour ■ Bear-country precautions pertain while camping and hiking ■ Contact Wapiti Ranger District, Shoshone National Forest, 203A Yellowstone Ave., Cody, WY 82414; phone 307-527-6921. www.fs.fed.us/r2/shoshone

FROM ITS STARTING point near Livingston, Montana, the Absaroka Range marches south to Yellowstone, curves around its east side, and continues southward to Wyoming's Wind River Valley—a total distance of some 150 high and scenic miles. The word Absaroka means "crow" in the language of the Crow people, who have lived on the edge of these mountains for centuries. Locals pronounce it ab-SOR-kee, or ab-SAR-a-ka, but almost any variation is acceptable.

Stuck like a wedge into the Absarokas where they cross the Wyoming-Montana border is a smaller but strikingly beautiful range called the Beartooths. The two ranges merge so tightly that they seem one continuous chain. However, they are distinctly different in appearance and geology.

Absaroka Range

The Absarokas are volcanic in origin, made of ash and lava spewed out in periodic eruptions 40 million to 50 million years ago. During quiet times, vegetation recovered. Forests, including warm-weather species such as sycamore and magnolia, grew up only to be buried—and subsequently petrified—beneath the next eruption. The numbers are hard to grasp but worth citing: 6,000 cubic miles of volcanic material blanketed 3,000 square miles of present-day Wyoming, accumulating in some places to depths of 9,000 feet. Layer upon layer, the raw material of the Absarokas piled up to form a smooth-topped plateau 10,000 to 12,000 feet high.

At the south end of the range that old plateau surface is still present, and makes for fine high-altitude hiking. But for most of their winding length, the Absarokas have been deeply eroded, their rubbly volcanic rocks carved into sharp crests, steep slopes, and narrow valleys. In some places, the layering of repeated volcanic eruptions gives the mountains a stepped appearance. Water pouring down those ledges in hundreds of waterfalls supports hanging gardens of moss. In other places there is no sign of ledges; sharp ridges and outcrops rise above long slopes of crumbling debris.

Because volcanic material is porous, the Absarokas are well drained. Streams are numerous but lakes are not, which might explain why many backpackers go elsewhere—all the better for those who seek solitude. While Yellowstone bursts with summer tourists, the Absarokas are relatively peaceful. The peaks are grand enough to warrant anyone's attention. Streams offer good trout fishing. The forest breaks into meadows often enough to keep valley trails interesting. Wildlife is abundant, including elk, deer, moose, bighorn sheep, mountain goats, black bears, grizzly bears, and others.

The range spans a handful of administrative units. Yellowstone owns a big chunk of it. So do four neighboring national forests—**Custer, Shoshone, Bridger-Teton,** and **Gallatin.** Much of it is designated wilderness, including most of the Yellowstone section. In addition, the 704,822-acre **Washakie Wilderness** stretches to the park's southeast; the 350,488-acre **North Absaroka Wilderness** adjoins the park on its northeast corner; and immediately north of that lies the 943,626-acre **Absaroka-Beartooth Wilderness** *(contact Shoshone National Forest for information on wildernesses).*

Beartooth Range

Before the Absarokas erupted, the Beartooths pushed up as a solid block of Precambrian metamorphics—the ancient bedrock of the Rocky Mountains, some 3.2 billion years old. The block rose with a southward tilt. As a result, the southern aspect of the range is a relatively gentle slope, often nearly flat, strewn with lakes, and

Alpine Tundra

Alpine tundra is a world of miniature plants and hardy animals where winter is never far off. Survival means coping with ferocious conditions—high winds, severe temperatures, a short growing season, intense sunlight. Plants that in lower elevations grow tall are only inches high here. It's a place to explore gently on hands and knees, to see tiny flowers and dwarf shrubs, some of which are decades or even centuries old. Despite its toughness, tundra life is surprisingly fragile and slow to recover from damage. Thoughtless foot traffic can cause injury lasting many years.

Dark-throated shooting star

Beargrass

blanketed with tundra plants. In contrast, the northern side lurches above the rolling ranchlands of Montana in near vertical ramparts 6,000 to 7,000 feet high. Carved and polished by glaciers, the old granite forms soaring cliffs, rounded knobs, and deep canyons reminiscent of California's Yosemite Valley. Among the lofty summits is 12,799-foot **Granite Peak.**

Once covered by paleozoic sediments, the Beartooths were stripped of overburden in dramatic fashion. Most sediments were simply eroded away, but others moved en masse. As the mountain block rose it sent several giant slabs of limestone trundling southeast, sliding like books on an upended table. Near Cody you can see some of those sedimentary slabs where they came to rest on top of younger rocks. Heart Mountain, a regional landmark along Wyo. 120, was part of that movement and stands as a reminder that the earth is a dynamic place given to grand gestures. Perhaps grander than we know. The eruptions that built the Absaroka Range started just after the big slide. Did one trigger the other?

The whole story is dramatically evident along the Chief Joseph Scenic Highway (see p. 41), which follows the Clarks Fork River southeast of Cooke City. On one hand looms the smooth, bare slope of the Beartooths; on the other, displaced mountains of limestone jut out beneath higher volcanic summits. You see three classes of rock in a single view. Also prominent is the striking yellow mountain called **Beartooth Butte.** Near its summit a reddish band of Devonian siltstone contains fish fossils. A more recent example of zoologic preservation is found on **Grasshopper Glacier,** named for the millions of grasshoppers that were blown here some 300 years ago and remain frozen in the ice.

Trees in both the Absarokas and the Beartooths are typical of the region: Lodgepole pine, Englemann spruce, Douglas-fir, whitebark pine, and subalpine fir are dominant conifer species. Aspens favor moist hillsides, while cottonwoods crowd the river bottoms. Whortleberry, huckleberry, and shade-tolerant herbs make up the forest floor. Open meadows support grasses, sedges, shrubby willows, and a full array of wild-flowers, including beargrass, Indian paintbrush, and lupine. Sagebrush and occasional juniper trees indicate areas of drier soil.

Exploitable resources in the national forests are limited. Much of the land is at or above timberline, and only a small fraction of the forested zone supports commercial timber. With one notable exception (the area north of Cooke City in the Beartooths), the mountains are not a productive mining area. This translates to few roads and large expanses of pristine country.

What to See and Do

For such a large area, road access is good and every mile a stunner. US 26/287 passes the Absaroka Range at its south end, providing access to trailheads and recreation areas, notably the Brooks Lake area and Togwotee Pass. US 14/16/20 between Cody and Yellowstone NP parallels the North Fork Shoshone River, climbing from near desert on the edge of the Bighorn Basin to 8,559-foot Sylvan Pass. It's a famously beautiful drive through some of the Yellowstone ecosystem's best wildlife country. Two other highways, described below, magnificently showcase the region's rugged beauty.

Check on recent bear sightings at the **Grizzly Visitor Center** near the 1903-04 Wapiti Ranger Station. Buffalo Bill Cody built his hunting camp, Pahaska Tepee, at the head of the valley; it's now a resort and one of the many historic dude ranches along the North Fork *(307-527-7701).*

Chief Joseph Scenic Highway

Beginning a few miles north of Cody, the Chief Joseph Scenic Highway (Wyo. 120/296) is one of the world's great alpine drives. It is a less traveled route to Yellowstone's northeast entrance and to the old mining towns of Cooke City and Silver Gate. Toward the beginning, look for **Heart Mountain,** a chunk of paleozoic sediment that slid off the Beartooth Plateau. Then, on Wyo. 120, it climbs through steep grassy ranchland to a jaw-dropping view at **Dead Indian Pass.** At 8,060 feet in elevation, the pass affords a sweeping panorama of the Absarokas, the Beartooths, the Clarks Fork Valley, and beautiful **Sunlight Basin.** The road dives off the pass and crosses the black-rock chasm of **Sunlight Creek,** a good

Balsamroot

Rock climber

place to stop and gawk. To explore the Sunlight Basin, turn off on Forest Road 101 (just south of the highway bridge). Unpaved and rough in its upper reaches, the road pushes past ranches, campgrounds, and trailheads on its way to a historic mining district near the border of Yellowstone National Park.

Continuing northward, the Chief Joseph highway parallels the deep gorge of the Clarks Fork Yellowstone River, skirting its nearly inaccessible, rapids-filled canyon, heading toward the Beartooths. The river itself is hidden until you get near the junction with US 212, the end of the drive.

Beartooth Highway and Beyond

At the junction of US 212 and the Chief Joseph highway, a left turn leads to Yellowstone; to the right, the Beartooth Highway (US 212) begins its long spectacular ascent. This improbable, audacious route teeters across the high tundra. There are numerous campgrounds and stopping points along the way, which are popular jumping-off places for day hikes, backpacking, or climbing expeditions. The weather can be ferocious even in July, but generally summer is a fine time for rambling through a gentle terrain of glacier-polished rock and alpine lakes. (The road is closed in winter and during storms even in summer.) You don't have to go far to find rarified delights. Wildflowers crowd the roadway. Springbeauty, marsh marigold, and cinquefoil are the first to appear when the snow melts in June or July. Later in the summer, they are joined by pedicularis, aster, buttercups, and Indian paintbrush.

In the first mile of this spectacular road, the Absaroka panorama opens to the south. Next comes **Beartooth Lake,** shimmering at the base of Beartooth Butte; representing the same sediments found in Heart Mountain, the butte is a block that did not slide off.

A bit farther, trees give way to the rarified zone of alpine tundra, where lakes and open meadows stretch to the 10,947-foot-high pass. The last stage is a brake-stomping descent to Red Lodge, a vertical mile below.

In contrast to the high-altitude experience atop the Beartooths, a number of access roads penetrate from the north, ending deep in the shadows of towering glacially smoothed walls. The drainages of

West Rosebud, East Rosebud, and **Rock Creeks** are noteworthy, offering pleasant forested campgrounds and fishing in lakes and streams. The trails that start here climb all the way to the top of the plateau past waterfalls and chains of trout-filled lakes. The hiking is demanding, but the scenery is worth the effort. Any length hike is possible, from day trips to overnight loops and weeklong treks across the range.

North of Yellowstone, the Absarokas are cut by a central drainage, the **Boulder River Valley,** which essentially divides the mountains in two. Forest Road 6639, a cherry-stem road with wilderness on both sides, provides access to campgrounds, trailheads, and good trout fishing. At **Natural Bridge State Park** *(25 miles from Big Timber. 406-932-5131)*, footpaths lead to views of a 100-foot waterfall and natural bridge. ■

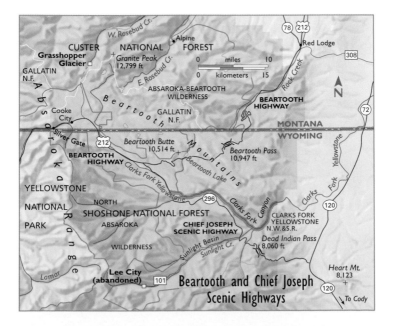

Island Park Area

■ Eastern Idaho, main access at Harriman State Park off US 20, near town of Island Park ■ Camping, hiking, boating, fishing, mountain biking, horseback riding, bird-watching, wildlife viewing ■ Adm. fee for Harriman State Park ■ Contact Harriman State Park, HC66 Box 500, Island Park, ID 83429; 208-558-7368

LOCATED ALONG THE western fringe of Yellowstone, the Island Park area encompasses a broad, nearly flat-floored volcanic crater cut from rim to rim by a handsome, trout-laden river called the **Henrys Fork.** It's a region of mostly gentle landscapes—restful, low-key, subtle yet seductive. Crystalline water bends across the wide sagebrush flats, passing shady copses of lodgepole pine. Marshy ponds nestle among the hollows and depressions, drawing moose, trumpeter swans, geese, and flotillas of young mergansers that dive in unison. Rolling hills and steep ridges, dark with evergreens, rise on all sides, and the distant but unmistakable crest of the Teton Range cuts across the southeastern skyline.

The volcanic crater, called the **Island Park Caldera,** was formed 1.3 million years ago during one of the periodic and massive detonations of the Island Park Volcano. The eruption hurled tens (perhaps hundreds) of cubic miles of finely shredded, viscous rhyolite lava across the land and released clouds of red-hot steam and ash into the atmosphere. Having emptied itself, the volcano collapsed, leaving a crater 20 miles in diameter. It's one of the largest and most symmetric calderas in the world, and its outline is clearly marked by the dark, semicircular ridgeline visible from Harriman State Park and from other open areas.

Through the caldera's heart flows the **Henrys Fork,** a tributary of the Snake. It begins as a small stream flowing out of **Henrys Lake** (to the north of the caldera) and surges to true river status after mingling with the abundant flow of bracing, glass-clear water from Big Springs, east of Macks Inn. It breaches the caldera's north rim near the town of Island Park, glides across the nearly flat calderic floor, then rushes through canyons as it breaks through masses of basalt along the caldera's south rim. Beyond, the river cuts through the rim of an older caldera, where it thunders over two major waterfalls, now included in the **Mesa Falls Scenic Area** *(208-558-7301. Closed Nov.-April to cars; open for cross-country skiing and snowmobiling).*

What to See and Do

Start 4 miles east of Macks Inn at **Big Springs,** a large, crystal clear pool tucked against a forested hillside. A prime spawning site for rainbow trout, the springs are among the 40 largest in the United States, putting out 120 million gallons of water a day. All that water flows as wide and as swift as a river over thick beds of monkey flower and watercress. An interpretive trail follows the glassy water downstream for at least a mile through open lodgepole-pine forests carpeted with lush grass and dotted with lupine, Indian paintbrush, and larkspur.

You can float over this luscious aquatic environment on the **Big Springs National Water Trail,** an easy, 4-mile trip that starts about a mile below the springs and takes out just above Macks Inn. Traffic is limited to hand-operated light craft; you can rent a canoe or arrange a shuttle in town.

At the caldera's center, **Harriman State Park** takes in some of the most enticing stretches of the Henrys Fork and offers a tremendous variety of habitat and wildlife. Hiking, biking, and horseback riding trails, which loop through forest, meadow, and sagebrush flat, climb to the caldera's western rim, and

hug the riverbank. At the end of the entrance road, an interpretive trail provides an overview of the region's geology and the park's major habitats: forest, marshes, wetlands, sagebrush flats, ponds, lakes, and riverbanks. Look for moose, elk, deer, pronghorn, beavers, muskrats, ospreys, bald eagles, and great blue herons.

A mile or so north of the Harriman entrance, pick up the **Mesa Falls Scenic Byway** (Idaho 47), a terrific 28-mile detour to Ashton that threads along the eastern slopes of the caldera and takes in Upper and Lower Mesa Falls—two of Idaho's few remaining undisturbed waterfalls. Separated by just a couple of miles and linked by a hiking trail, the two falls spill through a narrow gorge lined with colonnaded basalt walls. At **Upper Mesa Falls,** a network of walkways and viewing platforms zigzags down the cliffs to the very brink of the cascade, a wide curtain of concussive white water plunging 114 feet. **Lower Mesa Falls** is quite different, more of a funnel, with the full force of the river converging from three directions and dropping 70 feet through a narrow cleft. ■

Secrets to Successful Wildlife Observation

SEEING WILDLIFE in a natural setting is always a thrill, and the northern Rockies are loaded with good places for doing so. The best sites for large animals such as elk and bears are the national parks, where many species are more numerous than outside the parks; also, with few exceptions, they are not hunted in national parks and have grown accustomed to the presence of people. On the other hand, wildlife can be found throughout the region wherever conditions are favorable.

Canada geese

All three states covered in this guide have scattered wildlife-viewing areas, identified by special signs showing a binocular symbol.

Knowing wildlife habitat preferences is important to finding specific animals. Moose, for example, prefer marshy bottomlands dense with willow shrubs. Elk favor drier country of mixed meadow and forest.

The season also has an impact; animals migrate up and down mountain slopes or completely out of the area, depending on snow depth, food availability, and other factors. With experience, it's possible to predict where and when animals might be seen. Following are a few specific suggestions organized by species. All sites mentioned are described elsewhere in this guide.

Bald Eagles and Ospreys. Look along alpine rivers throughout the region, usually where there are sizeable nesting trees nearby.

Bighorn Sheep. In Glacier National Park, bighorns gather in autumn along the open slopes of mountains in the

Many Glacier area. In central Idaho, look for them in craggy areas at all elevations, including the banks of the Salmon River. In Yellowstone National Park the best spots are on Mount Washburn and in Gardner Canyon. Also on Wild Horse Island in Montana's Flathead Lake.

Bison. There are no free-ranging bison in the region; they are confined to specific reserves and private ranches. In Yellowstone National Park, they are found on the park's eastern side, especially Hayden Valley; as well as in the geyser basins and along the road from Tower Junction to Lamar Valley. Also at the National Bison Range north of Missoula and in Grand Teton National Park, usually east of the Snake River.

Black Bears. In Glacier NP, black bears are commonly seen during late summer in berry patches throughout the Many Glacier and Two Medicine areas, and along the Going-to-the-Sun Road. In Grand Teton National Park, they are sometimes seen along the Snake River between Jackson Lake and Pacific Creek. Tower Junction in Yellowstone is another likely spot.

Coyotes. Common, especially in open sagebrush-covered areas. Their high, yipping calls are easily distinguishable from the lower, throatier sound of wolves very often heard in Yellowstone during winter.

Elk. Watch for these large ungulates in Yellowstone National Park, at dawn and dusk, in almost any meadow on the park's west side between Old Faithful and Gardiner, Montana. Most commonly seen in the fall (during rut) and spring (calves are born in May and June). In Grand Teton National Park, they are found along the Teton Park Road between Moose Junction and Jenny Lake. The National Elk Refuge supports some 10,000 elk from October through April; sleigh rides take you into the herds. In central Idaho, elk are often seen in summer in forest openings and river bottoms; less often in fall during hunting season.

Gray Wolves. Always a rare sight, but glimpses are possible in Yellowstone National Park at Lamar Valley, northern Grand Teton National Park, and the adjacent National Elk Refuge. They are also occasionally seen in northwest Glacier National Park. Ask at visitor centers for recent sightings.

Grizzly Bears. In the spring, grizzlies are often spotted hunting elk in the northern sections of Yellowstone National Park and in Hayden Valley; other times of the year, they are more dispersed. In Glacier National Park grizzlies are most often sighted along the slopes above the Many Glacier area, on avalanche shoots, and occasionally

Bull elk

along the Going-to-the-Sun Road in the Logan Pass vicinity. Ask at visitor centers for recent sightings.

Moose. These big long-legged ungulates are fairly easy to spot throughout the northern Rockies. During summer they tend to hang out in marshy areas and tank up on aquatic vegetation rich in salt. In Grand Teton National Park, look for them at Oxbow Bend and among the vast willow flats near Jackson Lake Junction. In Yellowstone, check the meadows along Obsidian Creek north of Norris; the meadows of Lewis River south of Grant Village; and the mouth of Pelican Creek east of Fishing Bridge. In Glacier NP, look among the meadows off the Camas Creek Road west of Apgar.

Mountain Goats. In Glacier National Park, mountain goats are commonly seen on the rugged cliffs above the Going-to-the-Sun Road and along the Hidden Lake trail at Logan Pass; also in the Many Glacier and Two Medicine areas; and at Goat Lick on US 2 along the park's south boundary. In addition, look along Montana's Beartooth Highway, on the cliffs north of Beartooth Pass.

Mule Deer. Common in open areas and forest alike, usually alone or in small bands. They can be spotted in Glacier, Yellowstone, and Grand Teton National Parks; Sawtooth and Hells Canyon National Recreation Areas and the National Elk Refuge; along the banks of the Yellowstone, Missouri, Snake, and Salmon Rivers; and— especially at dusk and dawn—along many of the region's roadways. Deer make themselves scarce during fall hunting season.

Prairie Dogs. Once far more numerous than today, these intriguing rodents live in communities of burrows dug into the plains and prairies east of the Continental Divide. The region's finest prairie dog towns are found at Devils Tower National Monument in northeast Wyoming; at Greycliff Prairie Dog Town State Park east of Big Timber, Montana; and at Ulm Pishkun State Park near Great Falls, Montana. Wherever you find prairie dogs, you're likely to see their primary predators—hawks and coyotes, and perhaps a badger.

Trout. Trout are abundant at Fishing Bridge in Yellowstone National Park, as well as in Montana at Big Springs and in Idaho at Island Park. Also in The Rise, Sinks Canyon State Park, Wyoming. Visit the hatcheries along the Snake River in Idaho, especially at Niagara Springs State Park.

Trumpeter Swans. In winter and summer, these graceful birds congregate on Flat Creek north of Jackson, Wyoming, and on the rivers of Yellowstone National Park. Also at Red Rock Lakes National Wildlife Refuge and on Henrys Fork in the Island Park area west of Yellowstone.

White-tailed Deer. Less common than mule deer in the mountains, white-tails favor the marshland and shrubby country of eastern Montana's river breaks and wildlife refuges. Easily distinguished from mule deer by their smaller ears and bright white tails, which they lift like flags when fleeing from danger, you can look for them on the Charles M. Russell National Wildlife Refuge, and along the Upper Missouri Wild and Scenic River, and the banks of the Yellowstone River. ■

Howling gray wolves

Madison River Canyon Earthquake Area

■ 38,000 acres ■ Southwest Montana, west of Yellowstone NP on US 287
■ Camping, hiking, boating, fishing ■ Contact Hebgen Lake Ranger District,
Gallatin NF, P.O. Box 520, West Yellowstone, MT 59758; phone 406-646-7369

A VIVID REMINDER of Yellowstone's jittery seismic status, this deep, forested canyon still bears distinct scars from a 1959 earthquake that killed at least 28 people, stranded 250 more, and lifted the southern lobe of the Madison Range roughly 15 feet. The magnitude 7.5 quake triggered an immense landslide at the canyon's west end that peeled away the entire flank of a mountain and sent it crashing down into the bed of the Madison River. The rubble dammed the river and created **Earthquake Lake,** a small, serpentine body of water ringed with a band of dead trees that were killed as the lake level rose. Today, the trees offer prime roosting and nesting habitat for bald eagles and ospreys that feed on the lake's fish. Also during the quake, the northern bed of **Hebgen Lake** dropped 19 feet. Huge waves lurched back and forth across the lake and cracked the 1915 earthen dam. Homes were flooded and a section of the highway destroyed.

Drop by the visitor center at Hebgen Lake *(closed mid-Sept.–mid-May; adm. fee),* which stands atop the massive heap of slide debris overlooking Earthquake Lake. It faces the vast, semicircular scar left by the landslide on the mountain slopes across the road. An excellent film here tells the quake's story, clearly tying the event to volcanism throughout the Yellowstone region.

Next, pick up a tour brochure and head east through the canyon, stopping at various quake landmarks. As you drive, look for eagles and ospreys along Earthquake Lake, and for moose in the marshy bottomlands beneath the dam. At the **Cabin Creek Scarp Area,** walk along the steep, gravelly embankment that marks the fault line where the forest floor dropped and the mountain slope rose during the quake. Farther east, you can see a broken section of the old highway dip down into waters of Hebgen Lake. ■

Shaky Ground
Earthquake Lake and the Hebgen Lake are impressive indicators of Yellowstone's seismic instability. Major quakes periodically rock the region, the most recent being the 1983 Borah Peak Earthquake in Idaho, which measured magnitude 7.3. Lesser tremors too small to be felt occur frequently—sometimes many tiny shakes in a day. You can see the results on seismographs at several area visitor centers, including the one at Old Faithful. The activity is tied to the Yellowstone hot spot, whose movements and pressure have built dramatic landscapes for miles around.

Exploring at Lewis and Clark Caverns

Lewis and Clark Caverns State Park

■ 3,304 acres ■ Southwest Montana, 20 miles east of Whitehall off Mont. 2
■ Cave tours mid-May–mid-Sept. ■ Adm. fees ■ Contact the park, Box 949,
Three Forks, MT 59752; phone 406-287-3541

COOL, DAMP, ALIEN, this fascinating series of roomy chambers and
crooked passageways lies within the crest of **Cave Mountain,** high
above the Jefferson River west of Three Forks. Overgrown by slick dripstone formations and home to a colony of western big-eared bats, the
cave system meanders for roughly 2 miles and descends approximately
500 feet. Stalagmites, stalactites, and other globular masses of dripstone
crowd the caverns, and long, translucent ruffles of flowstone drape
the walls.

The park lies within the more spacious, eastern end of the **Jefferson
River Canyon,** where gentle grass hills rise to steep knobby mountains
peppered with juniper and streaked with bands of evergreen. Deer
often feed among the foothills at dusk, and red-tailed hawks and
golden eagles wheel among the pinnacles and cliffs.

Cave tours *(adm. fee)* begin at the historic stone-and-timber
visitor center, which stands at the end of a winding 3-mile road.
The trip lasts about two hours and leads through some three-quarters
of a mile of winding passageways. A short, downward slide on your
backside is necessary at one point, along with much bobbing and
weaving. But there is no crawling or squirming through the muck.
Interpretation is excellent, covering the formation of the caverns and
their beautiful structures as well as their history. ■

Missouri Headwaters State Park

■ 560 acres ■ Southwest Montana, off I-90 near Three Forks via Cty. Rd. 286
■ Camping, hiking, boating, biking, horseback riding, bird-watching, wildlife
viewing ■ Adm. fee ■ Contact the park, 1400 S. 19th St., Bozeman, MT
59718; phone 406-994-4042

WITHIN THIS SMALL state park, three muscular rivers join to form the
Missouri amid a seductive landscape of lush bottomlands, low cliffs,
semiarid grasslands, and shady cottonwood groves. From the west comes
the **Jefferson;** from the south the **Madison,** and from the east the
Gallatin. Each of them swift, clear, and inviting, the rivers bend lazily
across the open floor of the Gallatin Valley and converge on this point in
full view of the mountain ranges they drain: the Tobacco Root Mountains to the southwest, the Madison Range to the south, the Bridger
Range to the east, and the Gallatin Range to the southeast.

   Though small, the park's varied landscape offers good chances for
seeing a wide variety of wildlife. White-tailed deer browse in the meadows, moose wade in the bottomlands, hawks hunt for Richardson's
ground squirrels in the rocky uplands, and golden eagles nest among the
high cliffs overlooking the park from the north. Great blue herons and
double-crested cormorants nest along the Gallatin, and you're also likely
to hear the hoarse chuckle of sandhill cranes.

   Start your visit with a short stroll along the **Headwaters Trail**
(begins from the first Headwater Viewpoint, beyond the campground),
which leads across a grassy flat to the confluence of the Jefferson and
Madison—the official start of the Missouri.

Next, hike the 1-mile trail that
circles the rim of **Fort Rock,** a
promontory of elevated limestone topped with sagebrush,
prickly pear, and wildflowers. Its
southern end offers the park's
finest vista of the converging
river courses and surrounding
mountains. Its northern end
overlooks the verdant mouth of
the Gallatin and a narrow gap in
the hills where the Missouri slips
from sight on its journey to St.
Louis. Here, too, is a small exhibit
on Lewis and Clark, who rested
here for two days in late July
1805. While on Fort Rock, look
for yellow pincushion cactus and
western harvester ants; Lewis
noted the presence of both. ■

Red fox

Centennial Mountains

Red Rock Lakes NWR

■ 44,963 acres ■ Southwest Montana, northwest of Macks Inn ■ Access road usually passable June-Oct. ■ Camping, canoeing, bird-watching ■ Contact U.S. Fish and Wildlife Service, Monida Star Route, P.O. Box 15, Lima, MT 59739; phone 406-276-3536

REMOTE BUT REWARDING, this sprawling refuge for trumpeter swans and other birds stretches across a broad, open valley at the foot of the Centennial Mountains. Speckled with shallow lakes and crystal-clear ponds, carpeted with lush grasses and prairie wildflowers, the land was set aside in 1935 to help boost the trumpeter population, which had dwindled nearly to extinction. Thanks in large part to this refuge, the magnificent birds are making a comeback. The swans use the refuge mainly as a place to nest and raise their young, though some remain throughout the winter. Typically, some three dozen trumpeter families share the refuge from spring through autumn. Cygnets hatch in mid-June and learn to fly in October—just in time to follow their elders to wintering areas along the juncture of Montana, Idaho, and Wyoming.

You're free to wander by foot over much of the refuge, and you can see a fair number of birds by simply driving the roads. But the best way to explore the refuge's heart is to launch a canoe and putter around in the lakes and marshes. Besides swans, you'll see sandhill cranes, geese, ducks, great blue herons, avocets, long-billed curlews, and perhaps a moose or two.

To reach the refuge, go 5 miles north of Macks Inn on US 20 to a well-marked dirt road; take this west for 30 miles. ■

Cathedral Group, Grand Teton NP

Grand Teton National Park

■ 310,000 acres ■ Northwest Wyoming, on US 191 ■ Best months June-Oct.
■ Camping, hiking, rock climbing, boating, fishing, bird-watching, wildlife viewing
■ Adm. and user fees; permit required for boating ■ Bear-country precautions
pertain while camping and hiking ■ Contact the park, P.O. Drawer 170, Moose,
WY 83012; phone 307-739-3300. www.nps.gov/grte/

HEAVED AGAINST THE SKY as an unforgettable wall of pinnacles, crags, and
great hulking domes of gray rock, the central peaks of the Teton Range jut
6,000 to 7,000 feet above the flat sagebrush floor of the Jackson Hole valley.
They form the scenic heart of Grand Teton National Park, a wonderfully
diverse park that also takes in much of the valley floor, a fine stretch of the
Snake River, and a string of large lakes that hug the very base of the range.

Spacious canyons separate the peaks and lead far back into the wilderness beyond the park's borders. Icy streams pulse from the high country,
cutting across vibrant wildflower meadows, pooling in small alpine
lakes, plunging over the cliffs as waterfalls, and eventually flowing into
the Snake River. Major plant communities range from moist ribbons of
streamside foliage to semiarid sagebrush flats, and from mountain forests
to the nearly treeless realm of the alpine zone.

It's a stunning landscape, full of surprises and rich in wildlife. Grizzlies and black bears roam the length of the Tetons, as do herds of elk
and deer. Pronghorn race across sagebrush flats, occasionally flashing

past clusters of bison. Moose saunter among willows, river otters chase fish in the Snake, mountain lions track deer, and wolves haul down elk wintering in the valley.

Still, one's gaze keeps returning to the mountains, and especially to the glorious mass of fractured naked rock that stretches between the daunting fang of the 13,772-foot Grand Teton and the sawed-off summit of 12,605-foot Mount Moran. Largely composed of Precambrian gneiss, schist, and granite almost half as old as the earth, the Tetons are a very young mountain range, perhaps just five million years old.

They rose along a fault zone skirting the base of the range. As the mountains emerged, the valley floor tilted westward and sank. Movement came in fits and starts to the accompaniment of earthquakes large and small that, over millions of years, separated the two bodies of rocks to the amazing distance of roughly 30,000 vertical feet. The reason we see a mere 7,000 feet of relief is that erosion has carried off the thick, overlying mantle of sedimentary rocks that once capped the central peaks of the Tetons. Also, as the valley floor dropped, all manner of geologic debris piled in on top of it—rocks, sand, silt, boulders, gravel, and volcanic ash.

During the ice ages, glaciers formed along the crest of the range, gnawing out splendid little cirques and joining together to carve such great U-shaped canyons between the peaks as Death, Cascade, and Granite. Today, about a dozen small glaciers nibble away at the peaks, but they are not remnants of ice age glaciers.

What to See and Do

Visiting Grand Teton is almost always a pleasure, and its manifold joys range from the strenuous to the recumbent. On the more vigorous side of the ledger, you'll find mountain climbing, extended backpacking trips, and challenging all-day hikes that climb to the crest of the

Dogsledding in the Tetons

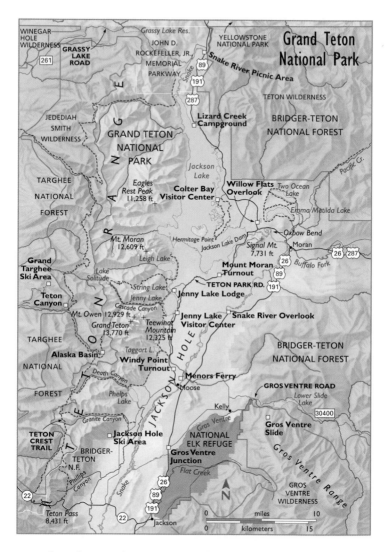

range through one major canyon and loop back through another.

But if that class of exertion isn't your idea of a good vacation, Grand Teton offers plenty of more sedate pursuits. You can get a good overview of the place from your car, as long as you get out now and then for a short stroll. The fishing is interesting, varied, and often excellent. And boating, whether on the river or one of the valley lakes, wafts you gently through a landscape that can make your heart sing for months.

The best place to kick off your visit is at the top of **Signal Mountain,** which rises from the east shore of Jackson Lake as an unpretentious hump of forested rock and offers a staggering vista of the Tetons, Jackson Lake, and the entire length and breadth of the Jackson Hole Valley. No mountain in the park is easier to ascend: A steady foot on the gas does it *(turnoff 4 miles S of Jackson Lake Jct.).* The summit is a good place to get your bearings and to appreciate the park's geology—the steep mountains rising without foothills, the valley floor tilted slightly to the west, the Snake River winding through glacial debris.

Next, head for the **Colter Bay Visitor Center,** with its excellent museum of Native American arts and crafts. Behind the building, you'll find the start of the easy, 1.5-mile **Colter Bay Nature Trail,** which circles a small peninsula in Jackson Lake and offers terrific views of Mount Moran and Eagles Rest Peak.

Heading south you might pull over at the **Willow Flats Overlook,** one of the most dependable sites in the park for spotting moose. If you strike out there, try **Christian Pond,** just to the north. Both of these sites lie within a short drive of **Oxbow Bend** *(about a mile E of Jackson Lake Jct.),* a cut-off meander of the Snake River frequented by moose, swans, ospreys, and bald eagles. When the water is calm, it reflects a classic view of the Tetons dominated by Mount Moran.

Take the **Teton Park Road** south past Signal Mountain and around the south shore of Jackson Lake to the **Mount Moran turnout.** This massive peak retains at its summit a thin layer of the sandstone that once covered the entire range before erosion stripped away the overlying rocks. A corresponding layer of sandstone lies 24,000 feet beneath the surface of the valley—carried down as the valley sank.

Aspen and maples in autumn   *Following pages:* Snake River Overlook at dawn

Farther south, the **Jenny Lake Loop Road** jogs west from North Jenny Lake Junction, winding through sagebrush meadows and pockets of forest to String Lake and Jenny Lake. Pause at the **Cathedral Group turnout** to admire the close-up view of **Mount Owen, Teewinot,** and the Grand Teton's north face. From here they look like a single mountain, with the north slope plunging dramatically into Cascade Canyon.

String Lake nestles against the flanks of **Mount St. John** and **Rockchuck Peak,** and warms enough by late summer for swimming. It's also the jump-off point for an easy, 2.2-mile trail that leads to a stunning beach on **Leigh Lake,** where the views of Mount Moran are unsurpassed. Paddlers reach Leigh Lake from a short portage at String Lake's north end.

Impounded by a terminal moraine, **Jenny Lake** lies at the mouth of Cascade Canyon beneath the awesome ramparts of The Grand, Mount Owen, Teewinot, and Mount St. John. Excursion boats shuttle between a boat dock along the southeast shore and the mouth of Cascade Canyon, accessing moderate trails (see p. 62) before climbing to the high country. Another trail loops around the shoreline, connecting to the north with String and Leigh Lakes. Perhaps the busiest spot in the park, Jenny Lake can get awfully crowded at the height of the summer.

South of Jenny Lake you can take a breather at the **Teton Glacier turnout,** which offers another fine view of **Grand Teton** with a long scar on its lower flank created by an ice age glacier. Today, the gulch harbors Teton Glacier.

If you're up for a relatively short hike, park at the **Taggart Lake Trailhead** and saunter 1.6 miles up through burned-over morainal hills to this lovely, deepwater lake at the mouth of Avalanche Canyon. **Bradley Lake** lies another half mile to the north, just over the hill from Taggart, at the mouth of Garnet Canyon.

Farther south, the **Windy Point turnout** offers a good view east across the valley to the **Gros Ventre Slide,** a prominent reddish scar on the side of Sleeping Indian Mountain. The 1925 slide impounded the Gros Ventre River with a dam 225 feet high and created a lake. Two years later the dam gave way, unleashing a flood that destroyed the town of Kelly and killed six people. (You can reach the site of the dam by following the park road that runs northeast from Gros Ventre Junction.)

Near Moose, take the spur road down to **Menor's Ferry Historic Site,** where an old cable ferryboat and a small cluster of buildings perch along the banks of the Snake and recollect the valley's settlement era. It's also a peaceful spot to watch the river's quick, clean current wash over its bed of cobbles. Exhibits at the **Moose Visitor Center** offer a primer on the park's geology, plants, and animals. This is also a place to pick up permits for boating and for backcountry camping.

From Moose Junction, US 191 heads northeast over the sagebrush flats, offering some nice vistas of the Tetons with the Snake River meandering along in the foreground (**Snake River Overlook** frames the classic Ansel Adams shot).

Hidden Falls, Grand Teton National Park

Field of arrowleaf and balsamroot in the Teton Range

More Activities

Hiking

Grand Teton is a terrific place for hikers of all abilities. Easy trails hug the base of the Tetons all the way from the mouth of Death Canyon to the north shore of Leigh Lake, winding through forests, traipsing past sagebrush meadows, skirting the lakeshores. Other easy trails explore the shores of **Jackson Lake** (the 9-mile loop around **Hermitage Point** is recommended), as well as Emma Matilda and Two Ocean Lakes. More difficult routes follow the major canyons into the high country, passing beneath waterfalls, rushing streams, breathtaking cliffs, and spires. The canyon routes (including Death, Garnet, Cascade, and Paintbrush) are rewarding even if you hike just a couple of miles into them. Finally, the **Teton Crest Trail** ambles along the spine of the range from the southern boundary of the park to Lake Solitude, far above and to the west of Jenny Lake.

Hike to Hidden Falls and Inspiration Point

This 2-mile classic outing starts with a boat ride *(fare)* across Jenny Lake, then climbs into the mouth of Cascade Canyon to a lovely waterfall and an overlook of the lake and the Jackson Hole Valley. Quite popular for good reason, the trip condenses into a leisurely 3-hour jaunt the essential elements of the Tetons—the morainal lake, cliffs soaring from the western shoreline, glaciers hanging among the peaks, cascading streams, a refreshing waterfall, deep forest, open meadows, wildlife, and a prominent viewpoint overlooking the valley.

Arrive at the Jenny Lake boat dock early to avoid the crowds. As you putter across the lake, the Cathedral Group of peaks (Teewinot, Mount Owen, and The Grand) rise to the left, Mount St. John to the right. It's a half mile through a forest of pine, spruce, and fir to **Hidden Falls,** where Cascade Creek tumbles for 200 feet down a ramp of boulders and rock ledges.

Just below the falls, the trail branches to the north and switchbacks for a steep half mile to **Inspiration Point,** a knob of bare rock with a great view of Jenny Lake and the terminal moraine that forms its eastern shore. The mountains across the valley are the Gros Ventres. From Inspiration Point, the trail climbs gradually into the mountains along one of the park's gentlest canyon ascents. It's a wonderful place to ramble— a wide open canyon floor carpeted with wildflower meadows and sheer rock walls rising more than 3,500 feet on either side. Go up the canyon as far as you like before turning around; the views keep getting better. Consider walking back to the ranger station along the south shore; the easy trail is nearly 3 miles long.

Boating

The park's large lakes and the Snake River are open to boating, with some restrictions. The Snake and all of the lakes except for Jackson, Jenny, and Phelps are closed to motors. All the lakes are gorgeous, but if you have time for just one head for **Leigh Lake** (via the portage at String Lake's north end).

But the park's greatest boating joy is a trip on the Snake. Several spur roads lead down to it from US 191, making possible a variety of partial-day or full-day float trips all the way from Jackson Lake Dam to Moose. Though this is known as the scenic stretch of the Snake (as opposed to the white-water section that roars through the canyon south of Hoback Junction), it is easy to underestimate. Alert paddlers should have no problem, but snags and other flood debris tend to pile up at the bends, creating tricky currents for unwary boaters. Cautious maneuvering is required. Paddlers should not take this river casually—especially when traveling between the Pacific Creek landing and Moose.

Still, floating the Snake is an incomparable experience. Without much effort it carries you far from the bustle of the roads, opens up tremendous mountain vistas, and presents abundant opportunities for seeing moose, otters, herons, swans, elk, deer, and the occasional bison.

Interpretive Programs

In summer and early fall, park rangers lead a variety of highly recommended walks and hikes, talks, demonstrations, and campfire chats. These programs enrich one's understanding of the region's geology, plants, animals, and history. A schedule is printed in the park publication "Teewinot." Those hungry for more instruction should check out the Teton Science School (307-733-4765), based in Kelly, which offers day- and multi-day seminars on natural history. ∎

Elk on the refuge

National Elk Refuge

■ 24,700 acres ■ Northwest Wyoming; visitor center 1 mile north of Jackson Town Square on Cache St. ■ Best months to see elk Nov.-April ■ Wildlife viewing ■ Contact the refuge, P.O. Box 510, Jackson, WY 83001; phone 307-733-9212

LARGELY DESERTED DURING summer but crowded with thousands of squealing elk every winter, the National Elk Refuge occupies a spacious

Elk Talk

Of all the ungulates that inhabit the Rockies, elk are the most vocal. During the autumn rut, males emit especially long, squealing calls that rise in pitch before falling away in a series of hoarse grunts. Year-round, cows and calves communicate through a variety of mews, squeals, and grunts that carry long distances through forest or across mountain basins. The sounds can be heard during a winter sleigh tour of the herds on the National Elk Refuge.

platter of grass that extends north from the town of Jackson to the boundary of Grand Teton National Park. The refuge, established in 1912, replaces crucial winter range denied to elk by ranching operations and the town of Jackson and its satellite communities.

Triggered by heavy snows, the annual migration of elk begins in late October or early November. Herds from Yellowstone and Grand Teton National Parks, as well as Bridger-Teton National Forest, filter down to the refuge for several weeks, eventually filling it with 7,000 to 10,000 elk. The animals forage for themselves for as long as possible, but elk in such numbers can not be sustained even on nearly 25,000 acres of prime grazing land. So, the refuge also feeds them alfalfa, like domestic livestock. In April, the herds begin moving back to their summer ranges.

November to April, elk are visible in large numbers from US 191 north of Jackson. In midwinter, you can get a much closer look from horse-drawn sleighs, which glide slowly into the midst of the animals. Besides elk, you may see trumpeter swans and other waterfowl on the open water of Flat Creek, just north of town. ■

John D. Rockefeller, Jr. Memorial Parkway

■ 8 miles long ■ Northwest Wyoming, US 89 between Jackson Lake and Yellowstone National Park ■ Contact Grand Teton National Park, P.O. Drawer 170, Moose, WY 83012; phone 307-739-3300

SET ASIDE AS a scenic corridor in honor of John D. Rockefeller, Jr.'s contribution to the expansion of Grand Teton National Park, this small tract of gently rolling lodgepole-pine forest lies between the northern end of Jackson Lake and the southern border of Yellowstone National Park. Though US 89 carries a steady stream of traffic between the parks, the lands beyond the road are left largely to the elk, moose, deer, and bears that live there.

When Grand Teton National Park was established in 1929, it included just the mountains and the morainal lakes at their base. During the 1930s, Rockefeller recognized the importance of preserving the area and bought up large amounts of private land in the valley. He donated it to the government in 1943, when President Roosevelt declared the valley floor a national monument. In 1950, Congress joined the monument to the park, creating a single national park comprising 485 square miles.

Traveling north from Grand Teton, the parkway leads through a lodgepole-pine forest that was burned during the great Yellowstone fires of 1988 and is now clearly on the mend. Soon, the road crosses the Snake River and plunges back into lodgepoles unaffected by the fires. Notice the difference in the understory of the forests—the relatively open floor of the mature forest versus the lush tangle of shrubs, wildflowers, and lodgepole saplings of the regenerating forest.

At the river crossing, you'll find the **Snake River Picnic Area,** a pleasant spot to relax or to launch a canoe for the 10-mile paddle down the Snake to Lizard Creek Campground on Jackson Lake. Totally unaffected by dams, the stretch above Jackson Lake is arguably the last truly wild section of the mighty Snake River.

Beyond the picnic area, a turnoff for Flagg Ranch leads to **Grassy Lake Road,** a 45-mile stretch of gravel that leads west into Idaho and makes for a pleasant day trip. It follows the Snake River for a few miles and then bounds through rolling lodgepole-pine forests that open occasionally around large meadows—look for elk, moose, and deer. ■

Jedediah Smith Wilderness

■ 123,451 acres ■ Northwest Wyoming and eastern Idaho, west of Grand Teton National Park ■ Camping, hiking, wildlife viewing ■ Bear-country precautions pertain while hiking and camping ■ Contact Targhee National Forest, P.O. Box 777, Driggs, ID 83422; phone 208-354-2312

PICKING UP WHERE Grand Teton National Park leaves off, this narrow corridor of wilderness runs along the western slopes of the Teton Range for roughly 50 miles. Though its trails lead to spectacular vistas of the jagged summits that have made the Tetons famous, the Jedediah tends to embrace a different, perhaps more soothing, type of landscape.

Unlike the abrupt east face of the range, the west slope slants down at a relatively gentle angle, ending in a rumpled margin of foothills. The peaks are rounder, even fulsome, and a deep, overlying layer of limestone forms vast open shelves and bands of high cliffs that wrap around spacious, glacially carved basins. Compared with the east side, there is little exposed rock and much more vegetation. Thanks in part to a wetter, warmer climate, dense evergreen forests cover most of the land, with brush, grass, and aspen groves along the lower slopes and great rambling meadows above tree line.

Walking distances into the high country of the Jedediah are short because the wilderness corridor is just 5 miles wide and lies right along the crest of the Tetons. Still, the area has nearly 300 miles of interconnecting trails, making it possible to traverse the range in a north-south direction. Unless you hike in from Grand Teton National Park, all access is from the west slope, often from the head end of spectacular canyons.

For a taste of the Jedediah, head for **Teton Canyon** (*from Jackson, go W on Wyo./Idaho 22 and north on Idaho 33; following signs for Grand Targhee, proceed 5 miles N of Driggs to a right turn on FR 009*), and park at the Alaska Basin Trailhead, which starts where the road ends. The 11-mile hike to **Alaska Basin,** which lies right behind the Grand Teton, is an overnighter, but the initial 3 to 4 miles of the trail makes an easy day trip, with excellent vistas of the three central Tetons.

A more strenuous day hike follows the Alaska Basin trail for 2.5 miles then climbs the **Devil's Stairs,** which rise 1,150 feet in less than a mile. ■

Beware: Bear Country

Bear sightings are on the increase throughout the Yellowstone region. Hikers should avoid walking alone, and they should make noise as they hike so they do not surprise bears. This is especially important when walking upwind or approaching blind curves or the tops of hills. Campers need to be wary of food odors and should never leave food unattended around a campsite. It should be packed away in a hard-sided vehicle or hung from trees or stored in bear-proof containers. A can of pepper spray may come in handy, but should never substitute for taking proper precautions.

Two Ocean Plateau, Teton Wilderness

Teton Wilderness

- 585,468 acres ∎ Northwest Wyoming, southeast of Yellowstone NP
- Camping, hiking, wildlife viewing ∎ Best months mid-June–mid-Oct.
- Bear-country precautions pertain while hiking and camping ∎ Contact
Bridger-Teton National Forest, Moran, WY 83013; phone 307-543-2386

THE TETON WILDERNESS protects the forests and mountains wrapped around Yellowstone's southeast corner. The Absaroka crest forms its eastern boundary (shared with the adjacent Washakie Wilderness), while a length of the Continental Divide cuts across its middle and Grand Teton National Park abuts it to the west. Its high country gives rise to both the Yellowstone and Snake Rivers, but there's really no dominant drainage. Small streams and novice rivers run every which way. In the wilderness's western part, the mountains are a jumble of ridges and plateaus and isolated high points. The eastern section, up against the Absaroka crest, is more rugged with narrow, steep-sided valleys and large areas above timberline. As in Yellowstone, a forest of mainly lodgepole pine blankets the wilderness, but it's broken up by frequent meadows and treeless ridges providing superb wildlife habitat.

The Continental Divide winds out of Yellowstone across country whose crest is so poorly defined that in one marshy area called **Two Ocean Plateau,** water comes together only to divide again, heading either to the west or east. When water is plentiful, it's possible that trout might swim up one side and down the other—surely one of the rarest phenomena in the Rockies.

If the wilderness has a heart, it must be the great wetlands of the Yellowstone River that run north into the park to Yellowstone Lake. That broad, mountain-rimmed marshland, called the **Thorofare,** is reputed to be the most remote spot in the lower 48 states. The isolation appears to suit the many elk and grizzlies that summer in the valley and adjacent alpine meadows.

Because the distances are long and valleys are broad, the preferred way to see this wilderness is from the saddle. Backpackers need lots of time to go any distance, and should know that main trails can be horse highways while the side routes shown on maps sometimes do not exist. Also, the fires of 1988 burned large areas of the wilderness, and deadfall in the burns can make for tough going.

That's not to say don't go. There are magnificent opportunities here, but they demand some creativity and plenty of skill. Three popular access points include: Pacific Creek from Grand Teton National Park, Turpin Meadows in the Buffalo Valley, and Brooks Lake near Togwotee Pass. The last of these provides the easiest chance for getting a high northward view across the wilderness. It would be a memorable bushwhack and trail-finding experience to follow the Absaroka crest to Yellowstone, then down to Yellowstone Lake and along its shore to the road. ■

Gros Ventre Wilderness

■ 287,080 acres ■ Northern Wyoming, northeast of Jackson ■ Camping, hiking, boating, fishing, bird-watching, wildlife viewing ■ Closed mid-Oct.–mid-June ■ In recent years, chances for bear encounters have increased; take all camping and hiking precautions ■ Contact Jackson Ranger District, Bridger-Teton National Forest, P.O. Box 1689, Jackson, WY 83001; phone 307-739-5400

PEOPLE HARDLY NOTICE the Gros Ventre Range because it rises opposite the Tetons and looks relatively tame. That's an illusion. The Gros Ventres (grow VAHNTS) may lack gravity-defying spires, but their 287,080-acre wilderness area is rich in pleasing, wildlife-rich high country well suited for rambling. Most of the summits are 10,000 feet and higher, with **Doubletop Peak** at 11,682 being the high point. You can get an easy sample by driving **Gros Ventre Road** (Forest Road 30400). It starts 1 mile north of the town of Kelly and soon passes the impressive scar of the **Gros Ventre Slide.** In 1925 the side of the mountain collapsed, damming the Gros Ventre River and creating Upper and Lower Slide Lakes. The road continues some distance past trailheads and campgrounds through some of the sweetest summer landscape in Wyoming.

Another popular access is Granite Creek, off US 189/191 about 15 miles east of Hoback Junction. Forest Road 30500 leads 10 miles up the scenic valley of Granite Creek to a campground near the excellent Granite Creek Hot Spring. From the hot springs, hike to Bunker Creek on the **Granite Creek Trail,** a 10-mile round-trip that affords tremendous views of the glacial valley. Another good hike begins about a mile south of the hot springs on Forest Road 30500; the 7-mile (one-way) **Shoal Falls Trail** leads to Shoal Falls, providing scenic views of the Gros Ventre Range and of the falls. ■

Wind River peaks

Wind River Range

■ Western Wyoming, southeast of Jackson ■ Camping, hiking, boating, fishing, bird-watching, wildlife viewing ■ Contact Bridger-Teton National Forest, P.O. Box 220, Pinedale, WY 82941; phone 307-367-4326

A MAGNIFICENT CREST of bare rock peaks draped with glaciers and peppered with hundreds of lakes, the Wind River Range stretches southeast from the Jackson Hole area for roughly 100 miles and extends the Greater Yellowstone Ecosystem far into central Wyoming. Arguably the highest mountain range in the northern Rockies, it contains more than 20 peaks over 13,000 feet, including the region's highest summit: 13,804-foot Gannett Peak. It also harbors the largest glacial ice field in the lower 48 states.

Named for the river that drains its eastern slopes and protected by three wilderness areas, the range takes in an immense and sprawling landscape well-suited for day hikes or extended backpacking trips. Much of the terrain lies above tree line in a delightful, glacially carved realm of cirques, towers, and grand amphitheaters. Lower down, thick forests cloak the slopes, obscuring deep canyons swept by white-water creeks.

Like the Tetons, the Winds are composed of ancient rocks nearly 2.5 billion years old—gneiss, schist, granite—the very bedrock of the continent. Unlike the relatively young Tetons, the Winds rose 55 to 65 million years ago during the general mountain-building phase known as the Laramide Orogeny. The range heaved upward as a vast and coherent block that was moved 13 miles to the southwest along one of the biggest fault zones in the Rockies. During the past two million years, glaciers formed repeatedly throughout the range, biting deeply into the rock to form the beautiful canyons, basins, and sharp-pointed peaks the eye lingers over today.

What to See and Do

Skyline Drive

The most accessible portion of the Winds lies east of Pinedale, where Skyline Drive *(S end of town)* climbs through steep morainal hills to two beautiful lakes and then continues on to forests, meadows, and trails leading into the scenic heart of the range.

Though it may be difficult to resist the emerald waters of Fremont Lake, it's best to drive right past the turnoff for now and head for the **Elhart Park Overlook** *(follow FR 740 and FR 134)*, which offers a smashing vista of the lake, the forested midriff of the Winds, and an arresting line of 13,000-foot peaks that form the crest of the range. Perched some 2,000 feet above the lake, the overlook peers down into the great maw of **Fremont Glacier Canyon,** a vast bowl of glacially polished cliffs

that wrap around the head end of Fremont Lake. Far across the void, a ferocious ribbon of white water called **Miller Creek** cascades for nearly a mile down the face of the cliffs.

The road dead-ends at **Trails End Campground,** a good place for a picnic and a major staging area for backpacking and horse-back trips into the wilderness. From the Pine Creek Canyon parking lot, a steep but rewarding 2-mile trail descends to the shores of **Long Lake,** a veritable fjord glimmering beneath 2,000-foot cliffs. The same trail bends west around a lobe of magnificent cliffs and follows Fremont and Pine Creeks for 3.5 easy miles to the head end of **Fremont Lake** and Upper Fremont Lake Campground. It's a gorgeous place, with Miller Creek pouring down

Hikers at Wind River Range

Lonesome Lake and Cirque of Towers, Wind River Range   *Following pages:* Sinks Canyon,
Wind River Range

over the cliffs, but you'll have to share the hard-won shore with power boaters.

Also from Trails End *(lower parking lot),* the **Pole Creek Trail** bores through a deep forest of evergreen and tangled deadfall for 3.5 miles of easy walking before emerging at **Miller Park,** a large opening with views of the peaks along the Continental Divide. The farther you walk the better the view, as the trail ambles out onto the boggy meadows and round rock knobs of the high country. Make a day of it by adding a moderate, 3.5-mile walk from the Miller Park trail junction (take the left-hand trail) to the spectacular alpine meadows surrounding **Hobbs Lake.**

Within a few miles of Pinedale, a spur road breaks away from Skyline Drive and descends to the southeast shore of **Fremont Lake,** a large body of blue water occupying a spectacular glacial trough. The road dead-ends at a Forest Service campground and boat ramp. It's a lovely spot to car camp or to launch a canoe for the paddle up to the cliff-lined upper end of the lake.

Green River Lakes

Farther north along the range, northeast of Cora, lie the Green River Lakes, a pair of large alpine lakes that nestle against the base of high, bare rock peaks and form the headwaters of the Green River. Like Fremont Lake, these beautiful lakes occupy a vast trough gouged out by glaciers during the ice ages. Forested on one side, open and grassy on the other, the valley bears the unmistakable U-shaped track of the glaciers. **Squaretop Mountain,** one of the most distinctive peaks in the Winds, rises some 3,800 feet above the water as a grand, flat-topped stump of naked rock.

The lakes make a fine car camping destination full of

possibilities for day hikes and boating adventures. They are also a major jump-off for extended backcountry treks (one classic trip threads back along the crest of the range to Trails End, near Pinedale).

To reach the lakes, follow Wyo. 352 for 21 miles north from Cora, then bump along 17 miles of gravel and dirt roads to a forested campground and boat landing on the lower lake. The road hugs the **Green River** as it meanders across sagebrush and grass meadows, often breaking into foaming rapids that cascade over rounded boulders. The proximity of the road makes it easy to scout a section of the river, shuttle your boats, and take a second or third crack at a favorite rapids.

Moose, black bears, elk, deer, pronghorn, coyotes, and ospreys frequent the area, and in the meadows and forests surrounding the lakes and river grow spectacular wildflowers—fireweed, lupine, scarlet gilia, and many others.

A pleasant day hike runs along the east shore of the lower lake for an easy 1.5 miles, then heads 4.5 miles up magnificent **Clear Creek Canyon** to Clear Lake, tucked between 2,500-foot walls of rock. If you prefer flatter terrain, turn right at the Clear Creek junction and take the **Highline Trail,** which leads to the upper lake within a mile or so and then continues along the Green River bottoms for miles beneath the awesome walls of Squaretop Mountain. Even if you intend to hike the Highline, consider following the Clear Creek trail for at least a quarter mile, just to see Clear Creek Falls.

Paddlers can reach the head end of the lower lake in an easy 45 minutes, then thread upstream for a mile or so through wetlands (look for moose) to the upper lake, which is gripped by sheer 1,500-foot cliffs. ■

Sinks Canyon State Park

■ 600 acres ■ Central Wyoming, southwest of Lander on Wyo. 131 ■ Visitor center closed Labor Day–Mem. Day ■ Camping, hiking, wildlife viewing ■ Contact the park, 3079 Sinks Canyon Rd., Lander, WY 82520; phone 307-332-6333

SITE OF A PECULIAR disappearing river, Sinks Canyon bends through the eastern foothills of the Wind River Mountains southwest of Lander as a swerving, glacially carved trough lined with great brows of smooth limestone. Down its center flows the **Middle Popo Agie River,** a vigorous, crystal clear stream that cascades over a steep bed of round boulders and then rushes into the maw of a large limestone cavern known as **The Sinks.** Little is known about what happens underground except that the water trickles back to the surface a quarter mile down the canyon in a springlike pool called **The Rise.** Tests using dyes have shown that it takes more than two hours for the water to make its subterranean journey, indicating that the water must pass through many small underground channels and fissures.

The park itself stretches for about a mile along the canyon floor, taking in open, upland areas as well as pockets of evergreen and aspen.

The river corridor—with its shade, pools, and chilly mist—is a welcome respite from central Wyoming's summer heat. Mule deer, elk, moose, and bighorn sheep share the canyon with kestrels, blue grouse, pygmy owls, golden eagles, and lazuli buntings.

Stop by the visitor center for a summary of the canyon's geology and wildlife, and an explanation of the river's vanishing act. Have a look at The Sinks, then drive down the canyon to The Rise, where you can stand on a platform overlooking the quiet water and toss fish food to lunker trout. ■

Salt River and Wyoming Ranges

■ Western Wyoming, south of Alpine ■ Camping, hiking, boating, wildlife viewing ■ Snow can close forest roads, including Greys River Road, from mid-Oct.–mid-June; lower elevation areas have a longer season ■ Contact Greys River Ranger District, Bridger-Teton National Forest, P.O. Box 339, Aspen, WY 83110; phone 307-886-3166

RUNNING SOUTH FROM the Tetons for about 80 miles, these parallel mountain ranges are among Wyoming's most undeservedly overlooked wild patches. With summits over 10,000 feet and Wyoming Peak topping out at a respectable 11,378, the two ranges offer many of the same back-country pleasures of better-known places but without the crowds. Both ranges are part of western Wyoming's Overthrust Belt. In effect, the land was shoved east until it crumpled in parallel corrugations, creating not only high mountains but gas and oil fields—and the environmental controversy that arises wherever the two occur together.

Between the ranges runs a long valley draining the Greys River, which flows into the Snake River near Alpine. **Greys River Road** (Forest Road 10138) parallels the river 58 miles to its source at **Tri Basin Divide.** Both the river and the road cruise through meadows, forest, and narrow canyons, often beneath fine views of the high peaks, passing numerous trailheads, side roads, a handful of campgrounds, and frequent trout pools.

The river's lower end challenges kayakers during spring runoff with Class III, IV, and V white water between Bridge Campground and Lynx Creek. Some Class II stretches exist between Lynx Creek and Sheep Creek, but be careful—the Greys can be blocked by logjams. Don't launch without asking someone who knows current conditions.

At Tri Basin Divide, the road splits in two directions. Both routes follow the **Lander Cutoff,** a branch of the Oregon Trail. Forest Road 10072 climbs west over hogbacked Commissary Ridge before dropping to Star Valley and the town of Afton. Forest Road 10138 continues southeast through the gentle meadows of La Barge Creek to the open ranchland around La Barge. To follow the Lander Cutoff, look for Forest Road 10128 (signed as Coyote Park Rd.) about 9 miles from Tri Basin Divide; it leads out of the mountains to Big Piney. ■

Wyoming's Basins and Mountains

Reflection of the Snowy Range at sunset,
Medicine Bow-Routt National Forest

WIDE OPEN AND LIGHTLY TRAVELED, this vast and varied
region takes in much of Wyoming and stitches together
a glorious patchwork of mountains, deserts, plains, deep
river canyons, fossil beds, sand dunes, trout streams, cool
evergreen forests, and high alpine lakes. Often overlooked
by visitors to the northern Rockies because it lacks trophy
destinations such as national parks, the region still offers
a great deal in terms of scenery, wildlife, and solitude.
It includes two fine national recreation areas, several

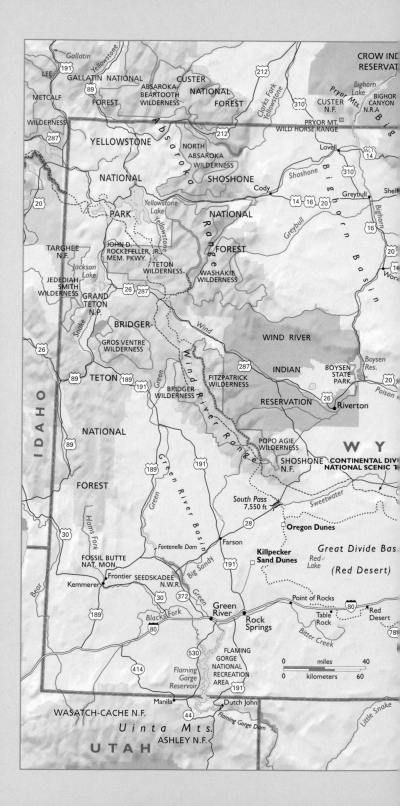

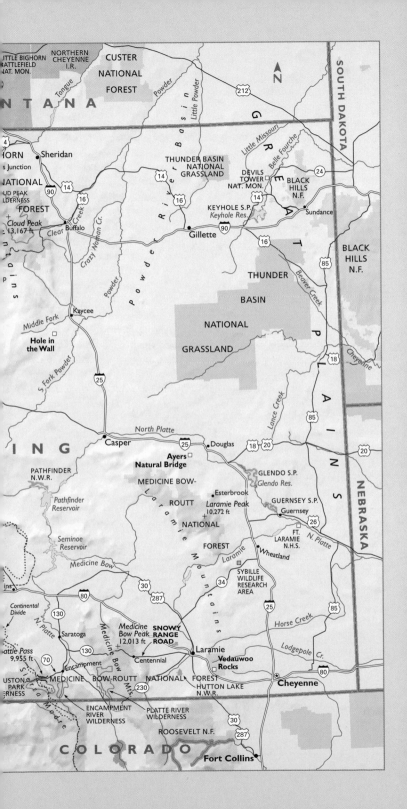

wilderness areas, one national monument, portions of three national forests, and a handful of intriguing archaeological sites.

Taking central Wyoming as its axis, the region stretches off in three directions. To the north it follows the broad, forested back of the Bighorn Mountains into Montana, where the Bighorns plunge into a spectacular desert canyon. To the southeast it encompasses a cluster of three mountain ranges that spill into Wyoming from Colorado: the Laramies, the Medicine Bows, and the Sierra Madre. There, some of the peaks rise well above tree line and beckon with glaciated cirques, crystalline lakes, and boundless tracts of alpine wildflowers. To the southwest lie Wyoming's desert lands, a seemingly endless tract of sagebrush plain, gravel hills, and crumbling rimrock. There you'll find a peculiar desert basin completely encircled by the Continental Divide as well as the region's most dramatic canyon, Flaming Gorge, which cuts a colorful gash south to the Uinta Mountains in Utah.

Flaming Gorge was formed by the Green River, which drains most of southwest Wyoming. It starts in the Wind River Range and flows through expansive sagebrush flats, gathering in tributary streams from the western mountains before carving into the beige, orange, and vermilion sedimentary rocks of the gorge. In the southeast portion of the state, the principle river is the North Platte, which enters Wyoming from Colorado through a narrow canyon of brawling white water, then bends placidly around the northern spur of the Laramie Mountains and heads east onto the Great Plains. To the north, the Bighorn River meanders across the desert floor of the Bighorn Basin, then punches a gap between the Pryor and Bighorn Mountains and flows northeast to the Yellowstone River.

Wildlife runs the gamut. Elk, deer, and moose inhabit the mountain forests and follow the shaded river corridors. Large herds of pronghorn drift across the billowing sagebrush sea. Mountain lions sun on rimrock cliffs. And birds of prey, including golden eagles and peregrine falcons, hunt among the plains and meadows.

Geologically diverse, the region includes mountains that rose in place as great masses of Precambrian basement rocks (the Bighorns and the southeast mountain cluster), as well as mountains that slid into place from the west as tilted slabs of sedimentary rock (the overthrust ranges along Wyoming's western border). Between the mountains lie vast arid and semiarid basins (the Bighorn, Great Divide, and Green River Basins), which accumulated all manner of erosional debris as the mountains formed around them.

A sense of vast emptiness pervades the land. Vistas are exceptionally long and often take in grand tracts of sagebrush stretching off to a distant rim of dark, forested mountains. Here and there a fence line intervenes, or an oil pump bobs slowly over the sand. Natural areas remain largely undeveloped, offer little by way of interpretation, and often seem deserted. After spending a day or more among these beautiful deserts, mountains, and rivers, it's not unusual to come away with the gratifying impression that you've had the entire place to yourself. ■

Mountain stream in the Bighorns

Mountain lion

Bighorn Mountains

■ 1.1 million acres ■ North-central Wyoming, west of Sheridan via US 14 or US 16 ■ US 14A closed in winter. US 14 and US 16 open year-round, although storms can close them temporarily. Snow lingers in the high country well into June, but foothill areas are pleasant by late May ■ Camping, hiking, fishing, mountain biking, horseback riding, snowmobiling, alpine and cross-country skiing, wildlife viewing ■ Contact Bighorn National Forest, 1969 S. Sheridan Ave., Sheridan WY 87801; phone 307-672-0751. www.fs.fed.us/r2/bighorn

CONSIDERING THEIR GREAT bulk, their impressive altitude, and their scenic beauty, it seems odd to think of the Bighorns as a little known sub-range of the Rockies. But they are all those things. Roughly 120 miles long, they arc southward from southern Montana to central Wyoming. With the dusty oil-rich **Bighorn Basin** on the west and the rolling cattle country of **Powder River Basin** on the east, they stand like a fortress island detached from the main chain of the Rockies.

About 60 million years ago, the Bighorns, riding a giant block of Precambrian granite, began shouldering their way up through deep layers of limestone and sandstone. The granite warped the sediments, tilted them edgewise, and eventually, with the help of glacial erosion, broke through. At the core of the range, 13,167-foot **Cloud Peak** presides over an assemblage of granite summits strewn with snowfields, alpine lakes, and wildflower meadows that comprise the 189,000-acre Cloud Peak Wilderness.

Two major highways—US 14 and US 16—cross the Bighorns.

Both are scenic routes traveled by thousands of visitors every day who can't help but be first impressed and, second, a bit surprised by what they see.

Most western mountain ranges were created along thrust faults that result in a steep side and a gentler side—that is, one side pushes up dramatically along a thrust fault while the other side rises less rapidly, or might even subside. The Tetons are a classic example. Their east slope is a striking rampart, while their west slope is a relatively gentle ramp. The Bighorns, however, rose along thrust faults on both sides. Both sides are steep. They go up emphatically, for thousands of feet, as if trying to create an isolated Lost World plateau. Driving across the mountains, your first encounter is with these steep, impressive ramparts that seem to promise great things ahead.

The surprise comes on the relatively gentle top, a broad plateau of mixed forest and meadow that is a pleasant but overall unspectacular landscape. Some might call it anticlimactic, without realizing how much scenic wealth lies hidden from the highways. These mountains reserve their best parts for people willing to explore farther.

The roads tell the story. At the range's northern end, US 14 struggles up 3,745 feet of switchbacks on the east side, opening tremendous views of the plains below. After a few miles of high forest and meadow, the highway splits at Burgess Junction. US 14A continues west about 20 miles through more forest and meadow punctuated by limestone cliffs before tipping off the western rim and plunging down another roadbuilder's fantasy of switchbacks to the Bighorn River. Meanwhile, US 14 slides south across the plateau for some miles before falling, as if someone pushed it, into the forbidding narrows of Shell Canyon. If you're looking for scenery, the feast is on the sides of the Bighorns.

At the range's south end, US 16 makes a similar traverse, but instead of switchbacking up a rampart, it follows a more broken route, climbing 4,400 feet from Buffalo to Powder River Pass at 9,677 feet. From there it lingers in forest and meadow for a time, until reaching **Meadowlark Lake**—a reservoir and popular fishing spot—where it turns south, dives into Tensleep Canyon, and drops 5,200 feet to the little ranch community of Ten Sleep. Again, it's the canyon on the flank of the range that travelers remember most vividly.

Flora and fauna

The plants and animals of the Bighorns are basically the same that live in the Yellowstone ecosystem, though without the grizzlies and wolves. Bighorn sheep are the signature species. There are also elk, deer, moose, black bears, mountain lions, lynx, bobcats, coyotes, porcupines, and on down the list. Two-thirds of the range is forested with lodgepole pine, Engelmann spruce, and Douglas-fir. There is tundra above timberline, wildflower meadows at all elevations, and arid sage desert around the range's base.

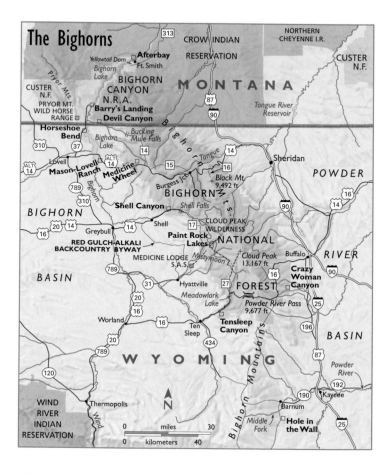

What to See and Do

Both major driving routes—US 14 and US 16—qualify as scenic highways. Both (and US 14A) are lined with campgrounds, trailheads, scenic viewpoints, picnic areas, and other good reasons to stop and spend some time. The **Burgess Junction Visitor Center** (*0.5 mile E of the US 14/14A junction*) is a good starting point for exploring the high country. Historic exhibits outline mining and logging in the Bighorns. Other displays provide a quick rundown of major natural history themes.

Perhaps the most famous site in the range is also the most mysterious. Perched on a high ridge 23 miles west of Burgess Junction, the **Medicine Wheel** is a circle of stones with 28 spokes radiating from a central cairn. Its origins are unknown, its age uncertain, its purpose the subject of controversy and speculation. The Crow Indians regard it as a sacred site. Some view it as a model of the medicine lodge in which Sun

Dances are held by Plains Indians. Others see it as a calendar marking astronomical and seasonal turning points. Clearly, it is a special place. Getting there requires a 1.5-mile walk along an old road. Interpreters are on duty during daylight hours in summer.

Geology of the Bighorns takes central stage in **Shell Canyon**, which cuts a neat transect through the up-tilted and twisted sedimentary strata sheathing the range's western slope. The scenic highlight is 120-foot **Shell Falls,** thundering through its narrow water-worn slot. A visitor center, paved walkways, and interpretive displays make it an easy place to see.

Back roads lead to a number of other interesting places. Forest Road 15 runs west about 20 miles from Burgess Junction, climbing to a high vista point before rejoining US 14A. Forest Road 17 provides access to **Paint Rock Lakes** from the upper end of Shell Canyon; this is an important trailhead for wilderness destinations

(see p. 88). The **Red Gulch-Alkali Backcountry Byway** rattles and rolls for 32 miles at the base of the range between Shell and Hyattville. Six miles east of Powder River Pass on US 16, Forest Road 028 leads to the **Sheep Mountain Fire Lookout.** You can also drive to the **High Park Lookout,** just south of US 16 near Meadowlark Lake. Also off US 16, on the eastern slope, Forest Road 033 plummets with wild abandon into **Crazy Woman Canyon;** it's an adventurous alternate descent route to Powder River Basin, if you're not driving an RV.

The mountains do not end at the national forest boundary. There's worthwhile exploring in the range's south end, notably along the **Middle Fork Powder River,** which flows through a canyon of red rocks near Kaycee. This is the original Hole in the Wall country, where Butch Cassidy and the Sundance Kid had a homestead. It's still a corner overlooked by most travelers, perhaps because a good portion of the

Colorado blue columbine   *Following pages:* Meadow of lupine and balsamroot, Bighorn National Forest

land is private and the main points of interest are hard to reach. But if you're looking for hidden corners, this one is worth some time; check with the BLM in Buffalo *(307-684-5586)* for a map and specific information on access.

Hikes in the Cloud Peak Wilderness

Cloud Peak Wilderness *(contact Powder River Ranger District 307-684-1100)* is the main hiking draw of the Bighorn Mountains. Its 189,000 acres, located in the mountains' southern reaches, contain a glaciated wonderland of sheer cliffs, rounded knobs, rock-rimmed lakes, high peaks, and loose boulder slopes, with all the attendant high country pleasures. Trails take off from several developed trailheads on both sides of the range; also from a number of undeveloped access points. One of the most popular is the **West Tensleep Lake Trailhead,** at the end of Forest Road 27 off US 16. Of two trails that depart from here, Trail 065 climbs 6.5 miles to **Lost Twin Lakes,** a pair of icy beauties shadowed by sheer, glacier-polished, 1,000-foot cliffs. If that seems long for a day hike, **Mirror Lake** is a reasonable intermediate objective, about 3 miles each way. Also beginning at West Tensleep, Trail 063 heads north to **Mistymoon Lake,** set in an alpine basin. One of the Bighorns' more popular hiking destinations, Mistymoon is also a good starting point for climbing Cloud Peak. The climb requires a full day from the lake and back—a demanding exercise in rock-hopping, but nontechnical. From Mistymoon Lake, it's possible to cross the range via Florence Lake and Medicine Cabin Park to **Hunter Trailhead** on the east side (also off US 16).

From US 14 at the head of Shell Canyon, Forest Road 17 winds south to the Paint Rock Lakes area. From here, loop trips can be designed that take in the Cloud Peak formation's northern end; or carry on northeast across the range to the **Coffee Park Trailhead.** Also from here, you can reach **Lake Solitude** on a trail that hooks up with Mistymoon Lake and the West Tensleep area.

Among day-hiking opportunities, the **Bucking Mule Falls National Recreation Trail** *(off US 14A, approximately 16 miles W of Burgess Jct.)* offers a strenuous 12-mile trip along the rim of a rugged canyon, or an easier 3-mile round-trip to the falls. The trail begins and ends at different trailheads far enough apart that hikers wanting to do the entire route will need a car shuttle. To reach the main trailhead, take Forest Road 14 *(off US 14A, 2 miles E of Bald Mountain Campground)* about 11 miles to its end. The trail follows the rim of Bucking Mule Canyon about a mile to a splendid view of the falls. From the falls, the trail continues for another 10 miles to a trailhead at the end of Forest Road 137 near Porcupine Campground.

Near Burgess Junction, the **Black Mountain Fire Lookout,** at 9,500 feet, offers sweeping vistas. To get there from Burgess Junction, take US 14 east 12 miles to Forest Road 16; follow to its junction with Forest Road 222. Drive a mile, then hike another 1.5 miles on Trail 011. ∎

Medicine Lodge SAS

■ 200 acres ■ North-central Wyoming, 6 miles northeast of Hyattville ■ Visitor center closed Nov.-April ■ Camping, hiking, fishing, mountain biking, petroglyphs and pictographs ■ Adm. fee ■ Contact the site, P.O. Box 62, Hyattville, WY 82428; phone 307-469-2234. www.commerce.state.wy.us/sphs/mlodge.htm

ONE OF WYOMING'S more pleasing state parks, Medicine Lodge State Archaeological Site lies at the foot of the Bighorns where Medicine Lodge Creek streams out of a limestone canyon. Yellow-and-red cliffs rise above the park. Willows and cottonwoods provide summer shade. In April, when winter still holds the high country in its grip, the peaceful glades of Medicine Lodge can be warm and green. Evidently, early residents also found it an attractive place. Since 1969, researchers have worked 26 feet into the surrounding soil and have uncovered thousands of artifacts from about 60 different cultural periods spanning 10,000 years. The discovery of fire pits, food storage pits, grinding stones, and projectile points has allowed archaeologists to study how life evolved in the Bighorn Basin. Some of these are on display in the small log visitor center, but the primary artifact remains in its original place. A 250-yard-long rock face, covered with petroglyphs and pictographs, serves as a newspaper to the ages.

The park itself is small, offering a campground, nature trail, and trout fishing. However, it is surrounded on three sides by public land and some worthwhile options. For a fairly easy hike along a beautiful creek, try the **Paint Rock Canyon Trail,** accessed through the Hyatt Ranch (and by kind permission of its owners) just southeast of the park. The trail follows an unpaved road closed to vehicles. Another option begins at the archaeological site and follows the bottom of **Medicine Lodge Canyon** northeast beneath increasingly high, colorful walls. The vegetation and rock shapes are similar to canyons in southern Utah.

If you keep walking you reach **Paint Rock Lakes,** a popular gateway to the Cloud Peak Wilderness (see p. 88). You can also drive that direction on Cold Springs Road, which starts climbing the limestone slabs just south of the park (this is the back way into Paint Rock Lakes). It's worth going part way for the splendid westward views. ■

Medicine Lodge wilderness

Bighorn sheep

Bighorn Canyon NRA

■120,284 acres ■ North-central Wyoming and south-central Montana, west of the Bighorn Mountains via US 14A or US 14 to US 310 N ■ US 14A closed in winter ■ Camping, boating, fishing, bird-watching ■ Adm. fee ■ Contact the recreation area, 5 Ave. B, Fort Smith, MT 59035; phone 406-666-2412. www.nps.gov.bica

THE SAME SEDIMENTARY ROCKS whose tilted and twisted slabs flank the Bighorn Mountains lie flat on the basin floor. Through these light-colored sandstone and limestone layers, the Bighorn River has carved a deep and winding canyon. In years past, the river carried a load of silt over rapids at the canyon bottom. But since the Yellowtail Dam was built in 1968, the river fills the serpentine, 71-mile-long **Bighorn Lake,** stretching from Wyoming into Montana and comprising the Bighorn Canyon NRA. At its deepest, the canyon's walls are over 2,000 feet high. Above them, the Bighorns loom large to the east, while the Pryor Mountains form a lower escarpment to the west.

No direct road connects the two ends of the reservoir, and a large portion is not reached by a road of any kind. Only with a boat can you see the entire canyon. The north end, at **Yellowtail Dam,** claims a visitor center, campground, and scenic drive and is used primarily by boaters and anglers. Those with powerboats head up the lake, while fly fishers launch drift boats below the dam. This 13-mile stretch of river is a world-famous trout fishery. It stays open all winter, making it a prime wintering spot for waterbirds. First birding choice is the **Afterbay,** a 2-mile-long mini-reservoir just below the dam that serves as a surge tank to temper fluctuating water levels.

The lake's south end offers more variety. The Lovell visitor center *(307-548-2251)* is on the outskirts of town at the junction of US 14A and US 310. From there, drive east 2 miles, then turn left on Wyo. 37 past sage flats and red badlands to the canyon's western rim. The lake has two access points. **Horseshoe Bend,** at the head of the canyon, has a boat ramp, marina, food service, campground, and swimming beach. **Barry's Landing,** 22 miles north, is primitive and less used. Although powerboats clearly own the lake, the canyon is narrow and intricate enough to hold some appeal for people in hand-propelled craft. Otherwise, you're limited to seeing the canyon from the road. Continuing north on Wyo. 37 stop at **Devil Canyon Overlook** just across the Montana border for a view across the 1,000-foot-deep canyon into the narrow mouth of Devil Canyon. If you visited the Bighorn Mountains and hiked the Bucking Mule Falls Trail (see p. 88), you've already seen the upper end of Devil Canyon in its alpine zone.

Down here, the climate is strongly affected by the Absaroka and Beartooth Ranges (see pp. 38-43), which, rising 100 miles to the west, throw a distinct rain shadow across the canyon. Horseshoe Bend is deep in the shadow. It gets only 6 inches of rain per year while Fort Smith, which lies north of the affected zone, receives about 20. Vegetation varies accordingly, from prickly pear, mountain mahogany, juniper, and yucca at the south end to prairie grasslands at the north end. Forest is scanty except on the high slopes of the Pryor Mountains and in moist pockets.

As for large mammals, look for mule deer and bighorn sheep. The bighorns are a conservation success story. Once common, the original populations both here and in the neighboring Bighorn Mountains were wiped out by hunting and domestic livestock diseases. Reintroduced to the mountains in 1973, the animals prospered and expanded their range to the canyon. The present herd ranges the west rim between the Pryors and the lake, and are often seen from the road. Speaking of reintroduction, the cliffs are obviously good habitat for raptors, including peregrine falcons—beneficiaries of a determined breeding and reintroduction effort.

The residents of the **Pryor Mountains Wild Horse Range,** located just outside the national recreation area's border, arrived on their own, as runaways from ranches or Native American herds. Their origins are disputed. Because some of them carry the marks of early Spanish horses—buff coats with dark stripes on their legs and a dark cross on the back and withers—they are viewed by some as historically important. Look for them along the Sykes Ridge and Tillet Ridge Roads, which leave Wyo. 37 a mile south of the NRA boundary. Both are rough, perhaps impassable, and directions are complicated; it's best to stop at the visitor center for advice and maps.

Most of Bighorn Lake is confined within canyon walls, but its southern, upstream end is a broad wetland—sometimes a mudflat, depending on water levels—frequented by waterfowl and designated the **Yellowtail Wildlife Habitat Management Unit** adjacent to the national recreation area. Rough roads and trails provide access for bird-watchers and, in season, hunters. ■

Near Vedauwoo, Medicine Bow-Routt National Forest

Laramie Range

■ Southeast Wyoming ■ Camping, hiking, rock climbing, fishing, mountain biking, cross-country skiing, wildlife viewing ■ Contact Laramie Ranger District, Medicine Bow-Routt National Forest., 2468 Jackson St., Laramie, WY 82070; phone 307-745-2300. www.fs.fed.us/r2/mbr

BULGING HIGH ABOVE grassy plains, this long, dark, and unpretentious hump of forested mountains spills across the Colorado line just west of Cheyenne and extends north as far as Casper. Broad-shouldered, cloaked in deep evergreen forests, and blessed with expansive shortgrass prairie meadows, the Laramies are a haven for wildlife. Pronghorn grace the foothills. Elk and deer wander the forests and meadows. Bighorn sheep live among the rocky highlands. And there are black bears, mountain lions, prairie dogs, endangered black-footed ferrets and a tremendous variety of birds.

Perhaps best of all, the Laramies—along with the neighboring Medicine Bows and Sierra Madre—tend to get bypassed by most visitors, who flock instead to the craggy peaks of northwestern Wyoming or to Yellowstone. Here, you can still go off on your own.

Geologically, the Laramies share with their neighboring ranges the same basic creation story. A long suture zone arcs diagonally across all three ranges, separating the underlying rocks into two distinct masses. North of the line, the rocks are 2.6 billion years old. South of the line, the rocks are 1.2 billion years younger. Geologists think the seam represents the juncture of two pieces of continental crust that joined together while the North American continent coalesced. All three ranges were pushed upward roughly 60 million years ago during the general mountain-building phase that created the Rockies.

Between Cheyenne and Laramie, I-80 climbs onto the broad back of the Laramie mountains and crosses a plain studded with the oddly shaped **Vedauwoo Rocks** (*Mem. Day–Labor Day; adm. fee*). For a closer look, take the Vedauwoo exit north to the short trails that thread through the **Turtle Rock** and **Devil's Playground** areas (see sidebar this page).

Farther north, southwest of Wheatland, you can get a look at North America's rarest mammal—the black-footed ferret—at the **Sybille Wildlife Research Area** (*28 miles W of I-25 on Wyo. 34. 307-322-4576*). Also consider taking the gravel loop road (Cty. Rd. 12) that traverses the foothills behind the facility. Pronghorn, deer, and elk frequent the slopes.

Continuing north on I-25, you can drive into the high country around Douglas and get a close-up view of 10,272-foot **Laramie Peak** from the tiny town of Esterbrook (*27 miles S of Douglas via Wyo. 94 and Esterbrook Rd.*). Beyond Esterbrook, the steep **Laramie Peak Trail** leads 5.5 miles from the Friend Park Campground to the summit. This is one of the richest wildlife tours in the Laramies, since it climbs from the banks of the North Platte River (golden eagles, deer, herons) through extensive grasslands (pronghorn, prairie dogs, grouse) and forests (mule deer, elk). Closer to Douglas, **Ayers Natural Bridge** (*12 miles W of town, off I-25 on Natural Bridge Rd. 307-358-3532. May-Oct.*) arches over the clear waters of La Prele Creek and makes a good picnic spot. ∎

Vedauwoo Rocks

The weathered piles, columns, and isolated boulders known as the Vedauwoo Rocks are composed of pink Precambrian granite that crystallized 1.4 billion years ago. The rocks formed from massive outcroppings that fractured and then eroded into strange, rounded shapes. Some resemble giant cairns, others mushrooms. Most are simply jumbles of interesting shapes with smooth pink surfaces that stand in vivid contrast with the rolling grass hills of the Sherman Summit between Cheyenne and Laramie.

Following pages: Immense boulders at Vedauwoo in the Laramie Range

Fall aspens and Sheep Mountain, Medicine Bow-Routt National Forest

Medicine Bow Mountains

■ Southeast Wyoming ■ Camping, hiking, fishing, mountain biking, snowmobiling, alpine and cross-country skiing, bird-watching, wildlife viewing ■ Contact Laramie Ranger District, Medicine Bow-Routt National Forest, 2468 Jackson St., Laramie, WY 82070; phone 307-745-2300 or Brush Creek-Hayden Ranger District, phone 307-326-5258. www.fs.fed.us/r2/mbr

CAPPED BY A magnificent crest of grayish white cliffs and spanned by one of the great scenic roads of the Rockies, the Medicine Bow Mountains lift their broad back against the skyline west of Laramie and stretch south into Colorado for roughly 40 miles. Though deep evergreen forests darken much of the range, some of the Medicine Bows rise well above tree line, topping out in that most splendid and fragile of mountain domains, the alpine tundra. Here, gently sloping wildflower meadows,

Fall leaves

flecked with tiny lakes and threaded by icy brooks, bowl along for miles and open up amazing vistas of northern Colorado's sea of peaks.

Descending from the high country, the slopes are covered with subalpine forests of Englemann spruce and fir that give way at lower, drier elevations to lodgepole pine, Douglas-fir, and groves of aspen. Along the very base of the range lie rolling sagebrush hills, shortgrass plains, and (on the west side) the priceless wetlands and riparian corridor of the North Platte River.

This wide spectrum of habitats supports a diverse wildlife community. Ospreys, ducks, geese, shorebirds, and moose live along the river. Pronghorn, deer, coyotes, and red foxes trot across the sagebrush foothills and prairies, while eagles, falcons, and hawks wheel overhead. Elk graze in the meadows and lay up for the day in the cool shade of the forests, and bighorn sheep amble among the rocky slopes of the high country.

It's a gorgeous place, easily visited, with plenty of casual trails that skirt the high lakes, loop through alpine meadows, and pass beneath soaring cliffs. ■

What to See and Do
Snowy Range Road

Wyo. 130, also known as the Snowy Range Road, climbs over the Medicine Bows between Centennial and the North Platte River Valley. The road usually opens in late spring, but because the range accumulates so much snow, some side roads and campgrounds can remain closed through midsummer.

Heading west from Laramie, the road crosses the Laramie Plains (coyotes, hawks, pronghorn, ground squirrels). Pick up a map and inquire about road closures at the Centennial Visitor Center, then make a leisurely ascent through the forest. Soon, the trees begin to give out, huddling in small thickets surrounded by wildflower meadows. And before long,

the range's distinctive crest bursts into view, looming over the meadows as a great high dome of whitish quartzite and granite. Luminescent in some lights, the dome has been carved by glaciers and erosion into sheer cliffs that sometimes rise 2,000 feet.

The heart of this high country scenic area surrounds 10,847-foot **Snowy Range Pass,** where a gently rolling meadow stretches off to the south and where the heady scent of wildflowers lingers in the air. **Libby Flats Observation Point,** a stone turret located at the very summit of the pass, overlooks the meadow and offers tremendous vistas of Colorado's mountains, including Longs Peak. The turret also provides an excellent view of the Medicine Bow crest. Here, too, a short

nature loop trail identifies some of the alpine tundra's showier wildflowers—sky pilot, fleabane, bluebells, alpine avens, and more.

A longer trail winds south from the turret, descending for more than a mile through this expansive landscape to small ponds and islands of stunted evergreens. Alpine tundra vegetation is easily damaged and takes many years to recover. Responsible hikers stick strictly to the trails.

Just east of the pass, a spur road trundles a mile down to **Sugarloaf Recreation Area** *(10 miles W of Centennial off Wyo. 130. Adm fee),* where a vast brow of bright white rock looms above two tiny alpine lakes. The lakes often act as mirrors, reflecting the quartzite edifice as well as the surrounding wildflower meadows and thickets of stunted trees. It's a great place for a picnic or a casual stroll.

About a mile west of the pass and right next to the highway, **Lake Marie** nestles against the soaring cliffs of 12,013-foot **Medicine Bow Peak.** Trout dimple the glassy surface, and easy trails hug the shoreline and wander among hillocks, knobs, and boggy meadows that surround the lake.

Elk frequent the forest-and-meadow landscape on both sides of the pass. If you're lucky enough to be camping in the area during the September rut, you may hear bull elk sending up their eerie squeals at dawn and dusk. In summer you're more likely to see mule deer, hawks, eagles, ground squirrels, and hoary marmots.

The road continues down the mountains into Saratoga. ■

North Platte River

■ Southeast Wyoming ■ Best seasons spring to fall ■ Camping, hiking, boating, white-river rafting, fishing, canoeing, bird-watching, wildlife viewing ■ Contact Brush Creek-Hayden Ranger District, Medicine Bow-Routt National Forest, P.O. Box 249, Saratoga, WY 82331; phone 307-326-5258. www.fs.us/r2/mbr

THE NORTH PLATTE—a wide, sometimes ferocious river—curves through the parched, semidesert lands that sprawl between the Medicine Bows and the Sierra Madre. A verdant ribbon of gurgling water, cottonwood groves, grassy banks, willow thickets, and occasional wetlands, it is a crucial riparian zone and top-notch trout fishery that attracts a wide variety of wildlife. Bighorn sheep, mule deer, moose, elk, and pronghorn can be seen along its banks, but birds are a more dependable sight. Great blue herons, bald eagles, kingfishers, swallows, blackbirds, and ducks live close to the water, while hawks and falcons glide overhead.

As it flows north from the Colorado border, the river crashes through **North Gate Canyon,** a narrow gorge gripped by cliffs, rock towers, and high, arid hills. Much of the canyon lies within the **Platte River Wilderness** *(Laramie Ranger District. 307-745-2300),* a small patch of protected lands in the Medicine Bow foothills. To get a taste for the country, hike a section of the **Platte River Trail,** which drops into the canyon at Six Mile

White-tailed deer

Gap Campground *(FR 492, off Wyo. 230, about 22 miles SE of Encampment)* and follows the river for about 6 miles. But the best way to see the North Platte is to float it. Most of the river in Wyoming is suitable for canoes, and a cinch for drift boats and rafts—except for the series of Class IV rapids between the Colorado border and Six Mile Gap. If you don't have a boat, book a guided float trip or rent a boat in Saratoga *(Chamber of Commerce 307-326-8855)*.

Whether you hike, boat, or wade the river with a fly rod, consider ending the day with a soak at **Saratoga Hot Springs** *(call the chamber)*, a steaming municipal pool open 24 hours a day, no charge. ■

Oregon Trail

The North Platte River served as guide and oasis for the hundreds of thousands of emigrants who headed west on the Oregon Trail during the 1840s, '50s, and '60s. They followed the river into Wyoming as it made its wide, northwestern bend around the Laramie Mountains, pausing at such landmarks as Fort Laramie and Register Cliff, both near modern-day Guernsey, and Ayers Natural Bridge, near today's Douglas. Most forded or ferried the river at modern-day Casper and then followed the Sweetwater River across central Wyoming.

Beyond the Trees: the Alpine Zone

GLANCE AT ANY major mountain range in the northern Rockies and you'll soon identify what appears to be a distinct horizontal line above which no trees grow. At first, tree limit, as it is sometimes called, seems almost exclusively tied to elevation: The higher you go, the colder, drier, and harder it is for trees to survive. But there's more. Latitude, for instance. As you travel north, mean summer temperatures drop and so does tree limit. In Colorado, it fluctuates between 11,000 and 12,000 feet; in Wyoming, around 9,500; in Montana, around 7,500. Deep lingering snowfields, desiccating winds, and poor soils also limit just how far up a particular mountain slope trees can live.

Perhaps the most reliable key to defining tree limit is cold. In the Northern Hemisphere, tree limit hugs a meandering line where mean summer temperatures average 50°F. Step across that line, and you begin to enter the alpine zone, where trees throw in the towel, and a deceptively lush carpet of wildflowers, grasses, and forbs stretches across the land. In summer, the alpine can seem like the sweetest place on earth, a bosky realm of endless vistas where nothing obscures the peaks.

But it is, in fact, a ferocious environment, an even tougher place for plants and animals to survive than the Arctic, where life can at least look forward to the midnight sun. In the alpine, the

growing season lasts just six to eight weeks. Snow can fall at any time during the summer. Winds, which often exceed 100 mph and sometimes reach 200 mph, intensify the cold and accelerate evaporation. Precipitation is abundant as snow and as rain. But when the snow melts, water quickly drains through gravelly soils and rushes downslope. Ditto with thundershowers. Here, too, the sun shines with far greater intensity than it does at sea level, beaming down twice the ultraviolet radiation and quickening evaporation.

Alpine plants tend to be small. Their diminutive size keeps them out of the worst of the wind and reduces their need for moisture and nutrients. Most are perennials, which eliminates the need to generate new leaves and stems each season. Many flower and set seed early, since flowering does not require the heat of high summer, while seed-ripening does. Others avoid the seed temperature issue by reproducing vegetatively. Many alpine plants can grow in temperatures barely above freezing, and they often contain anthocyanins, chemicals that warm plant tissue by converting light to heat.

Few animals live all year in the alpine. Those that do survive the winter in various ways. Many, such as marmots and ground squirrels, hibernate. Others, including pikas, spend the summer busily stocking a winter larder. Deer mice, active at night, huddle for warmth during the day and enter a torpor. Long-tailed weasels hunt all winter, caching dozens of rodent bodies in their burrows, to be eaten at leisure. ■

Old Man of the Mountain in the Snowy Range, Medicine Bow-Routt National Forest

The Sierra Madre

The Sierra Madre

■ Southeast Wyoming, south of Saratoga ■ Wyo. 70 closed in winter ■ Camping, hiking, boating, fishing, wildlife viewing ■ Contact Brush Creek-Hayden Ranger District, Medicine Bow-Routt National Forest, P.O. Box 249, Saratoga, WY 82331; phone 307-326-5258. www.fs.fed.us/r2/mbr

BROAD-BACKED, DARK, and rumpled, the Sierra Madre lie along the Continental Divide west of the Medicine Bow Mountains and overlook the seemingly endless sagebrush ocean of southwest Wyoming. Covered almost completely by evergreen forests and stands of aspen, the mountains rise to elevations of 10,000 to 11,000 feet. The forests give way to open valleys, wildflower meadows, alpine lakes, and mountain streams. Bighorn sheep live here, as do elk, deer, mountain lions, black bears, and pronghorn.

Drive over the range on deserted Wyo. 70, which climbs through sagebrush hills and deep forest to 9,955-foot **Battle Pass.** Here you'll find the abandoned mining town of Battle and a trailhead for the **Continental Divide National Scenic Trail,** which leads south through the tiny **Huston Park Wilderness** (*Maps available at Brush Creek-Hayden Ranger Dist. ofc. in Encampment, 307-327-5481*).

Just west of the pass, another trailhead accesses a north-bound section of the Continental Divide Trail that climbs 3 miles to the 11,004-foot summit of **Bridger Peak.** It's a terrific walk among thickets of stunted subalpine fir, snowfields, and rock outcrops that takes in Battle Pass, Battle Lake, the Medicine Bows, and the North Platte Valley.

Elsewhere in the range, the **Encampment River** rushes fast and cold along the eastern slopes, tumbling through a fine canyon of forest, cliff, and crumbling spire. One of the river's most appealing sections flows through the **Encampment River Wilderness,** where the 10.5-mile **Encampment River Trail** (Trail 470) hugs the bank from the outskirts of Encampment to a trailhead close to **Hog Park Reservoir** (*27 miles from Encampment via Wyo. 70 and FR 550*). ■

Eroded hills, Great Divide Basin

Great Divide Basin

■ 1.6 million acres ■ South-central Wyoming via I-80/US 30 ■ Hiking, wildlife viewing ■ Contact the Bureau of Land Management, US 191 N, Rock Springs, WY 82902; phone 307-352-0256. www.wy.blm.gov

LYING AT THE lonesome heart of southern Wyoming's high desert and completely encircled by the Continental Divide, this vast and largely unappreciated tract of desiccated land takes in 2,500 square miles of sagebrush, sand, parched lake beds, rimrocked plateaus, arid ridges, and crumbling hillsides. Overlooked by most people, it is a place of tremendous, if unconventional, beauty, full of rewarding vistas, peculiar landforms, and a surprising variety of wildlife.

Elk and mule deer summer along the basin's western side. Large herds of pronghorn sweep across the flats. Look, too, for mountain lions, bobcats, coyotes, foxes, wild horses, prairie dogs, and raptors.

Vistas are long, often topped by mountains, and especially beautiful at dawn or dusk when lengthening shadows set off every crack in the ground and the angled sunlight amplifies rich colors of rock and soil—gray, yellow, red, olive, and brown. Vegetation may look drab and uniform from a distance, but even a short springtime stroll among the sagebrush turns up various types of grasses, wildflowers, and blooming cactuses.

Much of the appeal of the Great Divide Basin (or Red Desert, as it is sometimes known) lies in how its plants and animals cope with the scarcity of water, the extreme temperature variations, the lack of protective cover, and the strong, persistent winds. Many of the smaller animals spend much of their time underground, rarely venturing out during the heat of the day. Larger mammals feed on dried grasses and shrubs, find cover in dry gulches or in the lee of large bushes, and drink from springs and small pools of meltwater. Plants often sink deep taproots to store nutrients and water, and sometimes grow fuzzy layers on stems and leaves to diffuse intense sunlight.

What to See and Do

First, a word about travel conditions. The handful of dirt roads crisscrossing the Great Divide Basin become slick as a hockey rink when wet. Keep an eye on the weather and don't venture more than a couple of miles on those roads unless you're prepared to spend the night or to walk out. That said, the basin and its surrounding deserts are wonderful places to roam for a couple of hours or even a week. They are solitary, peaceful, and completely removed from urban experience.

For a quick dip into the serenity of the desert, take any of the dozen or more exits off I-80/US 30 between Rawlins and Rock Springs. A short drive takes you out of sight and earshot of the freeway, and an amble of a quarter mile or so should turn up a pronghorn, hawk, or cottontail.

For a longer excursion, head to the **Killpecker Sand Dunes** area north of Rock Springs, part of an extensive body of scattered dune fields that stretches 100 miles across western and central Wyoming. Elk, mule deer, pronghorn, and sage grouse live in the area, and numerous spring-fed ponds in the dunes support an abundance of birds. To get there from Rock Springs, head north 8 miles on US 191, turn right on the Tri-Territory Site Road (Chilton Road), and drive to Fifteen Mile Knoll. The right-hand road, which may be very rough, leads into the dune field.

Other remote but interesting sites include the **Red Lake Wilderness Study Area,** a dry lake bed 30 miles north of Table Rock; the **Adobe Town Wilderness Study Area,** located south of the Great Divide Basin and offering an eroded landscape of colorfully banded cliffs, buttes, and small canyons; and the **Oregon Buttes** and **Honeycomb Buttes Wilderness Study Areas,** outstanding examples of badlands scenery partially visible from South Pass along Wyo. 28. Directions and good maps to any of these sites are available at the BLM office just north of Rock Springs. ∎

Wild horses in a desert canyon

Rabbithrush in Firehole Canyon, Flaming Gorge National Recreation Area

Flaming Gorge NRA

■ 201,000 acres ■ Southwest Wyoming and northeast Utah, south of I-80 via US 191 ■ Camping, boating, swimming, bird-watching, wildlife viewing ■ Adm. fee ■ Contact Flaming Gorge Ranger District, Ashley National Forest, P.O. Box 279, Manila UT 84046; phone 435-784-3445. www.fs.fed.us/r4/ashley

GRIPPED BY SOARING cliffs of yellow, orange, and vermilion stone, this titanic gash in the desert lands of southwest Wyoming cuts through the northern flank of the **Uinta Mountains** and impounds the **Green River** for 91 serpentine miles. Placid now, the river corridor roared with white water until the early 1960s when Flaming Gorge Dam was built south of the Utah border. The recreation area takes in the reservoir, adjacent lands, and a beautiful section of the free-flowing Green beneath the dam.

The gorge starts in the crumbling red- and peach-colored sedimentary buttes, bluffs, and chimneys near the town of Green River, then continues south, cutting a gap through layers of colorful sedimentary rock that were tilted when the Uinta Mountains rose 38 to 65 million years ago.

Huge, rounded highlands covered with sagebrush and hopping with pronghorn rise hundreds of feet off the water and offer grandstand vistas of distant desert lands creased with shadow. Narrow side canyons, stuffed with greenery, zigzag back from the gorge for miles, offering cool shade and safe haven for herds of bighorn sheep. Higher up in the Uinta foothills, ponderosa pines and other evergreens gather themselves into proper forests frequented by mule deer, elk, and moose. And then there is the plunging void of the gorge itself. As wide at its upper end as a large mountain valley, it eventually squeezes down into a precipitous alleyway lined with sheer walls of vermilion rock 1,300 feet high.

The dam, the visitor center, and most of the campgrounds lie at the

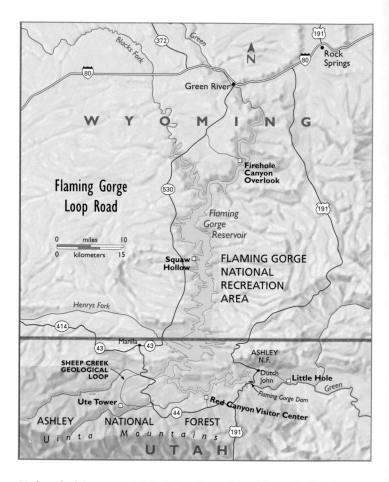

Utah end of the reservoir. The Wyoming end is wilder and offers fewer access points to the reservoir. But even when the roads lie far from the edge of the gorge, there is the beauty of the desert. Boundless tracts of sagebrush hills roll off to the distance beneath an open sky while prickly pear cactus blooms at your feet.

What to See and Do

Paved roads form a ragged, 145-mile loop around the gorge, making it possible to get an overview of the area in a single day. Start at the town of Green River and head south on Wyo. 530 into sprawling, high desert lands that stretch to the western horizon and beyond. Stop

at the **Firehole Canyon Overlook** to appreciate the scale of the upper gorge and perhaps to spot a hawk or even a peregrine falcon.

Continuing south, the road crosses deep side canyons and drops to enticing arms of the reservoir—sinuous tongues of water reach up into the crooked side canyons. Just past the Squaw Hollow turnoff, you'll find a prairie dog town on the highway's east side. Social, vocal, nervous, the rodents attract a variety of predators, including badgers, coyotes, golden eagles, and hawks.

South of Manila, go south on Utah 44 and then turn right on the **Sheep Creek Geologic Loop.** More a scenic drive than a geology lesson, the loop explores a deep and spectacular side canyon where bighorn sheep and mule deer are often seen. Columns, pillars, and broad slabs of smooth sandstone and limestone crowd the road and rise bright and fractured against the deep blue sky. Cottonwoods and willows cram the narrow creek bottoms, forming a refreshing corridor of emerald green, cool shadows, and gurgling water. As the road switchbacks out of the canyon, look back at the rock layers in the opposite wall. Swirled, folded over, and tilted almost to vertical, they were deformed by the colossal forces that heaved the Uintas into place. Farther along, follow the road to Bourne Lake and Spirit Lake, which leads to **Ute Tower,** an old fire lookout that offers a terrific vista of Flaming Gorge and the Uintas.

Back on Utah 44, proceed east to the turnoff for the **Red Canyon Visitor Center** *(435-889-3759. Closed Labor Day–Mem. Day; adm. fee).* Perched at the very rim of the gorge's most spectacular section, the building's plate glass walls overlook a 1,360-foot drop into a meandering brick red chasm dotted with juniper and pinyon pine. Modest exhibits outline the geologic story of the Uintas and the gorge, sketch 10,000 years of human history, and tick off the major plants and animals that live within the gorge and the surrounding deserts and forests. Outside, a pleasant footpath winds along the rim from overlook to overlook. The terrain here is high enough, cool enough, and wet enough to support a sparse canopy of ponderosa pines, which rustle in the breeze like an echo of the canyon's submerged white water.

Farther east, US 191 crosses the Green River at **Flaming Gorge Dam,** which offers a fine vista of the river flowing far below and bending out of sight in yet another beautiful canyon. Beyond, a spur road leads down to the **Little Hole Recreation Complex** on the banks of the free-flowing Green. This tailwater section of the river offers some of the West's best trout fishing, so the boat launch is often crowded with drift boats, rafts, and people carrying fly rods. If you have the time, you can float the river yourself by renting a raft or arranging for a guided trip at Dutch John. Hiking trails also hug the banks.

If a swim seems in order, head north into Wyoming on US 191 and take the spur road west into Firehole Canyon, a grand trough of sagebrush that lies beneath high rimrock cliffs and leads down to the reservoir. Along the shore, you'll find a sun-baked campground that overlooks the water and faces a massive brow of peach-colored stone across the gorge. The beach is to the left. On weekends, locals crowd the sand and zip around on jet skis. ■

Seedskadee NWR

■ 13,812 acres ■ Southwest Wyoming, northwest of Green River via Wyo. 372 ■ Sage grouse court in April ■ Hiking, boating, fishing, bird-watching, wildlife viewing ■ Contact the refuge, P.O. Box 700, Green River, WY 82935; phone 307-875-2187. www.r6.fws.gov/refuges/seedskad

OUT ON THE vast sagebrush platter of the **Green River Basin,** this hot, windy, and largely deserted haven for upland birds, waterfowl, and other animals hugs the meandering banks of the Green River for more than 35 miles. Set aside to help offset the loss of scarce wetlands habitat caused by the construction of the Fontenelle Dam, the refuge takes its name from a Shoshone word meaning "river of the prairie hen" (sage grouse). Its semiarid uplands, shady cottonwood groves, willow thickets, and precious marshy areas provide homes for more than 200 bird species, as well as for moose, mule deer, pronghorn, coyotes, white-tailed deer, prairie dogs, tiger salamanders, and dusky shrews.

The river—deep, fast, and dark—winds through this dry land as a ribbony oasis, with the snowcapped peaks of the Wind River Range to

Cottonwoods along the Green River, Seedskadee NWR

the east and the overthrust ranges of Wyoming's border to the west. Herds of pronghorn race across the flats. Gleaming white pelicans flap overhead. Sandhill cranes and great blue herons stalk the river banks, and northern harriers and red-tailed hawks hunt for rodents on the bottomlands.

Pick up a map at the refuge headquarters, off Wyo. 372, and then dawdle along the gravel roads that parallel the river. Most of the refuge is also open to hiking, and several boat landings make casual float trips possible. Though this is desert country, the place is remarkably comfortable if you can make or find shade, and you can always cool off in the Green.

During summer, look for moose calves in the willow thickets along the river and for mule deer fawns and nursery groups of pronghorn among the upland hills and hollows. Many types of songbirds, waterfowl, and raptors also raise their young on the refuge. During April, the impressive courtship displays of sage grouse take place among the sagebrush. Groups of both sexes gather at traditional sites called leks. The males strut about. Females choose from the group of males, mate, then leave to nest and rear the young alone. ■

Researchers prospecting for fossils at the Engelo Ranch, next to Fossil Butte NM

Fossil Butte National Monument

■ 8,198 acres ■ Southwest Wyoming, 14 miles west of Kemmerer on US 30 ■ Hiking ■ Contact the monument, P.O. Box 592, Kemmerer, WY 83101; phone 307-877-4455. www.nps.gov/fobu

ONE OF THE world's great mother lodes of fossils, Fossil Butte preserves part of an ancient lake bed where the remains of a startling variety of fish, reptiles, birds, mammals, insects, and plants have lain for 50 million years. Dry today and rising roughly 1,000 feet from its surrounding high-desert landscape, the butte records one of the most exquisitely detailed views we have of an Eocene ecosystem. Fish fossils, for example, often retain not only skeletons and teeth, but also scales and skin. The delicately webbed veins of leaves, the wings of insects, even the feathers of birds remain visible.

The large freshwater lake responsible for the fossils lay at the foot of a range of mountains long gone. In its waters swam at least 20 different species of fish, including big, toothy gars, stingrays, paddlefish, catfish, and great schools of small fish similar to modern herring. Turtles and crocodiles wallowed in the muck, and small horses, early primates,

Fossilization

The animals and plants that now appear as fossils at Fossil Butte settled to the bed of an Eocene lake roughly 50 million years ago. There, the remains were quickly buried in moist sediments that prevented weathering and excluded the oxygen and bacteria that would otherwise have led to decay. Instead, successive sedimentary layers sealed the remains and applied an increasing amount of pressure. Over time, what was once living tissue became dark brown rock.

snakes, and birds lived among a shoreline forest of palms, figs, and cypress. Among the foothills grew willows, beeches, oaks, and maples, and a spruce-fir forest cloaked the higher mountain slopes.

The remains of these and many other plants and animals now lie as dark, rock-hard fossils between layers of pale shale, like flowers pressed flat between the pages of a book. The most common fossils found among the layers of shale are of freshwater fishes that died and settled into the carbonate ooze on the lake bottom. They include mioplosus, an ancestor of the true perch which ate smaller fish along the reedy lakeshore and in slow-moving streams that fed into the lake. Another, knightia, was a small, herringlike fish that seems to have moved about in schools. It is, by far, the most common and widespread of the fish fossils found here. For some unknown reason, millions of them died over a short period, leaving fossils in densities of five to the square foot within what was the central portion of the lake.

Knightia compose one of the most impressive fossil murals at the **visitor center**—a great slab of shale bearing the remains of dozens of fish. Other fossils include an immense crocodile, a stingray, North America's oldest known fossil bat, and the leaves, stems, and flowers of many plants. Films and exhibits explain how the fossils were formed, discovered and prepared for display. Daily in summer, park staff offer guided hikes throughout the monument as well as engaging lectures that explain the site's geology, paleontology, biology, and history.

Two interpretive trails leave from the visitor center. The 2.5-mile **Historic Quarry Trail** meanders to an old fossil quarry on the face of Fossil Butte. Plaques describe how different layers in the rock were formed over the eons, as well as point out fossils still contained in the rock. The 1.5-mile **Fossil Lake Trail** winds through a high desert landscape—with plaques highlighting the plants and animals—to the bottom layers of the ancient lake bed.

Nearby, you can dig your own fossils at commercial quarries (*$35-$55 a day*), or buy them. **Ulrich's Fossil Gallery** (*307-877-6466*) near the monument's entrance is worth the stop just to browse through the exhibits. Depending on the size of the fossil and the type of shale embedded within, a single specimen can require five to five thousand hours of preparation time. ■

Palm frond fossil, Fossil Butte NM

Snake River Plain

THE SNAKE RIVER cuts across southern Idaho in a sweeping arc from the high forests of the Yellowstone plateau to the sun-drenched gorge called Hells Canyon. It starts in mountains above 9,000 feet and ends in one of the roughest terrains on earth, but for much of its 400-mile trip across Idaho it skirts a smooth plain that stands out as one of the largest and most obvious geographic features in the northern Rockies. The Snake River Plain looks like someone swiped a heavy thumb across the mountains from one side of the state to the other, turning the rough landscape into a flat smear.

In fact, that's almost what happened. Whatever mountains, valleys, lakes, and forests existed on the plain were wiped out by a series of volcanic eruptions and collapses starting around 17 million years ago in northern Nevada and progressing violently northeast across Idaho. The

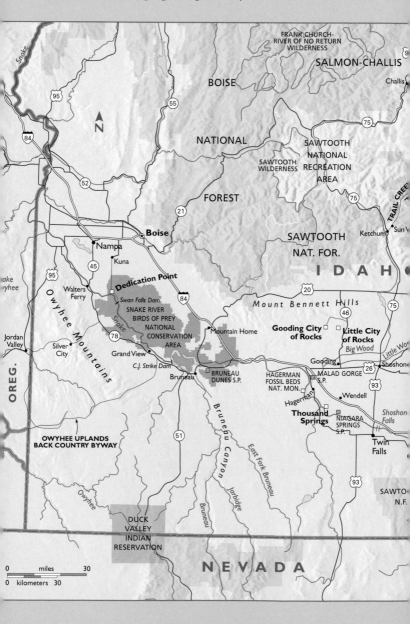

initial eruptions were all caused by the same phenomenon, a molten plume rising from the earth's mantle to just below the surface. It's called the Yellowstone hot spot because it currently lies under that national park (see pp. 21-22). When it bursts through the surface, its eruptions are the biggest ever known to have occurred in the world's history. The last one blackened the landscape 600,000 years ago. Once you know the story, you can see the

evidence of its passing in basalt formations throughout the region.

Although the hot spot appears to have migrated across Idaho, geologists tell us that it's actually a stationary body of molten lava over which the continent has drifted, rather like a sheet of plastic drawn slowly across the burner of a blowtorch. Uplift and earthquakes torture the earth's crust on the leading edge of the hot spot, while a burn trace lies in its wake. Yellowstone is the current active zone, and the Snake River Plain is the burn path.

One other big event left its mark on the modern landscape: the great Bonneville Flood. Some 15,000 years ago, at the height of the last ice age, prehistoric Lake Bonneville covered much of Utah; the Great Salt Lake is the shrunken remnant of that huge lake. Lacking an outlet, Lake Bonneville rose until it finally overtopped its rim at present Red Rock Pass north of Logan, Utah. Once it began flowing, the water swiftly cut an exit channel, lowering the lake level by 300 feet and sending a vast quantity of water rushing north to the Snake River. Flow levels reached 10 to 15 million cubic feet per second, three times the flow of the Amazon River. In its short but violent life, it carved channels, waterfalls, and narrow canyons in the basalt bedrock.

This chapter includes the Snake River, the volcanic plain through which it flows, and the neighboring mountains. The marquee site is Craters of the Moon National Monument, a strangely beautiful place where eruptions occurred a mere 2,100 years ago, and the ground seems hardly to have cooled. Almost everything in this region is off the beaten path—requiring some effort and maybe even some faith. Much of the year, this part of Idaho is a forbidding place. Summer heat can parboil your brain. Winter winds cut through clothing like razors. But if you spend a little time here, you come to appreciate a unique and sometimes strikingly beautiful geography.

Not all of southern Idaho is a volcanic plain. Sage-covered desert dominates much of the harsh upland landscape of the southwestern corner; it was built on basaltic outpourings that occurred long after the hot spot moved on. The Owyhee Mountains rise low and dry along the Oregon border, while the seemingly endless sage along the Nevada border is broken by deep canyons carved by the Bruneau, the Jarbidge, and the Owyhee Rivers. The southeastern corner, in contrast, is a green place with gentle mountain ranges, dense forest, and two important wildlife refuges, Grays Lake and Bear Lake. Also included are the fine but little known Lemhi, Lost River, and Pioneer mountain ranges northwest of Idaho Falls. Judging strictly from a map, it might seem that those mountains should belong to central Idaho, but in geologic terms they are part of the basin-and-range topography of Nevada and south-central Idaho.

The region has few grand displays of wildlife, but many small and interesting ones scattered across its many habitat types. Moose wade in the southeastern wetlands, pronghorn race through the sage near Arco, deer manage just about any environment. Migrating birds are seasonally abundant along the river corridors and at wetlands such as Mud Lake and American Falls Reservoir; nesting raptors draw visitors to the Snake River Birds of Prey National Conservation Area. Between horned lizards on the drylands and whooping cranes in the marshes, there's a lot to see. ■

Cove Creek near Hagerman

Craters of the Moon NM

■ 54,000 acres ■ Central Idaho, 18 miles southwest of Arco on US 20
■ Loop road closed to vehicles Nov.-March. Summer can be hot and windy;
most pleasant seasons are spring and fall ■ Camping, hiking, biking, bird-watching
■ Adm. fee ■ Contact the national monument, P.O. Box 29, Arco, ID 83213;
phone 208-527-3257. www.nps.gov/crmo

CRATERS OF THE Moon is a wonderful place to appreciate some of the
forces that shaped southern Idaho. Although the Yellowstone hot spot
passed through millions of years ago, the lava you see on the surface
spilled out within the last 15,000 years. During that time, a series of eruptions formed 25 volcanos and produced 60 different lava flows covering
618 square miles of the Snake River Plain. The most recent flows are only
2,100 years old—very young in geologic terms.

The eruptions are related to the tensional faulting that created, and
continues to create, the basin-and-range topography covering almost
all of Nevada and parts of surrounding states. The region is being pulled
apart. As it stretches, the crust breaks into long blocks along parallel fault

Big Crater, Craters of the Moon National Monument

lines. The blocks tilt, rising on one side to become mountains, sinking on the other side to form valleys. That process is evident on both sides of the Snake River Plain. To the north, it shows up in the Lemhi and Lost River Ranges, which stand as good examples of alternating basins and ranges.

As we've already seen, the Yellowstone hot spot destroyed the crust as it moved through. A 60-mile-long fracture zone called the Great Rift runs through Craters of the Moon. Here molten basalt made its strange and dramatic appearance through cracks in the earth's surface. Lava flowed, oozed, spattered, exploded, and shot upward in geyserlike fountains. It engulfed tree trunks, which burned out to form hollow molds. Ash and cinders fell like hard rain. The lava came up hot and glowing, cooled to a thin black skin, then broke open again to reveal its incandescent core. The skin shattered like pottery, or, if it stayed hot enough, it bent, stretched, and twisted like taffy before finally hardening. Rivers of lava pulsed beneath the hardening crust, and when the flows ebbed, they sometimes left behind long tunnels lined with drip structures.

More than 60 different lava flows make up the volcanic field at Craters of the Moon. Although the most recent in the area, they aren't by any means the only visible signs of volcanism. I-15 between Blackfoot and

Running on a lava field, Craters of the Moon NM

Idaho Falls and US 20 west of Idaho Falls are both cut through a young deposit called Hell's Half Acre. Nor can you help noticing Big Southern Butte, the distinctive landform directly east of the monument. It erupted some 300,000 years ago and is one of three such conelike domes of different ages and histories visible along US 20.

The names of lava formations are as interesting as the processes that made them: spatter cones, cinder cones, breadcrust bombs, spindle bombs, lava tubes, and more. All these are easily seen in the compact central zone of the monument, where a 7-mile loop drive winds through a sculpture garden of geologic special effects. Disney couldn't have designed it more efficiently.

Craters of the Moon is above all a geologic site focused on the weird and fascinating behavior of molten rock. But the monument also presents an interesting biological story. At best, life isn't easy here. It gets very cold in winter, with snows deep enough to lay a smooth white blanket that hides the rough lava. Summers are hot. Winds can be strong, and the 15 to 20 inches of annual precipitation vanishes quickly into the porous lava. Even so, what at first seems to be a slag-and-clinker wasteland turns out to be home to a sparse but thriving community of plants and animals. Lichens grow on smooth rock surfaces. Herbaceous plants send roots into the slightest of cracks. Miniature gardens sprout in the shelter of larger crevices. In areas of softer ground—cinder fields and places where windblown soil has accumulated—shrubs, grasses, and trees form the base of more complex communities that include limber pine, Douglas-fir, rabbit brush, big sagebrush, antelope bitterbrush, syringa, and cinquefoil. In spring, the black cinder fields are spangled with blossoms including dwarf monkey flower, buckwheat, bitterroot, blazing star, and Indian paintbrush. Owls roost in crevices and other shady places. Golden eagles, red-tailed hawks, American kestrels, and northern harriers hunt from above. There are coyotes, mule deer, marmots, chipmunks, voles, deer mice, ground squirrels, weasels—all told, 30 mammal species, 8 species of reptiles, 169 kinds of birds, more than 2,000 insect species, and about 375 different plants.

Craters of the Moon shows the amazing ability of living organisms to inhabit the harshest environments. However, it's worth pointing out that the soil covering much of the Snake River Plain—light colored and fine grained—is not the result of biologic action on hardened lava. Rather, it's loess, an unstratified deposit that, in this instance, is glacial sediment transported from the mountains by snowmelt and sorted by the wind.

What to See and Do

Monument Loop Drive

Start at the **visitor center** for a basic orientation to volcanoes and the behavior of lava. A film shows similar eruptions in Hawaii. Check the guided walk schedule if you'd like to take a ranger-led hike. Then head out on the loop road. First stop is the **North Crater Flow Trail,** which wanders over some of the younger flows. Among the more interesting features here are some large, jagged blocks of lava broken from a crater wall during an eruption and rafted by a lava flow to their current jumbled positions.

At **Devils Orchard,** a short loop trail wanders near more of these lava blocks in a field of cinders. Far from devilish, it resembles a naturally designed Japanese garden. Plants are few, but early summer wildflowers carpet the ground with a brief blaze of color.

For a high miles-wide view, climb the broad cinder-covered slope of **Inferno Cone,** or take the trail from Spatter Cones to **Big Crater.** From their summits, you can see a line of cinder cones that mark the Great Rift's northern end—probably the best and most instructive views in the park. Back on the loop road, and just over the

shoulder of Inferno Cone, another trail leads to the rim of a well-defined spatter cone. Peering into the vent, it's not hard to picture explosions throwing out blobs of lava tens of feet into the air to plop down around the periphery of the vent, building what appears to be a large-scale child's drip castle.

The loop road continues

Craters of the Moon
National Monument

Camping at Craters of the Moon National Monument

around the base of Inferno Cone to a 1-mile spur road that ends at a trailhead. There are two choices. One trail sets off southeast into the wilderness section of the park, which is open for camping (with free backcountry permits available at the visitor center); it's 3.5 miles following the line of the Great Rift to Echo Crater, and another mile to the trail's end. Then hikers must find their own way through the rough, broken volcanic cinders and flows. From the same trailhead, another route goes south to the **Tree Molds Area,** where you can see the hollow casts created when flowing lava enveloped trees.

From the last turnoff on the loop road, the **Caves Trail** leads to several lava tube caves within a half mile of the parking area. Take flashlights, good boots, and old clothes if you're interested in exploring underground. If not, it's still worthwhile to peer in from above, or to scramble in a short distance; the beginning of the trail is also a good place to see firsthand the differences between

types of lava. For example, the Hawaiian words *pahoehoe* and *aa* describe, respectively, ropy smooth lava and jagged, broken lava. **Indian Tunnel** has a stairway into its capacious interior—30 feet high and 80 feet wide. Breaks in the roof let in enough light that flashlights aren't needed. You can follow the tunnel 800 feet and climb out through a small opening at the other end, but watch your head—the lava stalactites are as sharp as daggers. **Boy Scout Cave** has a floor of ice, and **Beauty Cave** is big but dark.

More Exploring

If you crave further exploring, the opportunities are enormous. The monument occupies only the northern end of a huge lava wilderness stretched out along the Great Rift. Obviously, access is not easy, but with the help of the "Guide to the Great Rift and Snake River Plain," a detailed map available at the monument's visitor center or BLM offices, you can drive the Arco-Minidoka Road or the Carey-Kimama Desert Road to a number of interesting sites on the perimeters of the lava flows. Four-wheel drive isn't usually necessary for the maintained routes as identified on the BLM map, but this is not a place for RVs or for the unprepared. If you have a proper vehicle, you can go farther afield on numerous rugged side routes. One climbs to the top of **Big Southern Butte.** Another heads 8 miles south to the symmetrical crater called **China Cup Butte.** Among the more interesting and common features are *kipukas*—older vegetated areas surrounded by younger lava flows. Kipukas are the lava country equivalent of biologic islands—protected remnants of plant and animal communities that once covered much larger areas. Canoeing across the Pacific likely would be easier than struggling across an aa field to a kipuka.

One other site deserves mention. **Hell's Half Acre National Natural Landmark** (*on US 20 just W of Idaho Falls*) is an undeveloped curiosity stop with some interesting features. You park at the edge of the flow and climb up onto its broken surface. It takes only a few hundred yards to appreciate what an obstacle a flat lava field can be—and why so many plants and small animals do well here. It's a maze of fissures, caves, and broken passages that provide excellent shelter. A surprise on a hot day is the sight of green ferns growing 15 feet below the baking surface. But it's not impossible to move across; the surface here is mostly smoother, more negotiable pahoehoe. A trail sets off to a vent 4.5 miles south that was active just 5,200 years ago. At 750 feet long, it features a series of craters formed when lava receded back into the vent. ■

Airborne Hunters

Open, rugged terrain makes good country for red-tailed hawks that soar sky-high as they scan the ground for rodents, snakes, and lizards. However, not all raptors hunt by soaring. Peregrine falcons dive at speeds over 100 mph to strike birds in the air. The ferocity and speed of the attack makes it look as though the falcon has collided with its prey, which sometimes sends loose feathers flying. In fact, they strike with extended talons, ripping their prey and then picking it up off the ground or snatching it from the air before it hits. Kestrels, smallest of the North American falcons, hover several feet above the ground, holding themselves in one place with rapid, fluttering wing movements, then zipping off a hundred feet or so and hovering again; they move with the grace of hummingbirds and, while they occasionally take insects on the wing, they are generally looking for mice, grasshoppers, and sometimes small birds. Northern harriers exhibit low-flying aerobatics just above the ground—diving, swooping, and turning in an attempt to startle their prey. Yet much hunting is done from the vantage points of solid perches—high rocks and peaks, trees, telephone poles, even fences.

Life in the Lava Beds

HOT, DRY, AND RAKED by desiccating winds, the lava beds of the Snake River Plain confront animals and plants with a brutal environment where ground-level temperatures can reach over 150°F in summer. Survival demands adaptation. Most animals cope by laying low during the day and confining most of their activities to dawn, dusk, or the cool of the night. Some, such as the pocket mouse, require so little water that they obtain all they need from plants. Mule deer routinely live as far as 10 miles from open water and depend instead on water from forage, dew, fog, and puddles.

The best times to view wildlife on the lava beds are: one hour before sunrise and two hours after; late evening, up to three hours after sunset.

Plants tend to hug the ground, where wind velocities drop and where rocks cast small, protective shadows. Their short stature also requires less moisture, fewer nutrients, and (in the case of annuals) a shorter growing season. Some plants, such as dwarf monkey flower, remain dormant as seeds for 95 percent of the year and burst forth for a few sweet, springtime weeks to germinate, sprout, leaf, bloom, set seed, and die. Others, such as cactus, store moisture in fleshy tissues protected by a waxy coating. Dwarf buckwheat retains moisture and nutrients in a widespread root system. Hairy surfaces on scorpionweed and other plants reduce evaporation by diffusing sunlight and inhibiting air flow. A few surprising species, including ferns and mosses, find suitable microhabitats in deep cracks and crevices near persistent water sources such as potholes and ice caves. ■

Lava bed at Craters of the Moon National Monu

Pioneer Mountains and the Lost River and Lemhi Ranges

■ Central Idaho, northwest of Idaho Falls via US 20/26/93 ■ Best months May-Oct. Snow blocks the high country into July ■ Camping, hiking ■ Contact Lost River Ranger District, Salmon-Challis National Forest, Box 507, Mackay, ID 83251; phone 208-588-2224. www.fs.fed.us/r4/sc

AT 12,662 FEET, **Borah Peak** is the highest point in Idaho, but it is only one of nine 12,000-foot summits in the Lost River Range. These high peaks form an imposing rampart above the town of Mackay. Seeing them from there, you wonder why they aren't more famous. Only their relative remoteness can explain why so few people know about them.

The same is true of the neighboring mountains in this unsung corner of Idaho. The lake-strewn Pioneer Mountains (best known from the Sun Valley side), the mineral-rich **White Knob Mountains,** the colorful lava-painted **Pahsimeroi Mountains,** and the Lemhi Range all have areas of outstanding natural beauty. Together with the Lost River Range they form three parallel crests trending northwest-southeast, separated by broad sage-filled valleys. They contain no designated scenic attractions, wilderness areas, or parks, and the few people who know these mountains are just as happy for the lack of advertising.

This is classic old-time Idaho ranch country: hayfields in the bottoms, sage on the lower mountain slopes, timber on the higher slopes, and bare rock or snow on the summits. Mining has affected some areas, notably in the White Knob Mountains, but the boom days are long gone. Pronghorn and elk easily outnumber permanent human residents. The Pahsimeroi and Little Lost River Valleys (between the Lemhi and Lost River Ranges) are home to Idaho's largest pronghorn population. In addition to elk, mule deer, and black bears, the Lemhi Range also sustains a population of mountain goats.

These ranges represent the northeastern edge of basin-and-range topography—the repeating pattern of broad valleys slung between parallel mountain ranges. The process is still active, as demonstrated by a 1983 earthquake that pushed the Lost River Range a foot higher and

Pioneer Backcountry

For a scenic backcountry sample of the Pioneer Mountains, consider a driving and hiking combination to a subalpine lakes basin. Starting at Arco, follow US 93 north for 11 miles to Antelope Creek Road, then follow signs for 25 miles to a trailhead 2 miles beyond Iron Bog Campground. Getting to Iron Bog Lake takes one to two hours of moderate uphill hiking; Fishpole and several other small lakes are a short distance beyond.

Thousand Springs Creek, upper Big Lost River Valley

Pronghorn

The wide-open, sage-covered valleys of southern Idaho favor animals small enough to hide under bushes or fast enough to escape danger. Among the fast ones, no North American land animal is speedier than the pronghorn. They travel quickly by incorporating leaps into their running that can vary in length between 11 and 19 feet. With their front feet carrying most of the weight, they move at a top speed in excess of 53 mph and sustained speeds of about 29 mph.

caused the adjacent valley to drop 7.5 feet. Centered beneath Borah Peak, the magnitude 7.3 quake was big enough to shake the entire region. Witnesses at the epicenter heard a rumbling that sounded like a low-altitude flyover by jet planes and saw the fracture rip down the valley. A woman standing near the fault line suffered whiplash. Two children were killed by falling debris in Challis. The scarp runs across the base of the range and is dramatically visible north of Mackay. It looks like a crack in pottery.

Three peculiar rivers flow south from between the ranges. The **Big Lost River** begins like a conventional mountain stream high in the Pioneer Mountains, but strange things happen on its downhill journey. It flows northeast into the valley of its name, where it is fed by a large wildlife-filled marshy expanse called **Thousand Springs Valley.** Those uncountable springs never really develop a defined channel en route to the river. On a map the whole system looks like someone spilled a bucket of little blue worms. Crawling every which way, they don't connect. Tributary streams come out of the mountains and disappear into alluvial fans or irrigation ditches. Finally, beyond Arco, the Big Lost hits the lava fields of the

Cottonwood leaves in autumn

Preceding pages: Field of subalpine daisy and Indian paintbrush, Pioneer Mountains

Snake River Plain and meets riverine disaster. Spreading out across another marshy area, it completely disappears—sucked dry by the porous lava.

The same fate greets the Little Lost River on the east side of the Lost River Range; and Birch Creek, on the east side of the Lemhi Range. Of course the water of these three rivers is not forever lost. It goes underground to join the Snake River Plain aquifer, a vast reservoir fed by the runoff from 35,000 square miles of surrounding mountains and forest, and estimated by geologists to hold as much water as Lake Erie. The aquifer is heavily used—maybe overused—by pump irrigation. A substantial volume of its water returns to the surface at another Thousand Springs along the Snake River west of Twin Falls.

What to See and Do

These mountains are a place for self-directed exploring. Tips can be had from ranger stations in Ketchum, Mackay, and Challis, but the best thing to do here is pick up a forest service map and head out. Keep in mind that except for the Pioneer and White Knob Mountains, which run together, the ranges have narrow crests. It's essentially up one side and down the other, with few interior alpine valleys.

Hiking destinations are usually peaks or high ridges. Except in the Pioneer Mountains, lakes are few. Vigorous hikers might start with an ascent of **Borah Peak.** A climb of 5,100 vertical feet in 3.5 miles, it can be accomplished in a long day of hiking with some scrambling on steep rock near the summit. The trailhead is 21 miles north of Mackay on US 93. If you're in that area, don't pass up the **Borah Peak Earthquake Interpretive Site** (23 miles N of Mackay), where you can put your hand on the scarp and learn about the event from interpretive signs.

One of the most interesting backcountry roads climbs through **Pass Creek Narrows,** a gnarled slot between high walls of twisted limestone at the south end of the Lost River Range. The creek tumbles down the gorge in the shade of large Douglas-fir trees beside meadows of wildflowers. Colum-bine and iris mingle their roots with willows along the creek bed. Forget-me-nots and cinque-foil grow in drier areas. Up among the crags, rock wrens and junipers live in a vertical desert.

Conditions are quite different in the Pioneers. Most people see these mountains as a sharp line of high peaks above Sun Valley. They are more approachable on their less-steep eastern slope, via Trail Creek Road that runs over the range from Ketchum to US 93. About 10 miles east of Trail Creek Summit, Forest Road 135 (also called East Fork Rd.) follows the East Fork Big Lost River into **Copper Basin.** On its south side, there's a fine collection of alpine lakes among the sharp ridges of the Pioneers. Hike in from Bellas Canyon, Broad Canyon, or Starhope (which also has a campground). Distances are short enough for day hiking. ∎

Fishing on the South Fork

South Fork Snake River

- 64 miles long ■ Eastern Idaho, downstream of Palisades Reservoir
- Best months June-Oct. Best fishing at lower water levels Aug.-Oct.
- Boating, fishing, wildlife viewing ■ Parking fee ■ Contact Palisades Ranger District, Targhee National Forest, 3659 E. Pine Hwy., Idaho Falls, ID 83401; phone 208-523-1412. www.fs.fed.us/tnf/

SNAKE RIVER NOMENCLATURE is a bit confusing. In this case, the South Fork is the main branch, the one that starts in Wyoming and flows past the Tetons. In Idaho they call it the South Fork to distinguish it from the Henrys Fork, which begins in the Island Park area just west of Yellowstone (see pp. 44-45). The two forks join near Menan, and from then on, no one calls the river anything but the Snake. In Idaho, the South Fork flows between Palisades Dam and Menan. Clear and cold, it's a famous trout stream. It's also a good scenic trip with a strong current but no significant rapids. Cold and green, it passes through one of the country's largest remaining cottonwood forests, a rich bottomland inhabited by bald eagles, ospreys, deer, moose, river otters, beavers, and waterbirds.

Primary access ramps on the upper stretch include the Palisades Dam, Irwin, the US 26 highway bridge, and Conant Valley. Distances between these are short enough for day trips. Below Conant Valley, however, it's 24 miles through a near-wilderness canyon to a ramp at Byington Park. This stretch can be done in one long day, but the best plan is to camp out a night or two in the cottonwood bottoms; much of the land is publicly owned.

To float just a portion of the canyon, launch canoes and other hand-carried craft at numerous intermediate points. Fullmer boat ramp is located off Forest Road 206, which runs along the north bank for about 10 miles; get there via Kelly Canyon. It's wise to ask for directions and advice at local fly shops. ■

Grays Lake and Bear Lake National Wildlife Refuges

■ 18,300 acres (Grays Lake), 18,000 acres (Bear Lake) ■ Southeast Idaho, north and south of Soda Springs ■ Access to northern half of Grays Lake allowed mid-Oct.–March only, observation tower open year-round. Best seasons for bird-watching spring and fall ■ Hiking, canoeing, auto tour, and fishing at Bear Lake; restricted hiking only at Grays Lake ■ Contact Grays Lake NWR, 74 Grays Lake Rd., Wayan, ID 83285-5003, phone 208-574-2755. Bear Lake NWR, 370 Webster St., Montpelier, ID 83254, phone 208-847-1757

IF WILDLIFE REFUGES have signature species, then Bear Lake owns autograph rights for its great numbers of white-faced ibises. Medium-size wading birds, their long, curved bills give them an exotic appearance, like something you'd expect to see in Africa. At Grays Lake, the taller, stately sandhill cranes are the chief draw, but both refuges are treasure troves of flying, wading, nesting, and chattering waterfowl.

Grays Lake National Wildlife Refuge is the larger and more remote of the two. A big marshy area ringed by the Caribou and Gray Ranges, it's about 35 miles north of Soda Springs on Idaho 34, then 3 miles north on graveled Grays Lake Road. The observation tower at refuge headquarters is a good place to mount your spotting scope. Otherwise, drive the county roads that circle the giant wetland.

Sandhill cranes are among the spring wonders of Idaho's eastern mountains. Some 200 pairs nest at Grays Lake, while others nest in the surrounding region and even more pass through in spring and fall. On their spring migration, they gather in meadows and stream bottoms throughout the area, where they feed and practice their elaborate, graceful mating dances. In the fall you can hear their clattering calls sent down from great heights as they soar and wheel in the sky. In addition to cranes, look for trumpeter swans, Franklin's gulls, eared and western grebes, black terns, Canada geese, white-faced ibises, and various hawks including that low-altitude flier once called a marsh hawk but now officially the northern harrier.

Bear Lake National Wildlife Refuge occupies Dingle Swamp immediately north of the Big Lake Recreation Area. The lake is lined with cabins and doesn't feel very wild. That doesn't seem to deter the birds, many of which nest in the 18,000-acre refuge but feed throughout the valley. In addition to about 4,000 ibises are great blue herons, black-crowned night-herons, snowy egrets, avocets, willets, Canada geese, redhead ducks, cinnamon teals, Franklin's gulls, California gulls, three species of grebes, and white pelicans. Some nest here, some are seasonal transients. To reach the refuge headquarters, drive 2.5 miles west of Montpelier on US 89, then at the Bear Lake sign, go 5 miles south on a gravel road. You can view birds along the auto tour route and from hiking trails on refuge dikes. Canoeing permitted from September 24 until the lake is frozen. ■

Snake River near Massacre Rocks State Park

Massacre Rocks State Park

■ 995 acres ■ Southern Idaho, 12 miles west of American Falls on I-86
■ Camping, hiking, boating, fishing, bird-watching ■ Adm. fee ■ Contact Idaho
Department of Parks and Recreation, 3592 N. Park Lane, American Falls, ID
83211; phone 208-548-2672. www.idahoparks.org/parks/massacre.html

PINCHED BETWEEN I-86 and the Snake River, Massacre Rocks is an easy
place to speed past, thinking it's nothing but a rest stop. On the contrary,
it's an interesting natural and historic area. The history is a bit cloudy.
According to old journals, Massacre Rocks was the scene of an 1862 fight
between Shoshone and immigrants on the Oregon Trail. In fact, although
the rocks might have made a likely ambush site, the incident in question
happened 4 miles east in a less dramatic setting. These rocks are innocent.

They do, however, have a history. The bedrock is volcanic agglomer-
ate, a combination of ash and little chunks of basalt. On top of it lie big
angular basalt boulders torn loose from the canyon walls by the Bonneville Flood. They help illustrate the tremendous force of that epic
flood. The **visitor center** offers displays and publications relevant to natural history. The well-presented **Yahandeka Nature Trail** starts at the visitor center and winds a quarter mile through the rocks nearby. It points
out features of geology and identifies dominant plants and animals. Massacre Rocks is a well known birding site, with a list of over 200 species.
Bird-watchers should spend some time along the river, where riparian
and high desert habitats come together. Several islands within binocular
and spotting scope range provide cover for birds and other animals. ■

City of Rocks National Reserve

■ 14,300 acres ■ Southern Idaho, south of Burley on City of Rocks Road
■ Best months April-Oct., spring and fall storms can bring harsh weather
■ Camping, hiking, mountain climbing, rock climbing, bird-watching ■ Private
land interspersed with public land requires awareness on the part of visitors
■ Contact the reserve, P.O. Box 169, Almo, ID 83312; phone 208-824-5519.
www.nps.gov/ciro

IN A REGION dominated by dark volcanic deposits, the white spires at City
of Rocks provide pleasing visual relief. Sticking out like old bones at the
south end of the Albion Mountains, they rise from 100 to 600 vertical
feet in a variety of shapes, almost all of which are steep sided and craggy.
The stone is Cassia granite, about 25 million years old. When cracked and
exposed to weather, it erodes to form the rounded pinnacles, arches, and
overhanging shapes for which City of Rocks is famous. From a distance,
the formations look smoothly polished. But when you get close, you find
a rough surface covered with sharp quartz crystals. This combination of
clean lines and a high-friction surface makes for superb rock climbing. In
fact, the city was a climber's mecca long before 1988 when it became a park.

City of Rocks is a delightful place for hiking. It has the feel of
an eccentric garden, where footpaths of naturally white gravel wander
through a three-dimensional playground. Each alcove or canyon has
its own setting of trees and wildflowers framed by a unique stone
skyline. With more than 3,000 feet of vertical relief, the park sports
a wide range of vegetation types and their associated wildlife. Douglas-
fir, alpine fir, and lodgepole and limber pine dominate the higher areas.
Sagebrush, pinyon pine, and juniper occupy lower elevations. Aspens
and mountain mahogany live in the middle. Mule deer are commonly
seen. Elk are also present, along with mountain lions, badgers, bobcats,
coyotes, porcupines, and smaller mammals. As for birds, the mix
of vegetation—more than 450 plant species—and intricate stone
landscape provides excellent habitat. You don't have to go very far
to see a lot.

Administered jointly by the National Park Service and the Idaho
Department of Parks and Recreation, about half of the reserve is
privately owned. Camping is limited to designated, primitive sites.
Roads are gravel. The Almo Entrance Road splits with the right branch
climbing through a dense concentration of spires to **Emery Canyon.**
The left branch stays lower, following the approximate route of the historic **California Trail,** whose ruts are still visible in places. Immigrants
came this way beginning in 1843. Many remarked on the rocks' unusual
beauty, and some left inscriptions. Of special interest on this branch are
the **Twin Sisters,** a pair of fangs made from stone of vastly different ages.
The lighter one is Cassia granite, about 25 million years old, the darker
one is 2.5 billion years old. Side by side, they illustrate the great equaliz-
ing force of weather and time. ■

Niagara Springs State Park

■ 179 acres ■ Southern Idaho, northwest of Twin Falls, off I-84 at
Wendell ■ Closed Dec.-Feb. ■ Camping, boating, fishing, bird-watching
■ Adm. fee ■ Contact Idaho Department of Parks and Recreation, 1074
E. Hagerman, ID 83332; phone 208-837-4505 or 208-536-5522 in summer

NORTH AND WEST OF TWIN FALLS, the dark basalt cliffs along the Snake
River sprout a wonder of nature. The many rivers and streams absorbed
by the porous Snake River Plain miles to the north and east resurface in
terraced, frothing cascades called **Thousand Springs.** The number is no
exaggeration: Small rivers pouring from the canyon walls through dense
hanging gardens is something to experience, and it's a pity that more
of them were not preserved in a natural state. Niagara Springs is one
of America's largest cold springs by volume, and the Thousand Springs
network of which it is part may be the largest in the country. Unfortunately, much of the network's water has been claimed for irrigation,
power generation, and fish hatcheries. These development projects,
together with limited road access, have made it so difficult to appreciate
this natural treasure that few travelers realize that the springs exist at all.
However, at least one superb little site serves as an example of what might
have been. At Niagara Springs, about 250 cubic feet per second of pure,
clear water burst from the basalt cliffs and create a green, watery paradise.

The 179-acre state park adjoins a 957-acre state wildlife management
area. Together, the two areas contain a number of springs, about 3.5 miles
of Snake River frontage, and eight river islands. During some years,
irrigation demands can reduce the Snake to a tiny trickle above Twin
Falls, and the famous Shoshone Falls becomes Shoshone Walls. Then a few
miles downstream, water from Thousand Springs gives the river new life.

In summer, waterbirds crowd the river. The riparian woodland shelters
mule deer, skunks, bobcats, and small rodents. You can see steelhead trout
at a state hatchery and try catching other species in **Crystal Springs Lake.**
To get there, turn off I-84 at the Wendell exit. Head straight south several
miles to the canyon rim, where a narrow, steep road (not recommended
for large RVs) drops 350 vertical feet to the park. ■

Underground Reservoir

Flowing through porous
basalt and sedimentary layers,
the Snake River Plain aquifer
is one of America's most
productive. Its water, from
nearby mountain basins,
flows through an aquifer 200
miles long and 50 to 70 miles
wide. Some 800,000 acres of
cropland in central Idaho are
irrigated from deep wells.
Some water seeps back into
the earth, but the groundwater is being depleted faster
than natural sources can recharge it. In some places the
aquifer level has dropped 17
feet since 1987.

Niagara Springs, in the
Thousand Springs area near Hagerman

Malad Gorge State Park

■ 653 acres ■ Southern Idaho, north of Hagerman off I-84 ■ Hiking, biking,
bird-watching ■ Contact Idaho Department of Parks and Recreation,
1074 E. 2350 S., Hagerman, ID 83332; phone 208-837-4505

ABOVE THE SNAKE River just downstream from Hagerman, a deep gorge
slices through the high basalt cliffs. Within the gorge, clear springs add
their water to the upper reaches of the Malad River, which tumbles over
waterfalls and boulders on its way to joining the Snake. About 2.5 miles
long, the gorge narrows toward its upper end, where it becomes a forbidding slot 250 feet deep.

The state park occupies the rim. Roads and trails wander among
various overlooks. The best vantage point is from the middle of a steel
footbridge spanning the narrows. It's a very solid bridge, but a queasy
feeling comes naturally as you peer straight down into the **Devils Wash-
bowl,** a 60-foot waterfall plunging into a large round pool. Across the
footbridge, trails continue along the rim. Or follow the park road west
along the southern rim to the mouth of the gorge. From there you can
see an array of geologic features from interpretive overlooks. The most
direct way to get there is from the interstate, at the Tuttle exit. The more
interesting way is from the **Thousand Springs Scenic Byway** on US 30.
On the outskirts of Hagerman, take the Justice Grade Road to the top
of the bluffs and watch for signs to the park. ■

Hagerman Fossil Beds NM

■ 4,281 acres ■ Southern Idaho, east of Hagerman ■ Hiking, mountain biking,
horseback riding, auto tour ■ Contact the national monument, Box 570,
Hagerman, ID 83332; phone 208-837-4793. www.nps.gov/hafo

TODAY THERE ARE bluffs rising 600 feet above the Snake River, covered
with sagebrush, rabbitbrush, and other high desert plants. But three
to four million years ago these layers of shale, clay, and sand were being
deposited by ancient floods. It was a moist landscape of ponds, riverside
trees, and grassy plains inhabited by creatures long gone from North
America: saber-toothed cats, mastodons, camels, llamas, ground sloths,
and hyenalike dogs (also many familiar creatures like beavers, otters, and
frogs). Fossils of these and others—more than 120 animal species (including 8 found nowhere else) and 35 plant species—lie buried and preserved
in one of the nation's most important records of the Pliocene epoch.

A self-guided, 22-mile auto tour starting at the Hagerman visitor center *(221 N. State St. Closed Labor Day–Mem. Day)* visits the river, then
crosses it and climbs the bluffs. The tour, which takes about two hours,
provides views of the river valley, with the accompanying text telling the
story of fossils, the changing landscape, and local history. ■

Playing on the dunes at Bruneau Dunes State Park

Bruneau Dunes State Park

■ 4,800 acres ■ Southwest Idaho, south of Mountain Home on Idaho 78
■ Spring and fall are the best seasons; summer can be very hot ■ Adm. fee
■ Camping, hiking, boating, fishing, bird-watching ■ Contact the park, HC 85,
Box 41, Mountain Home, ID 83647; phone 208-366-7919

SHELTERED IN AN amphitheater of volcanic cliffs, the Bruneau dune field
is small—around 600 acres—but strikingly beautiful. Its 470-foot-tall
central dune is said to be the highest single-structured dune in North
America. This evidently refers to the way it rises in one unbroken slope
to its sharp crest. It is a lovely sweep of sand, and a worthwhile hike to
the top, but another feature makes these dunes truly unusual. Several
lakes and ponds, ringed by cottonwood trees and cattails, and filled with
bass and bluegills and waterfowl, shimmer at the base of the primary
dune. The combination of desert sand and cool water gives Bruneau
Dunes the atmosphere of a Saharan oasis, especially on summer days
when temperatures may rise above 100°F.

The dunes have been here for about 12,000 years, since the end of
the last ice age. The sand has been trapped in a dry meander of the Snake
River by winds that blow almost equally in opposite directions—from
the southeast and the northwest. The water, however, is a more recent
and not entirely natural development. It appeared after the nearby C. J.
Strike Dam was built across the Snake River in 1954. Its reservoir raised
the local water table, causing lakes to appear in the depressions around
the dunes. The park now augments water levels by pumping water from
the Snake River into the lakes.

Beyond the live dunes, the majority of this park is high desert dominated by sagebrush and rabbit brush, a prickly place inhabited by hardy

creatures. Among the reptiles: gopher snakes, blue racers, western hognose snakes, striped whip snakes, occasional Great Basin rattlesnakes, horned lizards, and western fence lizards. Mammals include black-tailed jackrabbits, coyotes, badgers, deer, kangaroo rats, and pocket mice. You don't see the ground animals very often, but there's usually a raptor somewhere in the sky. Red-tailed hawks, turkey vultures, ravens, golden eagles, northern harriers, burrowing owls, screech owls, and great horned owls are a few of the birds that hunt prey among the sagebrush.

To reach the park, follow Idaho 51 south of Mountain Home for 16 miles, then go east 2 miles on Idaho 78. Start at the **visitor center** near the park entrance, which offers good displays of native plants and animals, along with a collection of fossils. These include a huge mammoth femur, a saber-toothed cat skull, the bones of camels and giant ground sloths, and a 6-foot-long minnow; also turtle shells, pine nuts, pinecones, petrified wood, trilobites, and more. All but the mammoth bones were recovered from lake bed deposits within 50 miles of the park; they are unrelated to the dunes.

Climbing the dunes is a rewarding experience. Visually deceptive, they appear taller than they actually are, but because the sand slides down with every step, you end up climbing farther than you expected. Starting at the lake, you can be to the top of the large dune complex and back in about an hour. Although it looks like one long dune with an undulating crest, there are actually two primary dunes, joined at a low point. Here you'll find one of the park's more interesting features—a windblown crater, or funnel of sand, that goes all the way to the ground. If you hike to its bottom, you can look up and see nothing but a circle of sky.

Nature trails loop around the high dunes, the wetlands, and the surrounding desert, which includes areas of smaller dunes, some overgrown with vegetation. Blowing sand can hide the trails, and it's easy to get turned around, but the area is too small to get lost in. The big dunes are always in sight, and a relatively short hike will take you through a variety of micro-landscapes.

The lake is open to swimming, fishing, and nonmotorized boats. The picnic areas and campground have shade trees to provide relief in the blistering summer heat. ∎

Bruneau Dune Field

A dune field is a collection of dunes with sharply defined borders. Its growth and migration are dependent upon sand supply, wind power, wind direction, trap efficiency, and time. "Transverse" dunes form ridges perpendicular to winds that blow almost constantly from one direction. As they migrate farther from the original source of sand, the dunes break into smaller, crescent-shaped dunes called "barchans." You can see a few barchans at the Bruneau dune field in the area that is called Little Sahara.

Rafting in the Owyhee River Canyon

Owyhee Canyonlands

■ Southwest Idaho, via Idaho 51 and Idaho 78 ■ Spring is best season; summer can be very hot and dry ■ Undeveloped camping, hiking, boating, mountain biking, bird-watching ■ Contact the Bureau of Land Management, 3948 Development Ave., Boise, ID 83705; 208-384-3300

OWYHEE IS AN early spelling of Hawaii. If the name seems far removed from the tropical islands, southwest Idaho must have seemed like the other side of the world to the South Pacific islanders who disappeared here in 1818 on a trapping expedition. This is Idaho's lost corner, a windy, sagebrush-covered upland built on volcanic outpourings, the domain of hawks, bighorn sheep, coyotes, and pronghorn. Seen from the only paved road that crosses it, Idaho 51, the high desert rolls to the horizon. But the topography is far rougher than it appears. A network of sheer-walled canyons slices through the plateau. These are the handiwork of three main rivers, the Owyhee, Bruneau, and Jarbidge, and their numerous tributaries. With their many branches sunk like veins in a leaf, the canyons are riparian gems loaded with green vegetation and animal life. They're also nearly impossible to traverse. Hiking is difficult, and for most of the year there isn't enough water for boating. With challenging white water and a season that lasts only a few weeks, a run of the Bruneau is a rare treat, one that requires a combination of advance planning and flexibility.

The rough topography limits access to this area. Ordinary vehicles can make it to a viewpoint overlooking **Bruneau Canyon** on the rough gravel road that heads south from Bruneau. In dry weather the 101-mile **Owyhee Uplands Back Country Byway** is also suitable for most vehicles. It leads from US 95 at Jordan Valley, Oregon, to Idaho 78 near Grand View, Idaho, past sheer canyons and mountain slopes at the base of the Owyhee Mountains. Rocky back roads cross the Owyhees through ghost towns like **Silver City;** be sure to load up on supplies and detailed maps. ■

Following pages: Meadow of lupine and balsamroot, Bighorn National Forest

Hawk and babies at Snake River Birds of Prey NCA
Preceding pages:
Gooding City of Rocks

Snake River Birds of Prey National Conservation Area

■ 484,873 acres ■ Southwestern Idaho, south of Nampa ■ Peak birding in May and June ■ Camping, hiking, boating on the Snake River, fishing, bird-watching ■ Contact BLM, 3941 Development Ave., Boise, ID 83705; phone 208-384-3300

FOR 81 MILES near Idaho's western border, the Snake River flows beneath high basalt walls that make excellent nesting habitat for birds of prey. Several hundred pairs of raptors nest here in the spring. They include golden eagles, prairie falcons, peregrine falcons, ferruginous hawks, Swainson's and red-tailed hawks, northern harriers, American kestrels, burrowing owls, long-eared owls, great horned owls, and more. Many species nest in the cliffs, while other species nest on the ground; they hunt ground squirrels, black-tailed jackrabbits, and other small animals in the neighboring high desert rangelands.

Access points along the rim are limited. You can drive to **Dedication Point** *(16 miles S of Kuna on Swan Falls Rd.)* and from there down to the river below Swan Falls Dam. However, the most rewarding way to see the canyon is from a canoe or raft. The 20-mile float from Black Butte to Swan Falls is best done as an overnight trip; there are no rapids. From Swan Falls to Celebration Park *(10 miles)* or Walter's Ferry *(16 miles)* is a suitable day trip that includes two Class II rapids; the shuttle for this stretch is an easy 1.5 hours. Check with the BLM for maps.

The best way to see birds is on guided trips with local experts. Ask the BLM about them or better yet, get a recommendation in Boise at the **World Center for Birds of Prey** *(566 W. Flying Hawk Ln., Boise, ID 83709. 208-362-8687)*. The facility, headquarters of the Peregrine Fund, does work in research and breeding and operates an excellent interpretive center. The big attraction is seeing raptors that include Harpy eagles and a California condor. The docents bring live birds into the center for an up-close look; there are also many interactive exhibits oriented toward children. ∎

Checking a raven's nest

Gooding City of Rocks

∎ Southern Idaho, north of Gooding off Idaho 46 ∎ Spring offers best chance of finding surface water. All roads impassable in winter and wet weather ∎ Undeveloped camping, hiking, mountain biking, bird-watching ∎ Contact Shoshone Resource Area Office, Upper Snake River District, Bureau of Land Management, P.O. Box 2-B, Shoshone, ID 83352; phone 208-886-2206

TO SOME EYES, the strange shapes eroded from dark volcanic tuff resemble the abandoned, crumbling ruins of an ancient city. If so, its residents preferred fanciful architecture. Columns, spires, windows, flying arches, and bulbous monuments crowd canyon streets to form an eccentric badlands roughly 4 miles long and 8 miles wide on the south side of the Mount Bennett Hills. Fifty years ago, if the old guidebooks are right, this was a popular picnic site for locals. Today, raptors, snakes, and small mammals far outnumber visitors. Two gorges (**Coyote** and **Dry Creeks**) and their many canyons slice through the formations, and provide impressive panoramic views. Hiking is necessary to see the better parts, but there are no trails, so be careful to stay oriented. Rough roads lead around the perimeter but cannot penetrate far; they make for exceptional mountain biking and hiking. For a taste of similar topography at a more accessible and more frequently visited location, check out **Little City of Rocks,** 14 miles north of Gooding via Idaho 46 *(follow BLM signs at road junctions)*.

To reach Gooding City of Rocks, follow Idaho 46 for 18 miles north of Gooding; then, just past Flattop Butte, go west 9 miles on primitive roads *(follow BLM signs)*. ∎

Central Idaho Rivers and Batholiths

Marina at Redfish Lake, Idaho

CENTRAL IDAHO owns the most complex geography in this book. Unlike most places in the Rockies, where mountain crests are well defined and tend to run north-south, the only trend in this landscape is confusion. It's a country of convolutions, a great and delightful topographic puzzle, which, no matter how hard you study the maps, walk the trails, or float the rivers, never quite makes sense. Rivers and creeks take sudden, unpredictable turns. Even the region's main drainage, the Salmon River, scrapes its belly, grinds its teeth, and works up a white froth as it seeks a way through the wilderness. It flows north, then east, then north again before heading west. The region's complexities apparently confounded the efforts even of the pioneers, who tried to name the rivers in geographic order but failed in their search for clarity. For example, the South Fork Salmon begins north of headwaters for both the Middle Fork and main Salmon, and the East Fork is more southerly yet. Of course, there's also the East Fork South Fork Salmon, and what are we to make of the East Fork Lake Fork North Fork Payette, except to acknowledge the eccentric behavior of water in the company of hard old rock?

This region measures about 200 by 150 miles, from the dry desert rim of the Snake River Plain on the south to the misty forests of the Lochsa River Valley on the north. The continent's deepest gorge—Hells Canyon—marks its western boundary, and for reasons of shared geology, the region also includes a slice of western Montana.

Within those perimeters, three wilderness areas—the Frank Church-River of No Return, the Selway-Bitterroot, and the Gospel Hump—comprise almost four million acres of virtually continuous pristine land. Other major protected areas include the Sawtooth and Hells Canyon National Recreation Areas, each containing substantial designated wilderness areas, and the Anaconda-Pintler Wilderness in Montana. Eight national forests (Clearwater, Nez Perce, Payette, Boise, Sawtooth, Salmon-Challis, Bitterroot, Beaverhead-Deerlodge)

FLATHEAD
INDIAN
RESERVATION

FLATHEAD
NATIONAL
FOREST

LEWIS & CLARK
NATIONAL
FOREST

BOB
MARSHALL
WILDERNESS

Continental Divide

287

CONTINENTAL
DIVIDE
NATIONAL
SCENIC
TRAIL

Clark Fork

200

90

NATIONAL
BISON RANGE

93

LOLO

SCAPEGOAT
WILDERNESS

HELENA

LOLO
NATIONAL
FOREST

83

RATTLESNAKE
N.R.A.

Missoula

200

ARWATER

NATIONAL

FOREST

Lolo

90

M O N T A N A

NATIONAL

ATIONAL
LOLO
RWAY

500

Lolo Pass
5,233 ft

12

Sapphire Mountains

12

FOREST

OREST

Powell

360

12

LEE
METCALF
N.W.R.

93

1

GRANT-KOHRS
RANCH
N.H.S.

15

Lochsa

arwater

Selway Crags

Bitterroot

Hamilton

Georgetown L.

BEAVERHEAD-

Anaconda

ANACONDA-
PINTLAR
WILDERNESS

W. Goat Peak
+10,783 ft

Butte

SELWAY-
BITTERROOT
WILDERNESS

429

L. Como Darby

BITTERROOT

ay
alls

Selway

untains

RCE
k City

Paradise

Trapper Pk.
10,157 ft

Anaconda Range

DEERLODGE

Wise River

43

Pioneer Mts.

Wise

468

OREST

NATIONAL FOREST

BIG HOLE NAT.
BATTLEFIELD

NATIONAL

Big Hole

Coolidge

Beaverhead

almon

North
Fork

Shoup
Corn Cr.

Elkhorn
Hot
Springs

484

FRANK CHURCH-
RIVER OF

NO RETURN

WILDERNESS

SALMON-CHALLIS

Salmon

FOREST

278

Dillon

Salmon

River

NATIONAL

FOREST

Middle Fork

93

28

Lemhi Pass
7,373 ft

324

Clark
Canyon
Reservoir

15

N

Mountains

Salmon

SALMON RIVER
SCENIC BYWAY

Lemhi

Leadore

Red Rock

I D A H O

Challis

75

28

TARGHEE

21

Sunbeam

93

Borah Pk.
12,662 ft
+

NATIONAL

FOREST

Stanley

SAWTOOTH

CAMAS
N.W.R.

75

NAT.

SAWTOOTH
WILDERNESS

REC.

AREA

E. Fk. Salmon

SALMON-CHALLIS

NATIONAL

Big Lost

33

ise Mts.

S. Fk.

SAWTOOTH

Ketchum

75

FOREST

93

Arco

Snake River Plain

20

NATIONAL FOREST

Anderson
Ranch Res.

20

CRATERS OF THE MOON
NAT. MON.

93

0   miles   50

0   kilometers   50

26

15

Sawtooth peaks

share administration of the area's wildlands. Paved highways nibble at the edges, while rough forest roads burrow deeply into the interior.

If one aspect of central Idaho serves as a symbol for it all, it has to be the rivers. The Lochsa, Salmon, Middle Fork Salmon, Selway, Payette, Bitterroot, Big Hole, and others are primary gems in the crown of America's wild rivers. Some, like the Big Hole, are renowned for their fishing. Others, like the Middle Fork, are wilderness white-water runs. Sections of the Salmon afford enjoyable day runs for families, while the North Fork Payette will leave you slack-jawed in astonishment that anyone could launch a kayak into that boiling froth and survive.

Mountain ranges include the Sawtooth, Bitterroot, Anaconda, Pioneer, Salmon River, Clearwater, and Boise. Some of these sport craggy, snow-covered crowns in the best tradition of the Rockies, but overall, the landscape appears less spectacular than some other places. This relative lack of shining summits belies the extreme ruggedness of the interior. If you've been down in the canyons, if you tried traveling across this country, you know the truth. Central Idaho is a delightful, sometimes maddeningly rough old, cob.

The landscape owes its complex shape to a rather simple geology centered on several rock masses called the Atlanta, the Bitterroot, and the Boulder batholiths. Batholiths are large bodies of magma that well up from beneath the crust, melting and transporting surrounding rock as they rise like viscous bubbles until they harden some distance below the surface. Idaho's batholiths were formed about 75 million years ago. They hardened miles beneath the surface but are now exposed to view—partly by slow erosion, but primarily by another of those marvelous large-scale earth movements that occurred in various parts of the Rockies. In this

Along the Salmon River Scenic Byway, near Challis, Idaho

case, it appears that the overlying layers slid eastward to form mountain ranges on the edge of the batholith. Surface erosion then tore into the exposed granite. Volcanic eruptions added layers of ash and rhyolite that crop up here and there, but a dominant theme of central Idaho is batholithic granite. This explains the shape of Idaho canyons in contrast to, say, the Grand Canyon. Idaho canyons are in many cases just as deep—several are deeper—but they tend to be V-shaped, without the vertical cliffs or horizontal steps characteristic of southwestern canyons cut into sedimentary strata.

Seen from high vista points throughout the region, the country is a rumpled sea of forested ridges, dark and often misty, with occasional higher peaks and treeless ridges. Seen from below along the river corridors, it seems a country of steep angles where smooth granite slabs alternate with craggy gnarled outcrops and long sweeps of talus. At lower elevations, as along the Salmon River, which sweeps through its great canyon at between 2,000 and 3,000 feet above sea level, dryness and heat limit the growth of trees; slopes are covered by grass with sparse stands of ponderosa pine. But higher, the forest of Douglas-fir, limber pine, and lodgepole pine covers the mountains with a dense blanket.

The occasional open view, the rare glimpse of high summits as in the Sawtooth Range, gives a feeling of being inside the landscape—not skimming across it but burrowing deeper into it, beneath it, swallowed by it. It is precisely that character that makes this region such a good place for exploring. There are few geographic focal points, but thousands of personally rewarding nooks, crannies, and beauty spots. Whether you stick to maintained roads or strike off into the backcountry, the range of options is enormous, and it's completely impossible to take in. ■

Sawtooth National Recreation Area

■ 756,000 acres ■ Central Idaho, north of Ketchum via the Sawtooth Scenic Byway (Idaho 26/75) ■ Best months June-Sept. ■ Camping, hiking, boating, white-water rafting, fishing, mountain biking, horseback riding, bird-watching, wildlife viewing, backpacking, swimming ■ Adm. fee ■ Contact the recreation area, HC 64, Box 8291, Ketchum, ID 83340; phone 208-726-7672

CROWNED BY A splintering crest of jagged granite peaks, the Sawtooth National Recreation Area encompasses nearly 1,200 square miles of spectacular alpine terrain. That's more territory than you'll find in many national parks, and the scenery is of national park caliber. The borders take in four mountain ranges, two beautiful valleys, the Salmon River headwaters, several large mountain lakes, a handsome river chasm, and dozens of inviting hot springs.

At its heart stands the Sawtooth Range, a gloriously fractured spine of bare rock crags, razorback ridges, pinnacles, cirques, and towers that extends south to north for roughly 30 miles. This ragged line of rock and forest forms the western wall of the Sawtooth Valley, a broad prairie trough that parallels the range and cradles the infant Salmon River as well as spawning grounds for endangered salmon. Large morainal lakes

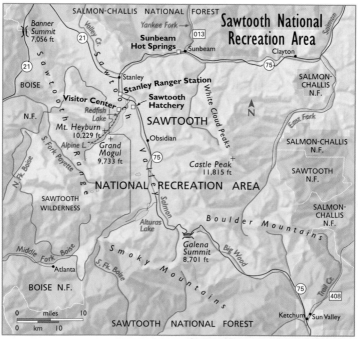

Opposite: Hiking in the Sawtooth Wilderness

Foxtail barley

lie along the base of the Sawtooths, reflecting the gleaming peaks.

The core of the range is made up of pink granite that welled up through the earth's crust 50 million years ago and spread over the surface of the great Atlanta batholith. Later, this core of granite rose slowly into place along a fault line while the floor of the valley slipped downward. Then, during various ice ages, glaciers carved the peaks as we know them today—an abrupt rampart of summits that rise as much as 4,000 vertical feet above the valley floor.

Across the valley, but obscured by foothills, rise the **White Cloud Peaks,** an even higher mountain crest composed of limestone. The Salmon River flows from south to north between the ranges, quickly gathering force. It turns abruptly east near the town of Stanley, then barrels down a rocky chasm dotted with hot spring pools. The Sawtooth Valley's south end is walled off by two more mountain ranges—the **Smoky Mountains** to the west and the **Boulder Mountains** to the east. Between them, the **Big Wood River** flows south to Ketchum through the recreation area's second major valley.

Throughout the high country, tiny alpine lakes nestle in glacial basins and cirques where mountain goats and bighorn sheep graze among verdant meadows. At lower elevations, dense forests provide daylight cover for deer, elk, and black bear. Owls, hawks, and other birds of prey hunt the high meadows and the open prairie landscape of the valley floor. Though wildlife thrives here, most of the big game animals tend to give humans a wider berth than they might in a national park, where hunting is prohibited.

Not all wildlife thrives. Years ago, the Salmon River and parts of Redfish Lake clogged annually with sockeye and chinook salmon that migrated 900 miles up the Columbia, Snake, and Salmon Rivers to spawn and die in the waters of their birth. Today, a pitiful few make the journey.

Lady ferns

Fishery biologists blame dams for the long-term decline in sockeye and chinook numbers. Between 34 and 57 percent of returning adults are killed while passing through an obstacle course of eight hydroelectric dams on the Columbia and Snake Rivers. Far worse, 77 to 96 percent of juveniles, called smolts, die on the downstream journey because of dam-related problems. Idaho sockeyes became so rare during the early 1990s that biologists began trapping the few returning adults as well as the ocean-bound smolts for use in a captive breeding program. They hope the program will eventually produce enough young fish to begin releasing smolts again from the Sawtooth Valley. The outlook for chinook, though alarming, is not quite so dire as for the sockeye—at least not yet.

What to See and Do

Start your visit in Stanley, a small mountain town at the north end of the Sawtooth Valley, and drive south along Idaho 75 with the serrated crest of the Sawtooth Range cutting across the western sky. The peaks you see from the road are part of the **Sawtooth Wilderness,** which follows the spine of the range and accounts for nearly a third of the recreation area. An intricate landscape, its maze of knife-edged ridges and crumbling peaks divides the water

courses into chains of small lakes and bone-chilling streams. It's a popular hiking area, where distances are short and the views gratifying. For maps and advice about the many trails and destinations throughout the recreation area, drop by the Stanley Ranger Station (*2.5 miles S of town. 208-774-3000*).

Just a bit farther south, take the turnoff for **Redfish Lake,** a long, narrow body of turquoise water surrounded by beaches and lodgepole pine forests. Two immense peaks, **Mount Heyburn** and **Grand Mogul,** rise abruptly from the lake's far end. Roads wrap around the lake's near end and lead to the **Redfish Lake Visitor Center** *(208-774-3376. Closed Labor Day–June),* a rustic flagstone building that offers a stunning water-and-mountain vista. Modest exhibits and a 20-minute slide show profile the area's terrain, plants, animals, and history. For a casual, interpretive stroll, look for the **Fishhook Nature Trail,** which starts behind the visitor center and loops an easy quarter mile out over the marshy bottomlands and spawning beds of Fishhook Creek. Excursion boats *(fare)* depart regularly from nearby Redfish Lake

Lodge *(208-774-3536. Mem. Day–Sept.)* and cruise the lake's length to a popular wilderness trail that follows a drainage for 5.5 moderate miles between Mount Heyburn and Grand Mogul to **Alpine Lake.**

Back on Idaho 75 is the **Sawtooth Hatchery** *(1 mile S of the Redfish Lake turnoff. 208-774-3536. Tours Mem. Day–Labor Day or by appt.),* which releases more than two million chinook salmon smolts a year in an attempt to maintain that species' spawning run. Exhibits track the decline of chinook and sockeye salmon populations and explain efforts to revive their numbers.

From the hatchery, Idaho 75 continues south for the length of

The Sawtooths reflected in Redfish Lake

the valley, then climbs 2,000 feet to the **Galena Overlook,** which offers a full-length vista of the Sawtooth Range. Far below on the prairie floor, a thin line of willows marks the Salmon River headwaters.

Beyond the overlook, the road climbs to 8,701-foot **Galena Summit,** then plunges into the Big Wood River Valley. The high peaks to the east are the Boulder Mountains, remarkable not only for their height, bulk, and rugged shape, but also for their unusually coarse texture and vivid colors. The valley opens up farther south and follows the Big Wood River to Ketchum through rolling hills and benchlands, prairie meadows, and forests of lodgepole pine and Douglas-fir.

Next, double back to Stanley and follow Idaho 75 east. The road hugs the banks of the Salmon, which soon dives into a forested chasm studded with granite outcroppings. The Salmon drops 15 feet to the mile, rushing past large boulders, cliffs, and steep gravel slopes. It also sweeps by several riverside hot springs—some secluded, others exposed, all well known among locals. The largest and easiest to find is **Sunbeam Hot Springs.** Located about 11 miles east of Stanley, it bubbles down a high embankment into a series of pools overlooking the Salmon. Not far beyond the hot springs lies the small crossroads town of **Sunbeam,** where the river slows and forms enticing green pools warm enough to swim in by late summer. ■

Confluence of Loon Creek and the Middle Fork Salmon River

Frank Church-River of No Return Wilderness

■ 2.3 million acres ■ Central Idaho, north of Stanley ■ See p. 159 for seasons
■ Hiking, boating, fishing, mountain biking, horseback riding, bird-watching, auto tour ■ Contact Middle Fork Ranger District, Salmon-Challis National Forest, P.O. Box 750, Challis, ID 83226, 208-879-5204; or Krassel Ranger District, Payette National Forest, 500 N. Mission St., McCall, ID 83638, 208-634-0600

ENCOMPASSING 2.3 MILLION acres, the Frank Church-River of No Return Wilderness is the largest designated wilderness in the continental United States. Slightly larger than Yellowstone National Park, it is a huge tangle of rugged terrain and the core of an even larger wild area. On its northern border, only a primitive dirt road, closed most of the year, separates it from the 1.3-million-acre Selway-Bitterroot Wilderness (see pp. 172-73). The Gospel Hump Wilderness (see p. 171) weighs in with an additional 206,000 acres on the northwest, while Hells Canyon complicates things on Idaho's western border. In addition, all sides of Frank Church are buffered by national forest land managed for varying degrees of wildness.

Three of America's premier white-water rivers—the **Salmon,** the **Middle Fork Salmon,** and the **Selway**—flow through parts of Frank Church-River of No Return Wilderness. In addition, tributaries like Chamberlain Creek, Big Creek, and the South Fork Salmon qualify as small rivers in their own right. They all flow through deep V-shaped canyons whose walls rise with unrelenting steepness to high forested ridges. The canyon bottoms are narrow. Flat land is uncommon. In places, the canyon walls are smooth slabs of gray granite. More commonly, the granite is broken. Craggy outcrops punch through steep, loose talus that even the deer try to avoid.

In this huge convoluted country, the spirit of wildness still breathes strongly. Creeks flow clear through deep forests of lodgepole and ponderosa pine. In August, sun-heated slopes are richly scented with the aroma of ripe huckleberries. High exposed ridges offer views of distant summits across deep valleys, some of which are 6,000 or 7,000 feet below. From the dry, warm canyon bottoms to the windy ridge tops, there's a place for just about any creature that lives in the Rockies. The list includes all the marquee species: elk, deer, mountain goats, bighorn sheep, moose, black bears (not grizzlies), mountain lions, lynx, bobcats, gray wolves, ospreys, golden eagles, bald eagles, hawks, falcons, great gray owls, and many more. The rivers are filled with brook, rainbow, and cutthroat trout, kokanee salmon, and dolly varden.

In the lower reaches, noble stands of yellow pine, or ponderosa, rise columnar and fine to look at. They share space with Douglas-fir and spruces. But the true beauty of the Idaho forest is western redcedar, which prefers areas of abundant moisture. Where it occurs in groves, it creates a cathedral atmosphere; you want to think only wise thoughts in the presence of such grand and ancient composure. Quaking aspens don't encourage such intellectual gravity, but maybe they should. Because they reproduce through their root systems, with all the trees in a single stand connected underground, a grove of aspen is actually a single plant with many tree-size shoots. It is conceivable that aspen root systems live for many hundreds, perhaps thousands, of years—placing them among the most venerable, long-lived plants on earth.

During the 20th century, some major forest fires altered the landscape. Terrain so rugged as this recovers slowly when denuded, but on the positive side, open areas increase

Seasons at Frank Church-River of No Return Wilderness

Snow can block the high country well into June. Streams in spring flood are hazardous, especially to hikers and wading fishermen who underestimate the power of moving water. Summer can be very hot at river levels; potentially dangerous for hikers. July brings a bloom of wildflowers. Late summer is the time for fruit: thimbleberries, huckleberries, wild currants, and more. Fresh snowfalls in September and October bring a risk of being trapped in the backcountry.

Following pages: Pungo Creek, Frank Church-River of No Return Wilderness

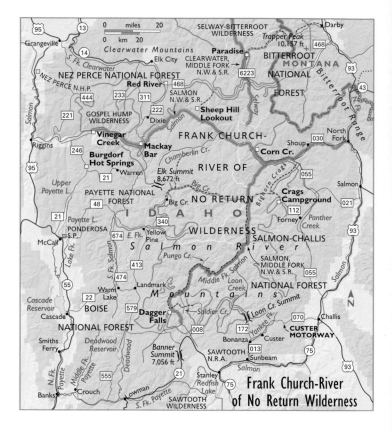

Frank Church-River of No Return Wilderness

diversity, which is good for wildlife and for providing breathtaking views of the countryside. In 1989, a particularly dry year, large forest fires burned through much of western Idaho, and you'll see the results around **Lowman** and **McCall.** More than a decade later, dead weathered trees standing in fields of wildflowers are surprisingly beautiful.

The price you pay for all these wild rewards is some pretty tough travel. Idaho's back roads aren't for everyone, certainly not those with an aversion to heights and dust; yet the roads are fairly well maintained, and many are suitable for passenger cars. They wander along creeks and little rivers beneath tall conifers, cross occasional meadows, top out on rocky ridges, then wind steeply down into the next drainage.

As for foot trails, some follow arduous up-and-down routes across the complex grain of the country. But there are many nearly flat trails that meander along creeks in the fragrant shade of conifers—ideal places for fishing, bird-watching, or relaxed hiking. It is certainly country to be appreciated slowly. A 50-mile drive can be an all-day, bone-jarring experience, worthwhile only if you make plenty of stops and end the day in a peaceful campsite or at one of the isolated lodges scattered on the edges of the wilderness.

If you're headed into the wilderness itself, choices are endless. You could walk all the trails and still see only a fraction of what's out there. Entire drainages and many prominent ridges are marked only by faint game trails; they remain as untraveled as they were a century ago—perhaps less, considering how energetically pioneer prospectors explored every nook and cranny. Because the miles are long, it's good country to see from horseback, but even so you pretty much have to stay on trails. Much of the country is simply too rough for anything but bighorn sheep and birds. Flat spots are rare; a step forward is usually a step up or down.

What to See and Do

With such a vast, sprawling complex, you can start from almost any direction. Much of the national forest and Bureau of Land Management land surrounding the wilderness is managed in a semiwild state, where vehicles are restricted to designated trails and roads. This means near-wilderness conditions exist in many areas while at the same time opening opportunities for mountain biking and motor touring. Both national forests publish a travel plan map with detailed regulations. The wilderness itself is limited to non-mechanized activities, which means you must walk, ride a horse, or float.

Driving

When it was established by Congress in 1980, the Frank Church-River of No Return was already penetrated by numerous backcountry roads leading to mines, ranches, airstrips, and ranger stations. By definition, a wilderness cannot exist where there are human developments. To purists, the area was already compromised beyond qualification as a wilderness. Yet the desire to set this place aside as one great contiguous unit was strong, and the rules were bent a little. Rather than leave out all areas near roads, planners drew the boundary in a complicated fashion that allowed narrow corridors. This means that for all practical purposes, and despite the contradiction in terms, there are roads through the wilderness. Rough and narrow, they can be frightening to anyone nervous about heights and steep drop-offs. There are neither guardrails nor caution signs. Maintenance is irregular, and deteriorating weather can quickly turn marginal roads impassable, especially in autumn when the chance of snow or freezing rain becomes a serious concern. Don't expect to see a snowplow. Main routes are generally suitable for high-clearance vehicles and sometimes for passenger cars, but trailers, motorhomes, and luxury sedans should stay near pavement. National forest maps (available at ranger stations) are essential for any travel beyond major routes; there's also an official wilderness map that shows contour lines and other important details. If you like that sort of adventure, or want to reach the more remote trailheads, these wilderness roads provide an unusual opportunity.

Circling the wilderness in a clockwise direction, a good starting point is at **North Fork,** where Forest Road 030, paved as far as Shoup, follows the Salmon River downstream into its canyon. You can drive to **Corn Creek** (several campgrounds along the way) and get a good feel for the rugged nature of the canyon. Only whitewater boats go beyond Corn Creek. About 9 miles downstream from Shoup, Forest Road 055 turns off to follow Panther Creek on a long backcountry excursion; it comes out to US 93 a few miles north of Challis. Don't be in a hurry; this is one way to **Bighorn Crags,** a towering set of white granite needles rising above alpine lakes on the edge of the Middle Fork Canyon. The crags are excellent for backpackers and day hikers alike, while the access road is a minor adventure in its own right.

From Challis, the **Custer Motorway** (Forest Roads 070 and 013) heads up the hill following an 1879 toll road to the **Yankee Fork** historic mining district, then down to Sunbeam. You can return to US 93 by heading east on Idaho 75. Before going, pick up a brochure and other information at the Land of the Yankee Fork Interpretive Center *(208-879-5244)* just south of Challis *(jct. of US 93 and Idaho 75)*. The road passes various historic landmarks as it works its way through forest and meadow beside cobble-filled trout streams. **Custer** *(for info call Land of the Yankee Fork Interpretive Center)* is a ghost town and state historic site that still shows the heavy impact of mining. The Yankee Fork flows south to meet the Salmon through a streambed devastated by dredging. A large strip mine still operates on the hill north of Bonanza, but you can leave it behind in a dramatic way by taking Forest Road 172 north over **Loon Creek Summit,** then dropping into the Loon Creek drainage and a mini-network of back roads and trails. Loon Creek Summit, which marks the wilderness boundary, is a worthy objective by itself.

On the south side of the Frank Church-River of No Return Wilderness, there are a couple roads of note. The old **Landmark Stanley Road** (Forest Road 579) predated modern Idaho 21; it takes off from Banner Summit west of Stanley on Idaho 21 and follows a forested path 82 miles to Knox and Warm Lake; there are many side roads.

Just west of Lowman, the **Scott Mountain Road** (Forest Road 555) climbs relentlessly above the South Fork Payette River, then bumps and twists its way to **Deadwood Reservoir.** The lake, ringed by forested hills, is warm enough for swimming in summer. Shaded campsites line the shore. It seems a long way to pull motorboats, but many people do just that. To get a sense of the pristine river canyon, take the gentle foot trail that follows the Deadwood River below the dam; mountain bikes are permitted. North of the reservoir, the road joins Forest Road 579 and continues north to Warm Lake, Yellow Pine, and other places.

One of Idaho's best backcountry loop drives—from Cascade past Warm Lake to Yellow Pine, to Big Creek and over Elk Summit to Warren, then back to Cascade

Rainbow trout

via McCall, on the west side of the wilderness—was disrupted by the rains of January 1997, which caused flash floods throughout the region, washing out numerous bridges and roads. Most were rebuilt in short order, but back-country roads have lower priority, and it's unclear when the road over Elk Summit between Big Springs and Warren will be repaired. Meanwhile, it's possible to drive most of the route without doing too much back-tracking.

Pavement extends from Cascade to Landmark, beyond Warm Lake. Forest Road 674 along the **South Fork Salmon** is also paved for 32 miles north of Warm Lake. It was paved to reduce silt runoff into the river; the silt clogged the gravel, destroying the nesting redds of chinook salmon. It remains a narrow, winding, one-laner that discourages anyone in a hurry, but is perfect for slow-moseying sightseers. The river itself is gorgeous. Near the junction with its named-to-confuse tributary, the **East Fork South Fork Salmon,** white sandbars invite a

dip on hot summer days. At the junction, you're back on gravel. Backtracking along the South Fork is the smooth way out. If you're up for some bouncing, take Forest Road 48 over **Lick Creek Summit,** where spectacular cliffs and rounded knobs of white granite are visible thanks to the 1989 fires. The weathered snags of fire-killed trees stand above lush meadows thick with wildflowers.

From McCall, another drive beckons for those who aren't too weary of wrestling the steering wheel. The **Warren Wagon Road** (Forest Road 21) heads northeast past Payette and Upper Payette lakes over Secesh Summit. Pavement extends as far as the Burgdorf Hot Springs junction. From there, it's 16 miles to Warren and 57 miles to Big Creek when that road gets repaired.

If you turn north at the junction, Forest Road 246 leads to Burgdorf Hot Springs *(208-636-3036),* an old rickety resort with a hot swimming pool; it's a local favorite. Beyond lie a series of lovely meadows and lodgepole forest and a gradual climb to a divide with expansive views to the north and east. You can see the gorge of the Salmon River far below, and as unlikely as it seems that a road can make it down there, this one does, in a rat's nest of curves and switchbacks called **The Fingers**. Check your brakes and your nerve before heading down. After 4,000 feet, you'll come out at the river, where you can drive on to Riggins.

Finally, on the north side of the Frank Church-River of No Return Wilderness, is the **Magruder Corridor Road** (Forest Road 468), a rough track right across the state—101 miles of up and down the mountains and through the forest. For much of the way, it runs between the Frank Church-Wilderness of No Return on the south and the Selway-Bitterroot Wilderness on the north. Built in the 1930s by the Civilian Conservation Corps, it roughly follows the old southern Nez Perce Trail. (It was the northern Nez Perce Trail, or Lolo Trail, that Lewis and Clark followed in 1805 and again in 1806.) The Magruder Corridor Road can be driven in a long day, but that would be a terrible waste of superb country. There are many reasons to go slowly. Highlights include several lookout towers, numerous vista points, plenty of campsites and the achingly beautiful Selway River. The road's western end is at Red River south of Elk City at the end of Idaho 14. The eastern end is south of Darby, Montana, on US 93. The Forest Service publishes a free driving guide available at ranger stations in Elk City and Darby.

While you're near Elk City, consider another option, the **Gold Rush Loop Tour,** a 62-mile route through a historic mining district. The route visits historic sites, as expected, but also some interesting natural areas and trailheads for the **Gospel Hump Wilderness**. From Dixie, Forest Road 222 drops nearly 3,000 feet south to the Salmon River at Mackay Bar. The Forest Service provides a free self-guided brochure.

These are the primary back roads in a network of farther-back roads. Driving them is not the pleasant part. It's where they lead that makes them worthwhile. Keep in mind that, in the buffer areas around the wilderness, hiking and mountain biking are permitted on many trails and closed roads. Pedaling or walking beside a wilderness trout stream on an abandoned logging or mining road is the real reward for the driving effort.

Hiking

Some 2,500 miles of trails crisscross the wilderness. Only the major ones are routinely maintained, and large chunks of country remain unmarked by any trails except those of deer, elk, and other animals. You can stand on a narrow footpath deep in the wilderness and gaze out over whole valleys of even deeper wilderness. Considering the rough roads, you may find it worthwhile—even cheaper—to plan backpack trips around backcountry airstrips. Air taxis operate from McCall, Cascade, Salmon, Challis, and other towns on the periphery. Roads are long, but flying times are short.

Rafting the Salmon River

Roads Less Traveled

THROUGHOUT the northern Rockies, modern highways, byways, and back roads open up magnificent scenery while taking the most direct route possible through an often rugged land. They are easily found on any road map. But there are also the forgotten ways, rough unpaved roads winding through wild corners of the mountains. Many of the latter began as important trails and mining roads—major thoroughfares of their time—but were preempted by shifting population centers and modern construction techniques. When roads and trails were built with hand tools, builders had to follow the natural contours of the landscape more closely; this often meant taking less direct routes. Where modern highways punch through mountains and span canyons on high bridges, the old roads mosey at a more relaxed pace, often through scenery the paved roads pass up.

Custer Motorway (see p. 164). Built in 1879 to supply mining camps, the one-time toll road runs between Challis and Custer City, Idaho.

Magruder Corridor Road (see p. 166). A motoring adventure, this route parallels the historic southern Nez Perce Trail.

Grassy Lake Road (Forest Roads 3261 and 261). This route begins at Flagg Ranch (between Yellowstone and Grand Teton NPs) and makes for a pleasant day trip to Ashton, Idaho. Built in the early 1900s as a supply road, it now offers access to lodgepole-pine forests and meadows where visitors can spot elk, moose, and deer. Primitive campsites dot the road and boating is allowed on Grassy Lake, a reservoir.

Lemhi Pass Road. Spanning the Continental Divide between Montana and Idaho, the road closely parallels Lewis and Clark's 1805 route between the Missouri and Columbia river

systems. From Clark Canyon Reservoir southwest of Dillon, follow County Road 324 across Horse Prairie and up through forested mountains to a high open saddle (Lemhi Pass) overlooking the mountains of central Idaho. The road continues to the floor of the Lemhi River Valley. A pamphlet is available at Forest Service offices in the area. Camping along the way.

Lolo Motorway. Located in north-central Idaho, this high country road follows a section of the Lolo Trail, a traditional Nez Perce route that Lewis and Clark used in 1805 and 1806 to cross the Bitterroots. The motorway starts in Powell, Idaho, climbs to the crest of the mountains on Forest Road 569, and follows Forest Roads 500 and 100 to Weippe Prairie, where Lewis and Clark met the Nez Perce. The entire trip requires a few days, especially if you plan to hike to some of the landmarks mentioned in the Lewis and Clark journals, but long day trips are also possible. Maps and an invaluable pamphlet are available at the Powell Ranger Station (208-942-3113). ■

Along Medicine Lodge Creek in the western foothills of the Bighorns

For hikers, several areas are noteworthy: **Bighorn Crags** is a granite outcrop carved into dramatic pinnacles at 9,000 to 10,000 feet in elevation. Dozens of small lakes attract hikers and fishermen willing to hammer their way up the long bumpy road to Crags Campground, the standard access point. Take Morgan Creek Road (Forest Road 055), which begins 8 miles north of Challis, to Forest Road 112 at Forney, and follow the signs from there. Or take the Williams Creek Road 6 miles south of Salmon. It becomes Forest Road 021 and joins Forest Road 055 along Panther Creek; turn south past Cobalt to Forney. From Salmon to the Crags is more than 5,000 vertical feet. You can day-hike from the campground to numerous lakes and glacially smoothed summits. Backpackers

will find fewer people in the southern, trailless portion of the crags. Distance hikers should look at the **Clear Creek** and **Crags Trails,** both of which start at a trailhead on Forest Road 055 about 4 miles south of the Salmon River. On either trail, it's a long climb. So is the trail up **Waterfalls Canyon** from the Middle Fork—6,000 vertical feet; it also begins at the trailhead off Forest Road 055.

The **Big Creek Trail,** one of the main routes, meets the Middle Fork across the river from Waterfalls Canyon. If you followed it, you'd end up traversing the wilderness from east to west. Nearby, **Chamberlain Basin** is a world of its own, a plateau bounded on all sides by deep canyons; almost any trip here involves about 50 miles of hiking. At the wilderness's south end lies a cluster of lakes around the headwaters of **Soldier Creek.** There are several trailheads along Forest Road 008 off Idaho 21 near Banner Summit. Way up north, some good ridge-top routes take off from the Magruder Corridor Road, notably **Trail 575** from Dry Saddle to the Sheep Hill lookout.

Beyond these few suggestions, several minutes spent with the overall wilderness maps (two sheets, available from ranger stations), with trails, airstrips, and boundaries clearly marked, will reveal the enormous range of possibilities.

Horseback riding

Horseback riding is generally the domain of outfitters; addresses can be obtained through the Idaho Department of Commerce *(208-334-2470 or 800-635-7820).* ∎

Poor Man's Gold

The first miners in the northern Rockies were independent souls armed with simple gear—picks, shovels, gold pans, and little else. They dug for placer gold, loose flakes and nuggets eroded from bedrock and deposited in streambeds. Success required luck and muscle but not much capital. Later, when placer deposits were cleaned out, only well-financed companies could afford to develop the hard-rock underground mines. Men who earlier might have sought their fortune in placer gold went into company tunnels to work for wages.

White-tailed deer

Gospel Hump Wilderness

■ 206,053 acres ■ Idaho's central panhandle, southeast of Grangeville ■ Summer can be tolerably cool in high country, but canyon bottom can be deathly hot ■ Camping, hiking, fishing ■ Contact Nez Perce National Forest, Route 2, Box 475, Grangeville, ID 83530; phone 208-983-1950

WITH THE SALMON River on its south boundary and historic mining districts scattered around its periphery, Gospel Hump showcases classic Idaho canyon country. A high divide runs across the middle of the wilderness, separating the densely forested northern section from the drier, more open southern part. The high country is a relatively gentle terrain of forest and wet meadows filled with wildflowers—good habitat for moose, deer, and elk. Trails follow timbered creek bottoms, climbing occasionally to ridges at or above timberline. Several make their way into the arid, sparsely vegetated **Salmon River Gorge.**

There are three important access points for hikers and car-campers alike. On the east, a rough road (Forest Road 223) grinds up from Elk City to the historic mining district at the base of **Buffalo Hump Mountain.** The last few miles, beyond Orogrande Summit, are four-wheel drive only; roads and trails wander every which way. This is a good place for day-hiking. On the west side, distance hikers can strike out across the highlands from a trailhead at Square Mountain Lookout *(FR 103 to FR 221 to FR 444; improved roads).* Or, they can make a diagonal crossing of the wilderness from the Salmon River via Black Butte. This trek begins with a 4,000-foot ascent from **Wind River Bridge,** the only road access (Forest Road 103) at river level. ■

Selway-Bitterroot Wilderness

Selway-Bitterroot Wilderness

■ 1.3 million acres ■ East-central Idaho, southwest of Missoula ■ Camping, hiking, boating, fishing, wildlife viewing ■ User fee in summer at Lake Como ■ Contact West Fork Ranger District, Bitterroot National Forest, 6735 West Fork Rd., Darby, MT 59829, phone 406-821-3269; or Moose Creek Ranger District, Fenn Ranger Station, Nez Perce National Forest, HC 75, Box 91, Kooskia, ID 83539; phone 208-926-4258

IF WILDERNESS MEANS isolation, the Selway-Bitterroot qualifies in all regards. Surrounded by natural fortifications, it allows no easy entry. The imposing, snow-covered Bitterroot Range forms a 5,000-foot-high wall on the eastern flank. A few narrow valleys penetrate the wall, but even they require hikers to negotiate high passes. The northern rampart, called the **Lochsa Face** because it stands above the Lochsa River, is a similar barrier that rises in two steps. The first is about 2,000 feet high; it forms the wilderness boundary. The second is 2,000 to 3,000 feet higher yet. This crest reaches its climax in the lake-studded **Selway Crags** on the wilderness's northwest corner. The southern boundary adjoins the Frank Church-River of No Return Wilderness (see pp. 158-170), while the western side is buried in the mostly roadless lands of the Nez Perce National Forest.

Inside those defenses lie 1.3 million acres of hard granite carved into ridges and canyons with few flat spots. Interior streams all drain toward the Selway River; Moose and White Cap Creeks are the main collectors. Elevations range from about 1,600 feet along the Selway River to 10,157 atop Trapper Peak in the southeast corner. Supplied with abundant water, the forest is a rich blend of Douglas-fir, grand fir, old-growth cedar, ponderosa pine, and maple. Timber grows thick and tangled over most of the

wilderness but yields to glaciated granite on the high crests—which, inci-
dentally, and happily for hikers who love the alpine zone, harbor most of
the Selway-Bitterroot's lakes. Late summer brings an explosion of forest
fruit: huckleberries, thimbleberries, twinberries, wild currants, and more.
The wildlife roster includes all the familiar and wonderful animals of the
Rockies except for grizzly bears. Talk of reintroducing them has stirred
up a hornet's nest of opposition that may well be stronger than that
surrounding the recently accomplished reintroduction of gray wolves.
Meanwhile, black bears are common in the Selway-Bitterroot. They are
thrilling enough to see, and they warrant the same caution you would
exercise in grizzly country.

Because the mountains rise steeply above the Bitterroot Valley, there
aren't many recreation sites on the edge of the wilderness. The exception
is **Lake Como,** a popular reservoir and recreation area several miles north
of Darby. A few roads climb the lower slopes but only one (Forest Road
429) gets far. It follows Lost Horse Creek into a high basin near timberline. This is a scenic drive leading to two campgrounds and a pair of
alpine lakes. From here, it's an easy hop over Bear Creek Pass or Lost
Horse Pass into the wilderness area—the only eastside hiking access that
doesn't involve a stiff climb.

There's a similar access point on the **Lochsa Face.** From the Powell
Ranger Station, located west of Lolo Pass on US 12, forest roads climb about
3,000 feet to Elk Summit and other trailheads. Day-hikers can reach the
Diablo Mountain Lookout from Hoodoo Lake; also **Walton Lakes** from
Forest Road 362. Finally, Forest Road 319 climbs adventurously from the
Selway River near Selway Falls to **Big Fog Saddle,** 4,100 feet up in 14 miles.
This is the preferred (but still not easy) trailhead for the Selway Crags.

Clearly, one of the big differences between this wilderness and the
Frank Church-River of No Return Wilderness is one of road access.
Whereas the Frank Church-River of No Return Wilderness is surrounded
and often penetrated by backcountry roads—many of them spectacular
drives—the Selway-Bitterroot is a place for hikers. If you're looking for
auto-touring or car-camping, the **Lochsa River Valley** together with the
Lolo Motorway combine many of the same attractions that you'd find if
you could drive across the wilderness.

For backpackers, loop trips are possible from a variety of starting
points, particularly the **Big Fog Saddle** and **Elk Summit** areas. Planning
is a matter of studying the topographical wilderness map available from
ranger stations and keeping in mind that not all trails are maintained
regularly. On the other hand, the most satisfying routes, in the sense
of offering deep wildland experiences, may well be the ones that traverse
the wilderness. For example, starting near Darby, you can follow Tin Cup
Creek to the divide, over the bare granite crest, and down White Cap
Creek to the Selway at Paradise. Or from Elk Summit across to a branch
of Moose Creek, following that to the Selway and out through the river
canyon. These would be long trips—at least a week and easily more. It's
hard to find more complete solitude anywhere else in the Rockies. ■

Following pages: Mouth of Loon Creek, near the Middle Fork Salmon River

Upper Salmon River

Wilderness Rivers: The Salmon, Middle Fork Salmon, and Selway

■ Central Idaho ■ Best seasons late spring–fall ■ Car-camping along non-wilderness sections, hiking, white-water rafting and kayaking, fishing, wildlife viewing ■ Permits required to float wilderness sections ■ Contact North Fork Ranger District, Salmon-Challis NF, P.O. Box 180, North Fork, ID 83466, phone 208-865-2383 (Salmon and Selway). Middle Fork Ranger District, Salmon-Challis NF, P.O. Box 750, Challis, ID 83226, phone 208-879-5204 (Middle Fork Salmon)

THE RIVERS OF central Idaho are legendary, particularly the Salmon, which is often called the main to distinguish it from the Middle Fork. Its reputation for wild water and impassable cliffs goes back far before Meriwether Lewis and William Clark came this way. They wanted to float down it in dugout canoes, until the Shoshone chief Cameahwait told them the canyon was a bad route. After scouting it below present North Fork they gave up, choosing instead to go overland on the difficult Lolo Trail. Later, pioneers and prospectors called it the River of No Return because once you went down it, there was no simple way back. Even today, if you float through the roadless heart of the wilderness, getting back to your starting point involves a circuitous drive of 385 miles—one of the longest river shuttles in the country.

Access to all three rivers is rationed by the Forest Service, which gives out permits according to an annual lottery. Boaters must apply for float trips around the first of the year. The only guaranteed seat is on a professionally guided trip. Private companies offer a safe and enjoyable way for nonexperts to float the wilderness sections of these rivers. Generally, the main Salmon and the Middle Fork each take about a week; the Selway is a run of about five days. The Middle Fork and the Selway are best run in the first half of the summer. Both suffer from low water late in the summer and in dry years. Those who can't fit in a full expedition can nonetheless sample the fun of white water on day trips on the main Salmon, either in their own boats or with numerous commercial companies. For a list of companies, contact the Idaho Department of Commerce *(208-334-2470 or 800-635-7820)*.

Salmon River

From its headwaters on the east slope of the Sawtooths, the Salmon River flows north, paralleled by Idaho 75 and then US 93, to the tiny community of North Fork. Here it turns sharply west and enters its famous gorge. You can follow it part way into the canyon by car.

Corn Creek, the launch site for wilderness float trips, is 46 miles from North Fork and well worth the drive. Keep in mind that almost the entire distance from Stanley to Corn Creek offers fine boating, rich scenery, and the convenience of easy car shuttles. Permits aren't required, but as you can see from the highways, the Salmon is not a river for beginners. Never launch without getting updated local information. At high water levels the Salmon can be dangerous even for experts.

Of course, the wilderness float is the main treat. In 79 miles the Salmon falls nearly 1,000 feet, tumbling over numerous rapids, then gathering in deep green pools. The canyon walls rise steep and ragged, sometimes covered in timber, sometimes lurching upward over cliffs and outcrops. There are hot springs to sit in, sand beaches for the kids, campsites shaded by towering ponderosa pines, and always the chance of wildlife: black bears, moose,

Cedar Groves

Moist Pacific air masses that stall out against the western slopes of the Rockies support luxuriant groves of western redcedar. Some of the groves contain old-growth cedars with trunk diameters exceeding 8 feet. Most are found at relatively low elevations—less than 5,000 feet—along rivers, streams, and lakes. The trees thrive in mucky soils and often rise from a thick undergrowth of ferns and shrubs such as devils club. They often grow in the company of western hemlock (another shade-tolerant species), as well as with western larch, western white pine, and black cottonwood.

White-water kayaking

bighorn sheep, mule deer, mountain lions, ravens, ospreys, bald eagles, and, since their recent reintroduction, gray wolves.

The Salmon is rich in history—going back 8,000 years or more, as shown by pictographs, old campsites, and other artifacts. At the time of Lewis and Clark's expedition the entire area was familiar to the Shoshone, Nez Perce, and other Native Americans. Later in the century, prospectors, miners, ranchers, and resourceful eccentrics began moving into the canyon and its tributaries. Some people still live year-round along the river. Other historic homesteads are seasonal retreats for absentee owners. In the early years, all supplies had to be carried in on horseback or floated down the river in flat-bottomed wooden scows. The men who rowed those awkward craft through the rapids, and the people they served, were a tough and self-reliant breed. Today jet boats roar through the canyon in both directions while inflatable rafts drift downstream. It's not a tough trip these days, but it's an exciting and rewarding one.

The end comes at the **Vinegar Creek** boat ramp, served by Forest Road 9900, which turns into Forest Road 103 and winds 28 miles upriver from Riggins. Like the road to Corn Creek at the canyon's upper end, this road hugs the bank of a long and beautiful stretch of the river, offering campsites, beaches, and plenty of opportunities for short float trips that don't require permits. There are several boat ramps along this stretch of the river. The country is drier here, and warmer. The canyon remains deep and rugged, but its hills are smoothed by the velvety covering of grass and sparse timber. Below Riggins, the Salmon parallels US 95 for about 30 miles—good boating and frequent access—then slips away to another, shorter roadless stretch before joining the Snake River below Hells Canyon.

Middle Fork Salmon River

Many boaters consider this the jewel of Idaho rivers. The white water is challenging but not intimidating except during periods of high water. The river begins at the junction of Bear Valley and Marsh Creeks, just inside the southern boundary of the Frank Church-River of No Return Wilderness (see p. 158-170). It flows 104 miles through a variety of land-scapes including deep forest, narrow canyons, and small valley bottoms occupied by historic ranches. From the put-in at Dagger Falls to the river's junction with the main Salmon, there is no road access; no jet boats, either.

The river divides into three sections. The upper third features deep spruce and fir forest, hot springs, fast current, and numerous boulder-choked rapids. In its midsection, the canyon widens. The land is drier, the views longer. Stately ponderosa pines crowd the riverbanks, while treeless ridges climb to high forested summits. The final stretch squeezes into a gorge beneath smooth granite slabs. Throughout, the water is cool, clear, fast-moving, and filled with trout.

Trail 001 follows the river its entire length; considering how few people walk compared to those who float, hikers may well get the more authentic wilderness experience.

Selway River

There can be no better symbol for the wilderness of central Idaho than its most wild river, the Selway. Beginning in the Frank Church-River of No Return Wilderness on the northern edge of the Salmon River Canyon, it flows north into the Selway-Bitterroot Wilderness. For 96 miles it is a designated Wild and Scenic River. In that length, all its tributaries are wilderness streams, and only one rough gravel road touches its banks.

The water is cold, the current powerful, and during high water the river is a dangerous white-water run that demands the best of boaters who attempt it. **Ladle Falls,** a frothy collection of hydraulics and huge boulders, has killed at least two people who tried to navigate it during spring runoff. Even at lower levels, it's a tricky and exciting run; 47 miles long, it takes four or five days. Just seeing the river is a treat. Floating it is a privilege. A private permit is hard to get, but guided trips are readily available. *(Contact West Fork Ranger District, Bitterroot National Forest, 6735 West-fork Rd., Darby, MT 59829. 406-821-3269.)*

If you were to walk one of these three rivers, the Selway would be first choice; a hiking trail parallels its entire wilderness length. You can also drive to its remote, forested upper end on the **Magruder Corridor Road** (see p. 166). It's 67 miles from Darby, Montana, to Magruder Crossing, where a spur road (Forest Road 6223) parallels the river for 12 miles past several primitive campgrounds to the boat launch at Paradise. Anyone who likes forests and rivers would agree with the name. The takeout is above ferocious **Selway Falls,** 20 miles southeast of Lowell on Forest Road 223. This, too, is a beauty spot, complete with big overhanging cedars, sandy beaches, primitive campsites, hiking access to the wilderness, and catch-and-release fishing. ■

Lochsa River Valley

■ 1 million acres ■ North-central Idaho, between Lowell and Powell on US 12
■ Best months May-Sept. ■ Camping, hiking, white-water rafting and kayaking,
fishing, bird-watching ■ Contact Powell Ranger Station, Clearwater National
Forest, Lolo, MT 59847; phone 208-942-3113

THIS PLUNGING, STEEP-SIDED valley starts among the moist, western slopes
of the Bitterroot Range near Lolo Pass and cuts a deep, forested groove
across Idaho for nearly 80 miles. Down its narrow floor runs the breathtaking Lochsa River: a raging fury of silty white water during spring; a
seductive path of glass-clear pools, riffles, and cascades during summer
and fall. Moisture-loving trees such as western redcedar and grand
fir thrive in the mists of this damp corridor, where warm Pacific air
tends to stall against the Bitterroots. Thick layers of moss cover the
forest floor with a spongy mantle of iridescent green that envelops
fallen tree trunks and muffles all sound. Add ferny glens, hot springs,
grottoes, and shafts of angled sunlight. On some days, the Lochsa valley
can seem like Eden.

US 12 hugs the banks of the Lochsa from Powell to Lowell, where
the river joins the Selway to form the **Middle Fork Clearwater River.**
Campgrounds, picnic areas, and informal pullouts offer abundant opportunities to stop and admire the Lochsa as it washes over its bed of large,
rounded stones. Trails along tributary streams lead into the forest
primeval, where highway noise drops away and hot spring pools await.

For a short stroll among a remnant of the old-growth forest that
once lined the entire river corridor, stop at the **Devoto Memorial Grove**
(*4 miles NE of Powell*), where footpaths loop beneath gigantic cedar,
spruce, and fir trees. Some of the cedar trees are 3,000 years old and have
trunk diameters of 4 to 5 feet.

A longer, quieter walk begins about 10 miles down the road at the
Warm Springs Trailhead, where a footbridge crosses the Lochsa and
a 1-mile path leads along Warm Springs Creek to **Jerry Johnson Hot
Springs.** This is an idyllic setting. The trail winds through a forest of
cedar, larch, and Douglas-fir, mist rises from the forest floor, aerial-
feeding lichen hangs from the trees like druids' beards, and big owls
glide between the tree trunks. At the central hot springs, a ribbon of
muscle-melting water slips over a low cliff and collects in deep, rocky
pools with sand underfoot. If that particularly enticing hot springs
seems too crowded, keep walking up the trail. There are other, less
spectacular pools in the woods and meadows above.

In the autumn of 1805, the Lewis and Clark Expedition stumbled down
into the Lochsa River Valley after losing its way on the Lolo Trail. They
camped near the Powell Ranger Station and regained the trail by climbing
the valley's northern slopes. The **Lolo Motorway** (Forest Road 500), accessible via Forest Road 569 east of Powell, follows the expedition's route along
the crest of the mountains and down to Weippe Prairie (see p. 169). ■

Snake River winding through Hells Canyon

Hells Canyon National Recreation Area

■ 652,488 acres ■ Western Idaho and northeastern Oregon border ■ Spring comes to river bottoms in April, but not to mountain peaks until late May or even June. Summers are intensely hot and dry along the river, cool and moist in the mountains. October snows can close high country roads ■ Camping, hiking, white-water rafting and kayaking, fishing, mountain biking, horseback riding, bird-watching ■ Contact the recreation area, 88401 Oreg. 82, Enterprise, OR 97828, phone 541-426-5546; or the recreation area, P.O. Box 832, Riggins, ID 83549, phone 208-628-3916. www.fs.fed.us/r6/w-w/hcnra.htm

HELLS CANYON, NORTH AMERICA'S deepest gorge, straddles the border between Idaho and Oregon and plunges 8,000 vertical feet into some of the wildest, most remote terrain in the northern Rockies. Carved by the mighty Snake River, the gorge runs for nearly 100 miles through a landscape of desert chasms, forested ridge tops, and jagged mountain peaks. Much of it lies within Hells Canyon NRA, which extends south from the Washington border and also includes a long stretch of Oregon's Imnaha River.

To the east, a single dividing ridge separates Hells Canyon from the continent's second deepest gorge, the **Salmon River Canyon,** which reaches a maximum depth of roughly 7,500 feet. It parallels and then converges with Hells Canyon northwest of Riggins. The ridge dividing

Following pages: Lupines in bloom, Hells Canyon NRA

the canyons culminates in a ring of crags called the **Seven Devils Mountains,** which climb to elevations approaching 9,400 feet.

These extreme differences in elevation compress widely diverse habitats into a relatively small area. Summer temperatures on the sparsely vegetated floor of Hells Canyon often exceed 100°F. Meanwhile, melting snowfields up in the Seven Devils area irrigate lush wildflower meadows and forests of grand fir. Between the two extremes, bunchgrass and other sun-loving, drought-resistant prairie plants predominate among the ridges and hills, benches, bluffs, plateaus, and side canyons. Here and there, you'll find a shady pocket of Douglas-fir or ponderosa pine.

Wildlife abounds—more than 350 species are part- or full-time residents of the recreation area's habitat. There are mountain lions, deer, bighorn sheep, mountain goats, coyotes, lynx, black bears, and one of the largest elk populations in North America. The canyon also attracts a wide variety of birds of prey, including golden eagles and sharp-shinned and Cooper's hawks.

Geologically, the gorge is one of the region's most interesting spots. For roughly 700 million years, the area it now occupies formed part of North America's West Coast. Then, about 150 million years ago, the whole continent began to creep west. Over a period of millions and millions of years, the floor of the Pacific Ocean slid gradually beneath the leading edge of the continent. Everything attached to the oceanic plate moved with it—tropical volcanic islands, coral reefs, pieces of continental crust, even whole micro-continents. All approached the West Coast slowly and were eventually grafted onto what is now western Idaho. There are places in Hells Canyon today where white-water rafters bob past the remains of coral reefs that once lay hundreds of miles off the coast.

Long after this same tectonic plate collision helped to build the Rocky Mountains, a staggering volume of magma welled up from the earth's mantle and spilled over much of Oregon, Washington, and western Idaho. The lava flows began about 16 million to 17 million years ago, continued intermittently for millions of years, and built up the Columbia Plateau, an irregular heap of basalt that occupies much of eastern Oregon, Washington, and western Idaho. Both the Snake and Salmon river canyons cut right through its eastern margin.

1877 Nez Perce War

The Nez Perce War began in western Idaho, shortly after Chief Joseph's band arrived from the Wallowa Valley. The conflict stemmed from the 1860 discovery of gold on Nez Perce land near Pierce. Whites, demanding free access to the goldfields, succeeded in forcing an 1863 treaty that reduced the tribe's land holdings by 90 percent. In 1877, as the last of the "non-treaty" Nez Perce prepared to settle on the reduced reservation, embittered warriors killed 19 whites. The Army retaliated and pursued the Nez Perce across the West, eventually wringing Joseph's surrender in Montana.

Snake River rafting in Hells Canyon

What to See and Do

Visiting Hells Canyon requires time and effort. Few roads penetrate to the Snake River, and those that do are narrow, rugged, steep, and usually unpaved. Interpretative facilities are nearly non-existent, trails generally difficult. Still, the rewards are great.

On the Idaho side, Forest Road 517 *(dirt)* climbs 6,500 feet from just south of Riggins to an outstanding vista from **Heaven's Gate** in the Seven Devils area. The road starts in the desert bottomlands of the Salmon River Canyon and ascends 19 miles to the trailhead for **Heaven's Gate National Recreation Trail.** The view from the parking area takes in Hells Canyon and Oregon's Wallowa Mountains, but the moderate, half-mile hike to **Heaven's Gate Lookout** leads to an even better vista. There, you can trace the courses of both Hells Canyon and the Salmon River Canyon as they bend 50 miles to

the northwest and converge.

North of Riggins, Forest Road 493 *(gravel)* climbs over the dividing ridge between the Salmon and Snake Rivers, dead-ending after 17 miles at **Pittsburg Landing** in the desert heart of Hells Canyon. From Riggins, Forest Road 9900 *(paved)* follows the **Salmon River** east past rapids and seductive beaches. It's not part of the national recreation area, but it's well worth the visit.

Paved highways lead into the recreation area's southern end from Cambridge, Idaho, and end at **Hells Canyon Dam.** Farther south, at **Oxbow Crossing,** Oreg. 86 climbs out of the gorge and intersects with Forest Road 39 *(paved)*, which winds north along the rim, in Oregon. Forest Road 3965 *(paved)* runs 3 miles to **Hells Canyon Overlook,** which offers a marvelous vista of the gorge's southern end. ∎

Payette Lake at Ponderosa State Park

Ponderosa State Park

■ 1,470 acres ■ South-central Idaho, 1 mile east of McCall off Idaho 55
■ Best months June-Sept. ■ Camping, hiking, boating, fishing, mountain biking,
bird-watching, swimming ■ Contact the park, P.O. Box 89, McCall, ID 83638;
phone 208-634-2164

PONDEROSA STATE PARK occupies a narrow, wooded peninsula that
rises from the crystalline waters of **Payette Lake** to a high, open bluff
overlooking the region's gently rolling mountains. Groves of immense
ponderosa pine, as well as fir, lodgepole, and larch, shade much of the
peninsula, but the parklands also take in grassy meadows, boggy marshes,
even small sagebrush flats. Mule deer browse along the forest edge; foxes,
hawks, and owls hunt for mice and other rodents in the meadows; and
frogs send up their creaking chorus from the marshes.

For a quick overview of the park, drive (or bike) about 3 miles to
the end of the peninsula and follow the short footpaths to **Osprey Cliff
Overlook** and the **Narrows Overlook.** The basalt lava that composes
the bluff was deposited about 16 million years ago as part of the vast
lava flows that formed the Columbia Plateau. Later, glaciers covered
this area, smoothing the mountains and scooping out the lake bed to
a maximum depth of 304 feet.

Elsewhere, watch for ducks and other waterfowl on **Lily Marsh,**
or head for the picnic area and take a quick dip in **Payette Lake.** Stroll
through the campground to admire the park's largest specimens of ponderosa pines, or stretch your legs on the 1.4-mile loop trail that tours
Meadow Marsh (*maps available at the park visitor center*).

If you have time, drive around the lake to the **North Beach Area,** an enticing stretch of warm sand. From the parking area, an interpretive boardwalk leads over a marsh to the beach. Paddlers can float down to the beach on the gentle **North Fork Payette River,** which meanders through forest and marsh and attracts moose, ducks, herons, and beavers. The trip from the Fisher Creek bridge can take a half-day if you dawdle. ■

Payette River

■ South-central Idaho, north of Boise ■ March-Oct.; season depends on water levels and dam releases ■ White-water rafting and kayaking ■ Contact Lowman Ranger District, Boise National Forest, 7359 Idaho 21, Lowman, ID 83637; phone 208-259-3361

THE PAYETTE IS a complete river, possessing every aspect of a river realm—from peaceful canoeing water to the liquid madness of the Banks run. There are three branches. The **South Fork** comes out of the Sawtooth Wilderness and gradually grows from a mountain stream to a river with moderate to difficult rapids. Although the Banks-Lowman highway follows it closely, the canyon's depth keeps the river out of sight for much of the way. The South Fork is a popular, challenging white-water run. The **Middle Fork,** above Crouch, offers a 13-mile quiet-water stretch appropriate for canoes. As for the **North Fork,** here's where it gets really interesting. It starts out peacefully from Upper Payette Lake, Payette Lake, and Cascade Reservoir, offering stretches of good water for canoes. For 10 miles above Smiths Ferry it runs over moderate rapids and one waterfall, and then it goes nuts. In the 15 miles from Smiths Ferry to Banks, the river drops 1,700 feet down a nearly continuous staircase of hydraulics and frothy waves. When the current is cooking, it looks impossible to run. But highly skilled kayakers do it. Idaho 55 follows it closely, providing a fine grandstand when boaters are in action. If you want some of your own, 24 miles of the main Payette below Banks are a good training ground with moderate rapids. ■

South Fork Payette River, Boise National Forest

Hiking in Anaconda-Pintler Wilderness

Anaconda-Pintler Wilderness

■ 158,656 acres ■ Southwest Montana, west of Butte ■ Best months June-Sept.; lakes can remain frozen into July ■ Camping, hiking, fishing, mountain biking ■ Contact Dillon Ranger District, Beaverhead-Deerlodge National Forest, 420 Barrett St., Dillon, MT 59725; phone 406-683-3900

Good Fire, Bad Fire

Late summer is fire season in the northern Rockies, and great effort and expense goes into fighting and preventing fires each year. Forest ecologists point out that not all fires are bad. They can serve as agents of rebirth, releasing nutrients back into the soil, opening ground for new growth, clearing diseased timber, and creating a mosaic of young and old growth that provides habitat for a greater diversity of wildlife than mature forest alone can offer. Forests are adapted to fire as they are to any natural force.

THE ANACONDA-PINTLER is a relatively small but venerable wilderness. Among the original properties included under the 1964 Wilderness Act, it had long been recognized as an outstanding natural area, and has enjoyed protection as a primitive area since 1937. Not much has changed since then. It remains a little-known, often overlooked corner of the Rockies. The wilderness centers on the **Anaconda Range,** a high glaciated crest generally above 9,000 feet in elevation that also carries about 30 miles of the Continental Divide between the Big Hole Valley to the southeast and the Bitterroot Valley to the northwest. The highest point is 10,783-foot **West Goat Peak.** It stands a couple of miles apart from the crest, but seen from below, the peaks all blend together in a classic uplift of timbered slopes, bare rock, and snowy summits. The work of glaciers is evident in U-shaped valleys, cirque lakes, and knife-edged ridge tops.

Although located in Montana, the range is included here to acknowledge its position as the easternmost exposure of the great Idaho batholith, whose rocks occupy the lower, western portion of the wilderness. The high peaks are granitic intrusions involved in the movement of a big block of sedimentary rocks—the Sapphire block—which opened the Bitterroot Valley in its wake. It's part of the bigger story of how the Idaho batholith was denuded when overlying rock layers slid off toward the east millions of years ago. The Anaconda Range is a sort of narrative cross section, with batholith at one end, intruded granites on the crest, and bulldozed sediments piled up against the northeast corner.

For hikers, the wilderness is a compact landscape. Distances are not long and elevation differences are not extreme. A strong hiker could cross the range in a day. Trails generally head up streambeds toward alpine lakes tucked beneath the high peaks. There are dozens of lakes, most of them overshadowed by steep, glacially carved cliffs inhabited by mountain goats. Loose talus can make the alpine zone a hard place to hike across, but once you get to a ridge top, the going is reasonable.

The range's north side is a confusion of roads and development spilling out from Butte and Anaconda. **Georgetown Lake** is popular, the fishing is said to be good, and local weekenders are numerous. That's not to say it should be avoided, but in comparison the south side feels like classic old-time Montana. The mountains rise above the **Big Hole River Valley,** a green gem and one of the best natural hayfields in all the Rockies. The **Big Hole River,** a blue-ribbon trout stream, offers excellent drift-boat fishing. On the edge of the wilderness, several quiet campgrounds—Mussigbrod Lake, Pintler Lake, Lower Seymour Lake—share space with trailheads at the ends of access roads. National forest lands immediately to the east, along with the **Mount Haggin Wildlife Management Area** *(either side of Mont 274, some seasonal restrictions. Contact Montana Fish, Wildlife & Parks 406-494-1953),* are good places for back-road sight-seeing and mountain biking. ■

Black bear

Pioneer Mountains

■ 157,993 acres ■ Southwest Montana, southwest of Butte, west of I-15
■ Pioneer Mountains Scenic Byway closed in winter ■ Camping, hiking, fishing, bird-watching, auto tour, mining ■ Contact Dillon Ranger District, Beaverhead-Deerlodge National Forest, 420 Barrett St., Dillon, MT 59725; 406-683-3900

THE BIG HOLE RIVER VALLEY forms a crescent on the west side of the Pioneer Mountains. The two were created by a sort of landscaping partnership. As part of the general movement of sedimentary layers off the Idaho batholith, the Pioneers slid eastward, opening a gap behind them. The gap is **Big Hole River Valley,** one of Montana's hidden gems and surely one of its most pleasing landscapes.

The Pioneers, a rough circle some 30 miles in diameter, are split neatly down the middle by the Wise River, which in turn provides a natural travel route. Recently, the old backcountry road between the town of Wise River and County Road 278 has been rebuilt, paved most of the

Big Hole River Valley

way, and dubbed the **Pioneer Mountains Scenic Byway** (Forest Road 484). This is progress, of a sort. The driving is easier, but there are many more people sharing what was once a local hideaway. The byway travels for the most part through Beaverhead-Deerlodge National Forest, passing through the Wise River Valley before topping out at 7,800 feet above sea level. Along the way, trails take off in all directions, with the more interesting ones located on the east side, where the higher peaks congregate. Many of the trails are open to off-road vehicles for at least part of the year, which might discourage hiking. On the other hand, mountain bike options are numerous. Interesting sites include the ghost town of **Coolidge,** location of the historic (now abandoned) **Elkhorn Mine.** If you'd like to do a little mining of your own, check out **Crystal Park,** 26 miles south of Wise River. The digging is free since it's on national forest land. Families are encouraged to bring shovels and sifters to dig for amethyst and quartz crystals. At the byway's south end, the road drops steeply into Grasshopper Valley past **Elkhorn Hot Springs,** a rustic lodge with a steaming outdoor pool *(406-834-3434 or 800-722-8978).* ■

Great Plains

Sandstone formation at Medicine Rocks State Park, Montana

RARELY FLAT, AND MONOTONOUS only to those bent on
making time, the Great Plains drift away from the eastern
slopes of the northern Rockies and follow the general
course of the mountains from northwest to southeast
across Montana and Wyoming. It is a dry, windswept, and
often broken landscape where immense rolling hills alternate with broad prairie basins and where small plateaus,
crumbling ridges, and weathered escarpments expose
the rocky underlayment of the plains to view. The land

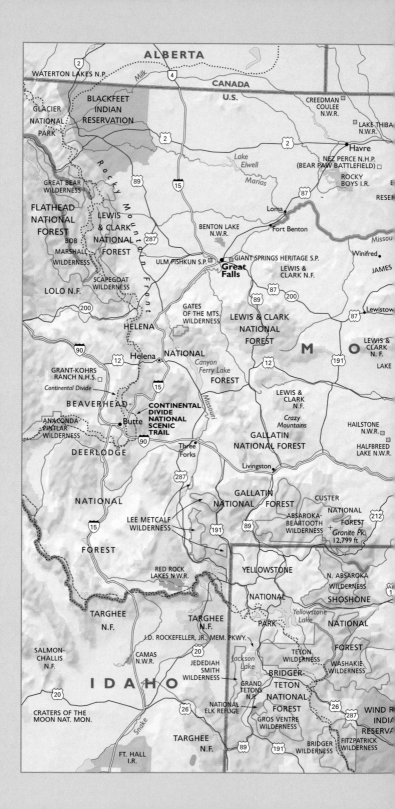

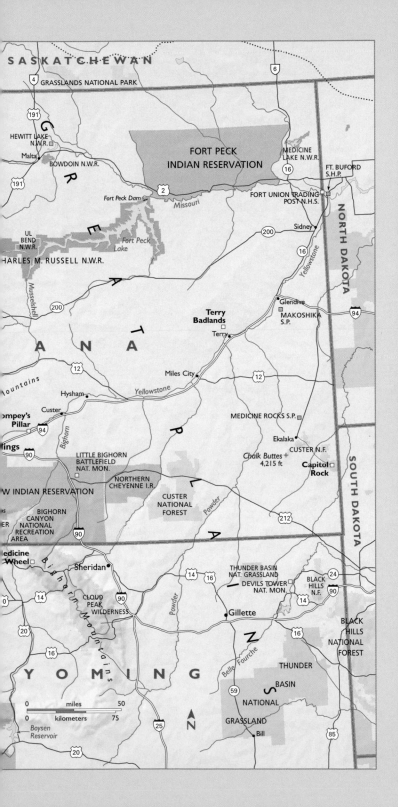

SASKATCHEWAN

GRASSLANDS NATIONAL PARK

4

191

6

HEWITT LAKE
N.W.R.

Malta

BOWDOIN N.W.R.

191

UL
BEND
N.W.R.

CHARLES M. RUSSELL N.W.R.

G R E A T

FORT PECK
INDIAN RESERVATION

MEDICINE
LAKE N.W.R.

16

FT. BUFORD
S.H.P.

FORT UNION TRADING
POST N.H.S.

Fort Peck Dam

Missouri

2

Fort Peck
Lake

Musselshell

200

Sidney

200

16

Yellowstone

NORTH DAKOTA

A N A

T

Glendive

MAKOSHIKA
S.P.

94

Terry
Badlands

Terry

P

Mountains

12

Yellowstone

Miles City

12

Hysham

Custer

MEDICINE ROCKS S.P.

ompey's
Pillar

94

Bighorn

Ekalaka

Chalk Buttes +
4,215 ft

CUSTER N.F.

L

ings

90

LITTLE BIGHORN
BATTLEFIELD
NAT. MON.

NORTHERN
CHEYENNE I.R.

CUSTER
NATIONAL
FOREST

Capitol
Rock

W INDIAN RESERVATION

s

BIGHORN
CANYON
NATIONAL
RECREATION
AREA

90

Powder

A

212

SOUTH DAKOTA

edicine
Wheel

Bighorn Mountains

Sheridan

14

16

THUNDER BASIN
NAT. GRASSLAND

DEVILS TOWER
NAT. MON.

BLACK
HILLS
N.F.

24

90

0

14

20

CLOUD
PEAK
WILDERNESS

90

Powder

14

Gillette

BLACK

HILLS

16

NATIONAL

FOREST

16

Y O M I N G

Z

THUNDER

BASIN

59

S

NATIONAL

85

miles   50
0

0   kilometers   75

25

N

GRASSLAND

Bill

Boysen
Reservoir

20

Belle Fourche

erodes easily. Even tiny, seasonal creeks bite deeply into the ground, and major drainages such as the Missouri and Yellowstone river systems carve across the plains as grand troughs lined with shortgrass hills, colorful badlands bluffs, and sandstone cliffs.

Often placed at opposite ends of the topographic spectrum, the mountains and plains of the northern Rockies are in fact intimately related. The plains rivers all start in the mountains. Many species of wildlife shuttle back and forth. And, until quite recently in geologic time, today's mountains and plains were parts of the same basic structure—a vast expanse of ancient metamorphic rocks covered by deep layers of sedimentary rock. Most important, though, it is the very presence of the mountains that make the plains as we know them possible. About 100 million years ago, much of what we now call the Great Plains was covered by a tropical forest. As the mountains rose into place 60 to 80 million years ago, they forced the entire region into higher, cooler elevations and wrung most of the precipitation out of moist Pacific air masses that had supported the tropical forests. As the climate grew colder and drier, the tropical forests died and gave way to a newly evolved family of plants—grasses.

Dryness is the fundamental characteristic of the plains all the way from the 100th meridian west to the foothills of the Rockies. Nowhere is that climate more punishing than on the Great Plains. It's not just the paucity of rain and snow that accounts for the semiarid nature of the Great Plains. Desiccating winds often blast across them at 60 miles an hour, and daytime highs hover in the 90s throughout the summer. Grasses survive—indeed thrive—by retaining a large proportion of their biomass underground as roots. Years of drought, fire, or passing herds of bison might destroy what grows above, but with an intact root system grasses quickly send up new shoots.

Prior to settlement, the Great Plains were dominated by shortgrass prairies characterized by such species as blue grama, buffalo grass, junegrass, and needle-and-thread. These grasses mixed with lovely wildflowers, sagebrush, and prickly pear cactus. Much of the native cover is gone, plowed under and replaced with wheat, flax, alfalfa, and other crops. But remnants of the shortgrass prairie lie scattered across the most arid, broken, and visually appealing areas of the country. Other pockets of native vegetation are found along the banks and bottomlands of the rivers and streams.

When Lewis and Clark passed through Montana's high plains in 1805 and 1806, the region teemed with bison, pronghorn, elk, deer, Audubon's bighorn sheep, grizzly bears, and wolves. Today, the vast herds of bison are gone. So are their attentive companions, the wolves. Audubon's bighorn is extinct, and populations of other ungulates— especially pronghorn—have plummeted. Still, to modern eyes, the Great Plains seem to abound with game. Elk and Rocky Mountain bighorn sheep have been reintroduced along some of the river corridors. Grizzly bears, which are making a comeback in the mountains, have

Bull elk

begun to make seasonal forays onto the Montana plains. Mule deer are common and pronghorn so numerous in some areas that you can hold your breath between sightings and drive 50 miles or more without feeling winded. During migratory seasons, vast numbers of snow geese, tundra swans, shorebirds, and ducks descend on the major river corridors and among the thousands of pothole ponds and small lakes that dot the plains of northeastern Montana.

The region's natural areas tend to follow the water, turning up among prairie potholes and along the Missouri and Yellowstone river systems. Starting in Great Falls, they stretch eastward along the Missouri and include the Upper Missouri Wild and Scenic River corridor and an immense wildlife refuge surrounding Fort Peck Reservoir. To the north of the Missouri lies a handful of rich birding sites. Working east along the Yellowstone from the Billings area, sites take in rock formations of historic and archaeological interest, as well as fine examples of river bottomland, badlands, and wind-weathered sandstone columns. Devils Tower protrudes from the prairies of northeastern Wyoming, which include the sprawling Thunder Basin National Grassland.

Though the beauty of the landscape offers sufficient reason for spending time on the plains, solitude may be the region's greatest reward. It is a constant and welcome companion that taps out a quiet accompaniment to the soothing procession of grassland swells and the vast thunderheads gathering on the horizon. ■

Buffalo jumpsite at Ulm Pishkun State Park

Great Falls Area

■ West-central Montana ■ Best months May-Sept. ■ Hiking, boating, biking, bird-watching, buffalo jump ■ Contact the visitor center, 15 Upper River Rd., Great Falls, MT 59401; phone 406-771-0885. www.city-of-great-falls.com

LOCATED ALONG THE western fringe of the Great Plains, the Great Falls area lies within sight of the Rocky Mountain Front and straddles a deep gorge carved by the Missouri River. Despite obvious changes in the landscape (the city, the dams, the wheat fields), the area still typifies the rugged, semiarid nature of the western plains and offers several easy opportunities for exploration.

The city Great Falls takes its name from a series of five major waterfalls that once thundered within the Missouri River gorge. Most have been dammed, but the reservoirs behind them extend for limited distances, leaving much of the river as a relatively free-flowing, surprisingly uncluttered riparian corridor. This is true even within portions of the city, where pelicans, cormorants, egrets, herons, and ducks frequent the Missouri and its banks at Giant Springs Heritage State Park.

Though grainfields now dominate the flatter areas surrounding the city, remnants of the shortgrass prairie still cling to steeper slopes along the gorge. There, with the Missouri washing over its stony bed, the mix of prairie grass, prickly pear cactus, yucca, and wildflowers offers a glimpse of the land as the Lewis and Clark Expedition saw it in 1805.

Gone, though, are the grizzly bears, wolves, and bison that so densely populated the area when Lewis and Clark spent three weeks portaging around the waterfalls. The bison were so numerous then that when herds came down to the river to water, many of the animals were pushed out beyond their depth and were swept over the falls. Their mangled remains collected on the banks below and attracted the bears and wolves.

Out among the sprawling plains surrounding the city rise various flat-topped buttes and crumbling ridges—harbingers of the mountainous terrain that lies just to the west. For thousands of years, Native Americans used some of cliff elevations as buffalo jumps. Today, Ulm Pishkun State Park preserves the largest known in Montana and offers one of the finest prospects of the Great Plains anywhere in the northern Rockies.

What to See and Do

Start in Great Falls at **Giant Springs Heritage State Park** (*4600 Giant Springs Rd. 406-454-5840. Adm. fee*), which hugs the Missouri's south bank for several miles. Trails wind along the river through prairie grass and tall shrubs. In the middle of the park, **Giant Springs** wells up through a bed of aquatic vegetation, then flows as a crystalline stream into the silty Missouri. Giant Springs Road (as well as the city's excellent **River's Edge Trail**) continues east for a mile or two to an overlook of **Rainbow Falls.** If Lewis and Clark interest you, don't miss the outstanding **Lewis and Clark National Historic Trail Interpretive Center** (*406-727-8733. Daily Mem. Day–Labor Day, Tues.-Sat. rest of year; adm. fee*).

To see what remains of the **Great Falls,** head north on US 87 and follow Ryan Dam Road east. The road descends through short-grass prairie to a shaded park at the base of the falls, which are capped by Ryan Dam. During high stream flows one can still get a sense of the power of this waterfall. Even with the falls at half strength, the view down the canyon remains much the same as always—of a mighty river sweeping between high rocky walls dotted with shrubs and trees.

Southwest of Great Falls, **Ulm Pishkun State Park** (*Off I-15 at Ulm. 406-866-2217. Adm. fee*) occupies the top of a high bluff overlooking the Missouri and a vast, broken expanse of the high plains. You can walk the trail that leads above and below the buffalo jump, and visit the prairie dog town at the top of the bluff. A visitor center at the base of the bluff (*closed Labor Day–Mem. Day*) describes how the site was used. ■

Buffalo Jump
Ulm Pishkun, or "buffalo jump," is named for the high, sheer cliffs that tower within the state park. Between 900 and 1500 A.D., prehistoric men and women stampeded herds of bison over these cliffs—which, at 30 feet tall and stretching for more than a mile, comprise one of the largest bison jumps in the world. Below the cliffs, compacted bison bones have been uncovered nearly 13 feet deep. On top of the cliffs, you can still spot stone piles marking the drive lanes where the animals were funneled.

Sandstone bluffs along the Upper Missouri River

Upper Missouri Wild and Scenic River

■ 149 miles long ■ North-central Montana, between Fort Benton and James Kipp SRA ■ Best months March-Sept. Summers are very hot ■ Camping, hiking, boating, swimming, fishing, bird-watching, wildlife viewing, river trips (one of the finest in the West) ■ Contact Lewistown Field Office, Bureau of Land Management, P.O. Box 1160, Lewistown, MT 59457; phone 406-538-7461

CARVING A DEEP trough across the Great Plains, this remote section of the Missouri River stretches eastward from Fort Benton for 149 glorious miles, sweeping past voluptuous prairie hills, towering sandstone cliffs, and furrowed badlands bluffs. It was set aside as an irreplaceable legacy of the historic West, but its interest extends far beyond Lewis and Clark and

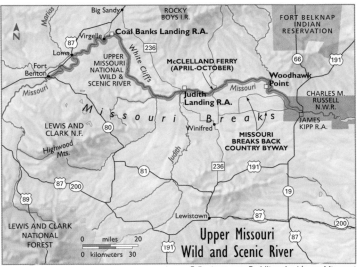

Following pages: Paddling the Upper Missouri

the fur trappers, steamboaters, and settlers who followed them upriver. Its incomparable scenery, abundant wildlife, and priceless ribbon of riparian habitat make for one of the most compelling landscapes on the Great Plains.

Starting in Fort Benton, the Missouri flows as a taut, muscular sheet of water through a spacious valley lined with shortgrass hills. Along the bottomlands, large groves of cottonwood, ash, box elder, and willow crowd the banks. The groves practically disappear out near the magnificent **White Cliffs** area, where massive blocks of creamy sandstone rise directly from the water or form protruding ledges and intricately weathered pinnacles, columns, and arches. These rock formations sometimes rise to a fringe of ponderosa and limber pine and often overlook expansive prairie bottomlands and narrow strips of riverside cottonwoods. Farther downstream, ranks of badlands bluffs stand shoulder to shoulder above the river.

Cut by the Missouri, its tributaries, and myriad seasonal streams, the eroded landscape reveals a layer cake of shale and sandstone deposits laid down over a period of ten million years by shallow inland seas. Volcanism built the neighboring Highwood Mountains and injected molten rock into the sedimentary layers. In some places, the softer sedimentary rocks have fallen away from the igneous intrusions, leaving dark plugs and dikes that stand in sharp contrast to the lightly colored shales and sandstones.

When Lewis and Clark traveled through this region in 1805, they encountered bison, deer, pronghorn, and elk that were so unconcerned about humans that the men had to throw rocks at the animals to move them out of the way. Today, you'll see no bison (no grizzly bears or wolves, either), but plenty of deer, elk, and even bighorn sheep. In addition to these there are 49 species of fish, even 140-pound paddlefish, and 233 species of birds, including pelicans, prairie falcons, golden eagles, grouse, swallows, and various songbirds.

What to See and Do

A few roads access the Wild and Scenic corridor, but the best way to see it—by far—is with a paddle in your hand. Depending on how often one stops to ramble among the cliffs and bottomlands, it takes seven or eight days to make the entire journey from Fort Benton to the US 191 crossing at the James Kipp Recreation Area. Prior back-country camping experience is a must for those wishing to make the trip on their own, but the river itself, which is fast but mostly flat, requires a minimum of boating skills. Area outfitters rent canoes and camping gear. Some run shuttle services between the far-flung landings and run posh guided trips replete with historical and natural history commentary. For maps and information contact the Bureau of Land Management (see p. 200).

One of the great joys of running the river lies in retracing the route of Lewis and Clark. They traveled upriver during the summer of 1805, weary but deeply appreciative of the beauty of the land and amazed by the abundance of animals. Here, they shot their first bighorn sheep, saw the Rockies for the first time, and continued their notorious battles with grizzly bears. River maps from the Bureau of Land Management mark and date the approximate sites of the expedition's campsites, making it easy to correlate the landscape with excerpts from the Lewis and Clark journals.

Fort Benton, a historic steamboat port and agricultural hub, stretches along the banks of the Missouri and offers an expansive downstream vista of the river, its bottomlands, cottonwood groves, and the long line of steep, eroded bluffs that parallel the current. The landscape typifies the upper portion of the Wild and Scenic corridor.

At Loma, **the Decision Point Overlook** (*near Loma Bridge Fishing Access; follow short footpath to top of the hills*) offers a sweeping view of the confluence of the Missouri and Marias Rivers as well as the yellowish badlands bluffs that extend northwest along the Marias.

East of Loma, access by road gets harder and longer. You can drive in to small campgrounds at **Coal Banks Landing Recreation Area** (*near Virgelle, 8 miles of gravel off US 87*) and **Judith Landing Recreation Area** (*S of Big Sandy on Cty. Rd. 236, 44 miles of pavement and gravel*). Both offer a glimpse of the river, a bit of shade, and loads of peace and quiet. East of Winifred, about 40 miles north of Lewistown, primitive roads form the **Missouri Breaks Back Country Byway,** which loops through the badlands country, reaches the river at the Woodhawk recreation area, and becomes impassable during rainstorms.

The next, relatively easy river access is at the **James Kipp State Recreation Area** (*US 191 crossing. (406-538-7461. June–mid.-Nov.*), which offers a campground amid tall trees, a fine view of the Missouri, and access to the western reaches of the Charles M. Russell National Wildlife Refuge (see pp. 205-07). ∎

Missouri Breaks on the Upper Missouri Wild and Scenic River, Charles M. Russell NWR

Charles M. Russell National Wildlife Refuge

■ 1.1 million acres ■ North-central Montana, south of Fort Peck via Willow Creek Rd. ■ Many unimproved roads become impassable when wet ■ Camping, hiking, boating, fishing, mountain biking, bird-watching, wildlife viewing. Best canoeing is on the river at refuge's west end; a motorboat is useful on the big open eastern section ■ Contact U.S. Fish and Wildlife Service, P.O. Box 110, Lewistown, MT 59457; phone 406-538-8706. www.r6.fws.gov/cmr

WHEN LEWIS AND Clark came this way, the country now included in the Charles M. Russell NWR was a virtual Garden of Eden. The abundance of wildlife astonished them. Clark wrote on May 11, 1805, "We observe in every derection Buffalow, Elk, Antelopes & Mule deer inumerable and So jingle that we Could approach near them with great ease." At times, they had to toss stones and sticks at bison to make them move out of the way.

The bounty did not last long. Before the century was out, bison herds across the Great Plains had been slaughtered. With them went the fearsome plains grizzly, wolves, and others—if not extirpated from the region, then greatly diminished in numbers. Even the Missouri River, with its lush cottonwood-filled bottomlands, was buried beneath the still waters of Fort Peck Lake, a flood-control reservoir that stretches for more than 100 miles behind the Fort Peck Dam. The loss of habitat created by the reservoir is difficult to measure or overstate. Yet there are compensations in the wildlife refuge established to protect the natural wealth that remains. With the notable exception of grizzlies, bison, and wolves, the Charles M. Russell accommodates nearly all the wildlife species that were here in 1805.

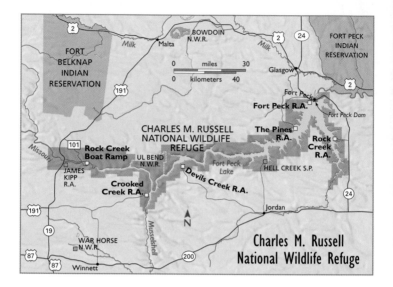

Charles M. Russell National Wildlife Refuge

    The refuge occupies 1.1 million acres on both sides of the reservoir and for some distance upstream. The river carved a winding channel between its banks, and, even full of water, the lake reflects some of that sinuous nature. The shoreline is complex with many inlets, peninsulas, and tributary drainages. The eastern end is characterized by upland prairie ending abruptly at mudbanks that drop steeply into the lake. There's not much of a transition zone between the prairie and the open water, but the uplands, with their rumpled hills, coulees, and badlands, are interesting in their own right.

    The western end is more diverse. The Missouri Breaks rise nearly 1,000 feet on both sides of the river, framing it with wooded coulees and high, grass-covered ridges. The refuge includes a 25- to 35-mile stretch of living river that flows through rich bottomland before hitting Fort Peck Lake. This piece of the Missouri resembles what Lewis and Clark saw in 1805—a powerful muddy river between dense stands of cottonwood trees. Of course, the lake itself is a huge body of water— good fishing, boating, and a stopover for migrating waterfowl.

    The refuge's wildlife list is extensive. Elk, reintroduced in 1951 from Yellowstone National Park, share woods and coulees with mule deer and white-tailed deer. Bighorn sheep live among the cliffs. Black-tailed prairie dogs congregate in towns covering hundreds of acres. Their burrows provide homes for mountain plover, cottontails, burrowing owls, salamanders, toads, and occasional rattlesnakes. The chirping rodents are hunted by numerous predators: golden eagles, hawks, bobcats, coyotes. Pronghorn race over the open prairie, stirring up sharp-tailed grouse. The lake attracts bald eagles, American white pelicans, loons, sandhill cranes, herons, and dozens of smaller species. Beneath the surface are walleye, sauger, smallmouth bass, catfish, lake trout, paddlefish, and others.

What to See and Do

Public access to the refuge is a bit complicated. Numerous local roads lead to refuge roads that in turn end at infrequently visited spots near the lakeshore. Most roads are impass-able when wet and maintenance is spotty. Having a four-wheel drive is helpful, but even that might not be sufficient when the top inch of soil turns to gumbo in a summer thun-derstorm. Before heading out, pick up a refuge map at the Lewistown office of the refuge *(Airport Rd., Lewistown. 406-538-8706)* and ask for a conditions update. And keep an eye out for storms—the danger of becoming stranded is real. Most visitors are content with designated campgrounds and boat ramps. The main ones, shown on the state high-way map and served by (usually) all-weather roads, are Fort Peck, Rock Creek, Hell Creek, Devils Creek, Crooked Creek, and The Pines.

For an excellent introduction to the **Missouri Breaks** landscape, take the 20-mile, all-weather self-guiding loop road (NWR Road 101) on the refuge's western end. For anyone who thinks of central Montana as a monotonous flat expanse, this drive is an eye-opener. It begins at US 191 on the Missouri's north bank, moseys along the river bottom, then climbs the Breaks and emerges on prairie. Brochures are available at the start or at the Sand Creek Field Station, located 4 miles south of the river on US 191. This section is above the reservoir; the river still flows strongly and offers a glimpse of how it must have looked when Lewis and Clark came through 200 years ago. Deer are common. Watch also for elk, coyotes, raptors, and waterbirds. At Stop No. 3, walk out to Jones' Island and wander through cottonwood trees and shrubby willows. Beyond Stop No. 5, where the improved road (NWR Road 101) starts climbing out of the river valley, NWR Road 201 continues a few miles downstream to the Rock Creek Boat Ramp and beyond. The ramp is a takeout point for float trips originating at the US 191 bridge, a fine day trip in a canoe. From the ramp, dirt roads continue along the river and up into the Breaks. If in doubt about conditions, stick to the designated loop road.

On the river's south bank by the US 191 bridge, **James Kipp State Recreation Area** *(406-538-7461. June–mid.-Nov.)* offers a pleasant campground, short trails beneath the cottonwoods, and a boat ramp. This is the usual termi-nus for multiday float trips down the Upper Missouri Wild and Scenic River (see pp. 200-04).

The **UL Bend NWR** is essen-tially part of the Charles M. Russell NWR and is administered by it. It occupies a peninsula opposite the mouth of Mussellshell River and includes a wilderness area attractive to the few hikers who get there. The CMR also administers four satellite refuges to the southwest: **Hailstone, Half-breed, Lake Mason,** and **War Horse.** These are small but impor-tant for migrating waterfowl and of interest to bird-watchers.

Guided fishing trips and lake excursions can be booked with outfitters in Fort Peck and sur-rounding communities *(Contact Travel Montana 800-847-4868)*. ∎

Prairie Potholes and Migrant Species

WHEN THE LAST great continental ice sheet melted back some 12,000 years ago, it left behind a rumpled landscape of low hills and shallow depressions called prairie potholes stretching across the Great Plains of the United States and southern Canada. Water, collecting in the potholes, supported marshes and wetlands ideal for all kinds of animals, particularly waterfowl and shore-birds. Migrating birds such as snow geese, plover, cranes, and sandpipers rely on the potholes as stopovers for rest and refueling on their long journeys between Arctic nesting grounds and southern wintering areas. Some birds travel the length of both continents. Other species, including white pelicans, avocets, phalaropes, herons, and numerous ducks, stay in the potholes all summer, raising their broods

Black-tailed prairie dogs, at Ulm Pishkun State Park

in one of the world's most productive and important wetlands. These places provide habitat not only for waterbirds but also for a range of other creatures from muskrats to deer to raptors.

Unfortunately, potholes and agriculture don't always mix. Roughly half of the region's wetlands have been drained and plowed smooth to accommodate row crops. As habitat disappears, birds are crowded into smaller areas and must compete for limited food supplies. Populations of transients and residents alike have suffered as a result of this and other factors. Although national wildlife refuges like Bowdoin and Medicine Lake compensate to some degree for the lost habitat, some 70 percent of surviving prairie pothole wetlands are privately owned. In addition to laws protecting the wetlands, coordination between landowners and management authorities is critical to the survival of many species. ■

American white pelicans, Bowdoin NWR

Prairie Wildlife Refuges

■ Northern Montana ■ Access depends on season and in some cases is limited to avoid disturbing nesting birds. Spring and fall are the best times for viewing migratory species, but enough birds and other animals are present at all refuges during summer to make a visit worthwhile then ■ Hiking, fishing, biking, canoeing, bird-watching, auto tours ■ Contact individual refuges (see p. 211)

STRUNG ACROSS THE northern part of Montana, three wetland wildlife refuges ring with the magic of migrating birds. Winged travelers by the tens of thousands appear in season, then move on, heading north in the spring, south in the fall. Some remain only long enough to rest and recharge for the onward journey. Others stay to build nests and raise their broods. They follow a global rhythm, as birds have done for eons. A few hardy species stay all year, joining the rich variety of nonmigrating mammals, reptiles, fish, insects, plants, and microorganisms that compose the living fabric of the ecosystem. The scenic beauty of these refuges is often subtle—the watery terrain is extremely flat—but the teeming array of wildlife can be overwhelming in spring and fall.

These prairie wildlife refuges are part of the northern plains' prairie pothole region—a land of rounded hills and depressions shaped by glaciers and supporting hundreds of small lakes and marshes (see pp. 208-09). Their importance to ducks, geese, swans, wading birds, and hundreds of other creatures cannot be overstated. The work of these refuges goes far beyond their immediate boundaries. Working with private landowners and various public agencies, refuge managers strive to protect numerous sites. Some are large and worth going out of your way to visit. Check with refuge offices about conditions and access. Each refuge also includes areas of upland prairie. Visitors, their eyes drawn to the dramatic congregations of waterbirds, often overlook these precious remnants of the once vast native habitat of the northern plains. All three refuges offer self-guided auto tour routes, along with recreational opportunities such as canoeing and hiking. To protect nesting waterfowl, regulations and access change with the seasons.

The 12,383 acres of **Benton Lake NWR** *(12 miles N of Great Falls on US 87. 406-727-7400)* were set aside in 1929. Early spring sees the arrival of up to 40,000 snow geese, 5,000 tundra swans, 50,000 shorebirds, and 100,000 ducks. Summer is nesting season for those who stay. Large numbers of Franklin's gulls and eared grebes are hard to miss. Look also for avocets; phalaropes; black-crowned night-herons; gadwalls; northern shovelers; lesser scaup; blue-winged, green-winged and cinnamon teal; and more. Northern harriers and Swainson's hawks are common raptors. Autumn is marked by the return of northern migrants, plus an abundance of raptors and bald eagles. The auto tour road is 9 miles long and curls around the lake's northern end. Limited canoeing and hiking are permitted. Photo observation blinds are available; these provide good views of sharp-tailed grouse dancing in the spring *(reservations required)*.

The 15,551-acre **Bowdoin NWR** *(1 mile E of Malta on US 2, then 6 miles E on Old US 2. 406-654-2863)* illustrates how refuges enhance conditions for wildlife through careful management. Bowdoin began as a natural wetland subject to severe water fluctuations. A combination of dikes and supplemental water from the Milk River have expanded the wetlands and created a more reliable situation for migrants and nesters—critical to their survival in a time when so many alternate sites in the region have been destroyed. In addition, most of the trees on the refuge have been planted to provide windbreaks and cover. The list of birds and their seasons is similar to what you'd see at Benton Lake, with the addition of nesting American white pelicans and great blue herons and lacking the great clouds of snow geese and tundra swans. White-tailed deer and coyotes are relatively easy to spot; mink, long-tailed weasels, badgers, raccoons, and the small rodents are not. The 15-mile auto tour road circles the 4,000-acre lake; boats are allowed only during hunting season.

Medicine Lake NWR *(24 miles N of Culbertson on Mont. 16. 406-789-2305)* covers 31,660 acres in two units, **Medicine Lake** and nearby **Homestead Lake.** The refuge features one of the largest nesting colonies of American white pelicans in the country. Occasionally, a whooping crane comes through in the company of sandhill cranes that appear by the thousands in autumn. Other important species: Canada geese, tundra swans, blue-winged teal, gadwalls, ruddy ducks, double-crested cormorants, and threatened piping plover.

A 100-foot observation tower stands at refuge headquarters. The 14-mile auto tour follows low hills on the lake's north side. These hills make for pleasant hiking and good views. On **Teepee Hills,** stone circles mark the campsites of Plains Indians. It's easy to understand why they chose these heights where meadowlarks sing and breezes keep the mosquitoes down. ∎

Yellowstone River

■ 671 miles long ■ From Yellowstone NP's southeastern boundary to Montana's northeastern border ■ Best months mid-April–mid-Nov. ■ Camping, fishing, bird-watching, canoeing ■ Contact Montana Department of Fish, Wildlife & Parks, 2300 Lake Elmo, Billings, MT 59015; phone 406-247-2940

THE YELLOWSTONE RIVER—671 miles long and nary a dam the whole distance from its headwaters southeast of Yellowstone National Park to its junction with the Missouri—is said to be America's longest free-flowing river. Without a doubt, it's one of the most beautiful. Its upper reaches, which include **Yellowstone Lake,** the two canyons, and the two big waterfalls, are admired by millions of people every year. Where it leaves Yellowstone National Park, it enters 50-mile-long **Paradise Valley,** whose very name is sufficient description for anyone who loves the Montana landscape.

And yet, there is that other river, the eastward-flowing Yellowstone beyond Livingston, where the mountains lie back against the horizon and the biggest objects in the landscape are clouds. Not so many people know the lower Yellowstone. As they hurry past on I-90 and I-94, the river affords little more than an occasional glimpse. It slides fast but smooth beneath cutbanks and bluffs, shaded by overhanging cottonwoods and lined with irrigated hayfields. In early years, the river was an important transportation route. Native Americans rode its current in skin bullboats long before 1806, when William Clark and his party sped downstream in two dugouts lashed together. Railroads and highways now follow its broad valley; unlike the meandering Missouri, the Yellowstone goes straight to the point and carries everything along with it.

Naming the Yellowstone

The term "Yellowstone" seems to have originated with a Siouan tribe that lived in what is now North Dakota. They described it to French trappers in the late 1700s as the Mi tse a-da-zi. The French wrote it as Roches Jaunes, or Yellow Stones. Ironically, the national park is mostly volcanic rhyolite—black rock. Although the park boasts a yellow canyon, the river's name more likely refers to yellowish sandstone bluffs on the lower river. The Crow tribe, which knew of the yellow canyon, nonetheless called it Elk River.

Several sites offer a chance to see the lower river close up. Public access points are conveniently spaced throughout its length. Pull off I-94 at almost any community or any side road, and you're likely to find a place to launch a canoe, have a picnic, set up camp, or walk beneath a bird-filled canopy. As for boating, the current is fast. Downed trees and strainers can be hazardous to inexperienced canoeists, but there's no white water. If you're looking for a scenic drive, a number of quiet back roads—some gravel, some paved—follow the river through small towns and ranchland. The main ones are shown on the state highway map, particularly between Miles City and Custer. ■

Bobcat pursuing a snowshoe hare

Pompeys Pillar NHL

■ 473 acres ■ South-central Montana, 28 miles east of Billings off I-94 ■ Walking, bird-watching, petroglyphs and pictographs ■ Adm. fee Mem. Day–Labor Day ■ Contact Billings Field Office, Bureau of Land Management, 5001 Southgate Dr., Billings, MT 59107; phone 406-875-2233 or 406-897-5253

THIS FLAT-TOPPED stump of yellowish brown sandstone rises 117 feet above the floodplain of the Yellowstone and overlooks an exceptionally appealing section of the river where rugged cliffs crowd the current and groves of cottonwood shade its banks. In 1806, William Clark carved his name on the formation and named it Pompeys Tower after Sacagawea's toddler.

Clark placed his signature amid the petroglyphs and pictographs that had been left before his time by Native American travelers. In later years, many others followed Clark's suit. Today, the rock—largely untouched by vandals—records a litany of 19th-century names. Fur trappers, missionaries, soldiers, railroad workers, and settlers all left their marks.

Exhibits at the **visitor center** *(Closed Oct.–Mem. Day)* summarize the site's history, and interpreters offer short walks and talks that focus on the region's ecology. Footpaths lead to the river and to a boardwalk that switchbacks up the northeast side of the pillar. Halfway to the top, you'll find Clark's name spelled out in sweeping cursive letters.

The vista from the top is very much the same as it was when Clark stood there. The Yellowstone meanders past the pillar as an inviting corridor of rushing water, cliff, and cottonwood. Across the plains to the south rise the Pryor and Bighorn Mountains; to the north stand the Bull Mountains. ■

Visiting the ancient drawings at Pictograph Cave SP

Pictograph Cave State Park

■ 23 acres ■ South-central Montana, 6 miles south of Lockwood exit off I-94 on Coburn Rd. ■ Closed Oct.-March ■ Walking, bird-watching, pictographs ■ Adm. fee ■ Contact the park, 2300 Lake Elmo Dr., Billings, MT 59105; phone 406-247-2940. www.travel.state.mt.us

LOCATED IN A shallow canyon that burrows into the plains east of Billings, Pictograph Cave preserves an ancient encampment where prehistoric hunters chipped stone tools, butchered animals, dried meat, rested, and painted the overhanging brow of sandstone with 106 images of animals, humans, and religious figures. Archaeologists estimate that people began using the cave at least 10,000 years ago.

Elevated a comfortable distance above the open canyon floor, the cave lies within a protective band of weathered sandstone that curves gently inward to form a sort of alcove that offered shelter from heat, rain, snow, and the incessant wind of the plains. A nearby spring provided water, and the site overlooked a rich plains hunting ground stretching north from the Beartooth Mountains to the Crazy Mountains.

From the parking lot, a 1,000-foot loop trail climbs a mild, boulder-strewn slope to **Pictograph Cave,** then traverses along the base of the sandstone cliffs to **Middle Cave** and **Ghost Cave.** Binoculars help pick out the smallest and faintest of the pictographs, which include a turtlelike creature painted 3,500 years ago, as well as bison, pronghorn, elk, and people carrying shields, spears, and guns.

Archaeological excavations during the late 1930s uncovered more than 30,000 artifacts representing four distinct prehistoric periods. They included arrow points, basket remnants, potsherds, and footwear. ■

Howrey Island and Other Bottomlands

■ 321 acres ■ Southeast Montana, 7 miles west of town at Meyers Bridge
■ Best seasons spring-fall ■ Hiking, bird-watching, wildlife viewing ■ Contact
Bureau of Land Management, 111 Garryowen Rd., Miles City, MT 59301;
phone 406-232-4333

WOOD DUCKS, THE most flamboyantly colored of waterfowl, perch in tall cottonwoods on Howrey Island. That in itself is a sight worth the effort of plowing through the dense vegetation of this mature bottomland. A short dirt spur road leads from the pavement near the bridge. Island is a relative term here; only a narrow marshy channel separates it from the mainland. Except during times of high water, you can walk to it with dry feet. There appears to be no maintained trail, but distances are short and game trails numerous. They lead through a riparian jungle beneath cottonwoods exceptional for the size and straightness—the result of growing undisturbed in such close proximity with their neighbors. Look for songbirds, woodpeckers, wild turkeys, bald eagles, hawks, owls, white-tailed deer, red foxes, beavers, and fox squirrels.

Several other bottomland sites are strung along the Yellowstone which, like Howrey Island, are undeveloped and wild. You won't find neatly cut trails or interpretive signs. Nor will you find crowds. They include (from west to east) **Pirogue Island** *(Miles City; cross the river on Mont. 59, go uphill to Kinsey Rd., and follow the binocular signs that indicate a wildlife viewing area);* **Elk Island** *(18 miles S of Sidney; watch for binocular sign);* and **Seven Sisters Island** *(10 miles S of Sidney; watch for a Fishing Access Site).* ■

Wood Ducks
Colorful male wood ducks sport orange bills and eyes, white bellies, spotted chestnut breasts, and green crested heads with flashy white lines. They live near water but prefer to nest in tree cavities. In addition to aquatic insects and small invertebrates, they eat berries, seeds, and acorns. Born with claws on their webbed feet, chicks can climb out of their tree nests 24 hours after hatching.

Great horned owl

Terry Badlands

■ 42,950 acres ■ Eastern Montana, northwest of Terry on Mont. 253 ■ Roads can be impassable when wet and confusing at any time ■ Undeveloped camping, hiking, mountain biking, bird-watching ■ Contact the Bureau of Land Management, 111 Garryowen Rd., Miles City, MT 59301; phone 406-232-4333

DOWNSTREAM FROM MILES City, badlands are a common feature of the Yellowstone River Valley. The bedrock in this region is a complex of sedimentary layers called the Fort Union Formation. Two to three thousand feet thick, it includes layers of sandstone, mudstone, shale, and a vast quantity of coal. The component layers vary in hardness and color, with light earth tones predominating (the Yellowstone River was likely named for the pale yellow sandstone in this area). Some of the sediments are nearly as unconsolidated as when they were laid down, and these erode easily to form badlands that, in general, occur along major drainages where the high prairie breaks into ravines and coulees. Marked by colorful clay soils, mushroom-shaped hoodoos, steep ravines, and small grassy plateaus, badlands appear to be landscapes in motion, dissolving as we watch. In fact, during rainstorms and times of heavy runoff you can actually see the erosion happening.

One of the better wild badlands, a 42,950-acre wilderness study area, is located near Terry. From the Terry exit off I-94, follow County Road 253 north for 1.5 miles across the river up onto the bluffs, then turn left on a marked road. Don't try it in wet conditions. Badlands appear within a few miles, and 6 miles take you to an overlook. Ponderosa pine and juniper provide scattered shade. Grass covers the gentler terrain. Owing to their rugged nature, the badlands are a good place for wildlife. Raptors, including golden eagles that nest here, sail past with the river valley as a backdrop. Look for pronghorn, mule deer, coyotes, foxes, desert cottontails, and white-tailed jackrabbits. Hiking is tough without a trail, but dirt roads wander through the area, and these would be fine on foot or mountain bike. Another access, from the river, is a dirt road called the **Calypso Trail;** you can drive on it if conditions are good, but they rarely are, and a mountain bike is ideal. Local directions are needed to find it. You start by crossing the Yellowstone on an old railway bridge west of Terry, then driving a short distance on an unnamed and unmarked road—a tempting Montana boondocks adventure. ■

Stealthy Hunters

Golden eagles prey mainly on jackrabbits, whose speed and strength make them challenging targets. The birds hunt from high in the air and sometimes attack directly, coming in from a steep angle, wings pulled in for speed. They have also been observed to cruise on past as if nothing was seen, then drop out of sight at a distance and return nearly at ground level, flashing into sight at the last moment and taking their quarry by surprise.

Makoshika State Park

■ 8,800 acres ■ Eastern Montana, southeast of Glendive on Snyder Ave.
■ Best months May-Oct. Warnings about wet roads being impassable apply
also to some hiking trails ■ Camping, hiking, mountain biking, bird-watching,
auto tour ■ Adm. fee ■ Contact the park, P.O. Box 1242, Glendive, MT 59330;
phone 406-365-6256. www.travel.state.mt.us

OF THE MANY Yellowstone River Valley badlands, none make for a better
visit than those within Makoshika State Park. Its name is a Lakota word
meaning "bad ground"—tough traveling, lousy grazing, good sightseeing.

In this case, the ground is soft sandstone and shale sculptured by
weather. The result would be interesting enough just for the shapes and
colors—but Makoshika is more than strange shapes. Hidden in the layers, and revealed by erosion, are fossil records spanning some 65 million
years. The lower levels contain the bones of *Triceratops, Tyrannosaurus,
Hadrosaurus,* and other creatures of the reptile age. They roamed a wet
subtropical plain at the edge of an inland sea. But this was near the end
of their time, and the transition is recorded at Makoshika. Above their
heavy bones lie the delicate fossils of early shrew-size mammals.

The park covers 8,800 acres of a larger badland area that begins on
the outskirts of Glendive. It consists of a pine-studded mesa and the
dissected badlands that drop away on all sides. Cavelike pockets and
crevices provide hiding places and nesting sites for coyotes, bobcats,
and many small rodents. Mule deer graze the natural prairie plants
that cover the mesa top. The edge of the mesa is a good place to have
a picnic and watch for raptors,
including prairie falcons and
golden eagles.

Start at the **visitor center** and
museum, where stone tools and
fossils are on display. From here,
the road heads up **Cains Coulee**
to the top of the mesa. Side roads
branch off in several directions,
leading to a number of viewpoints. Among them: **Eyeful
Vista, Pine-on-Rocks,** and
Artists Vista. It's good to have
a park map to identify these.

The 0.6-mile **Cap Rock
Nature Trail** provides an introduction to badlands erosion.
Nearby, the **Kinney Coulee Trail**
descends 300 feet and a half-mile
to the bottom of the canyon.
Don't go down unless it's dry. ■

Eroded badlands at Makoshika State Park

Southeastern Montana and Medicine Rocks State Park

■ 320 acres (state park) ■ State park is 25 miles south of Baker on Mont. 7
■ Best months May-Oct. ■ Primitive camping, hiking, bird-watching, wildlife
viewing ■ Adm. fee ■ Contact Montana Department of Parks and
Recreation, P.O. Box 1630, Miles City, MT 53901; phone 406-232-0900

MONTANA'S SOUTHEAST CORNER feels close to nowhere, but nowhere turns
out to be a surprisingly interesting and attractive place. High, wide, and
uncrowded, this is the Big Open, where the sky seems bluer than real, and
the horizon looks a mighty long way off. Unhindered by topography, it lays
the grasses down and strips moisture from the soil. There isn't much moisture to begin with—only about 14 inches of rainfall per year. Trees seek the
protection of coulees and the occasional river bottom. So do people. Towns
and ranch buildings are usually tucked into sheltered, timbered pockets.

The land is more rugged than it appears at first glance. The apparent
flatness is broken by badlands and flat-topped buttes that create numerous micro-habitats. Streams drain north toward the Yellowstone River,
chief among them the **Powder River,** fed by Wyoming's Bighorn
Mountains. William Clark, when he camped near its mouth in 1806,
named it the Redstone River for the reddish clinkers of burned coal
in the riverbed; it's not unusual for coal seams to ignite spontaneously
or from lightning strikes. Despite that, the Indian name is the one used
today. "Powder" is the translation of the Mandan or Hidatsa word "war-
har-sah." Both terms are descriptive of the actual river.

This region was prime bison country for the Plains Indians. By
the late 1800s, these giants were gone and cattle occupied the range. Vast
ranches, some of them owned by European nobility, ran enormous herds.
But cattle lacked the bison's natural toughness, and the enormous
ranches defaulted. Today's holdings are much smaller.

The region's natural focal points tend to be breaks in the prairie—
wooded river hollows and scattered bluffs. **Medicine Rocks State Park** is
a 320-acre prairie island featuring weirdly eroded outcrops. A small park
with a few primitive campsites, it was viewed by Indians as a sacred place,
hence its name. Legend has it that Sitting Bull camped here shortly before
the Battle of the Little Bighorn. It is not hard to see why Native Americans came here to pray. On a hot summer day the rocks seem to catch
and hold the cooling wind, which sighs through the long needles of ponderosa pines and lifts the wings of raptors. Mule deer and meadowlarks
are common, and owls hooting in the night are answered by coyotes.

The scene is much the same on the other side of Ekalaka, where
Custer National Forest *(Sioux Ranger District, Camp Crook, S. Dak. 605-
797-4432)* manages several tracts of piney woodland. These offer peaceful
wandering in summer; landmarks include the high white cliffs of **Chalk
Buttes** and the dome made of volcanic ash called **Capitol Rock.** ■

Yellowstone/Missouri confluence

Confluence of the Yellowstone and Missouri Rivers

■ Northwestern North Dakota ■ Contact Fort Buford State Historic Site, Rte. 3, Box 67, Williston, ND 58801; phone 701-572-9034

THE CONFLUENCE OF the Yellowstone and Missouri Rivers lies just a few miles east of Montana's border with North Dakota at **Fort Buford State Historic Site** *(Just east of Buford, off N. Dak. 1804. Closed mid-Sept.– mid-May; adm. fee. Camping).* There, a grassy bank overlooks the Missouri and faces the gravelly mouth of the Yellowstone, which stretches off into the distant plains as a wooded ribbon bending beneath a long band of low, broken cliffs. It's a beautiful setting, full of birds and history. Lewis and Clark camped on the point between the rivers nearby in April 1805, and Lewis wrote of the same "pleasing view of the country, perticularly of the wide and fertile vallies formed by the missouri and the yellowstone rivers, which occasionally unmasked by the wood on their borders disclose their meanderings for many miles in their passage through these delightfull tracts of country." In those days, the vast grasslands surrounding the rivers teemed with bison, elk, and pronghorn so gentle "that we pass near them while feeding, without apearing to excite any alarm among them."

As long as you're in the area, consider a stop at **Fort Union Trading Post National Historic Site** *(N. Dak. 1804, Buford. 701-572-9083),* a splendid reconstruction of an 1850s fur trading post that also offers a fine vista of the confluence. So do the prairie hills behind the fort, where the Swiss artist Karl Bodmer painted his 1833 landscape of the site. ■

Devils Tower National Monument

■ 1,347 acres ■ Northeastern Wyoming, east of Gillette via I-90, Wyo. 113, and Wyo. 24 ■ Best months May-Sept. ■ Camping, hiking, rock climbing, bird-watching, wildlife viewing ■ Adm. fee ■ Contact the national monument, P.O. Box 10, Devils Tower, WY 82714; phone 307-467-5283. www.nps.gov/deto

LOCATED IN WYOMING'S northeast corner, Devils Tower rises as an anomalous, flat-topped column of bare gray rock that punches straight up for 867 feet and overlooks a gently rolling landscape of grassy meadows, open ponderosa pine forests, and meandering riverbanks. Scored by hundreds of parallel grooves that rake its nearly vertical walls from top to bottom, it forms the centerpiece of the country's first national monument, established in 1906. It is a geologic curiosity, a sacred Native American site, a rock-climbing mecca, and a pleasant spot for a casual day hike.

The tower formed about 60 million years ago when a plume of magma forced its way up through thick layers of multicolored sedimentary rock and collected in a massive lump that lay buried beneath the surface or, perhaps, within the neck of an ancient volcano. In either case, as the magma cooled, the rock contracted and fractured into multisided (usually hexagonal) columns measuring roughly 4 to 8 feet in diameter. Over millions of years, the ancestral Belle Fourche River washed away the soft sedimentary rocks surrounding the hard igneous core and gradually exposed the tower.

Legend of Devils Tower

Long before a U.S. Army colonel named the rock formation Devils Tower, various tribes knew it as Bear's Tipi, Bear Lodge Butte, and other related names. The bear connection stems from a Native American legend in which a bear chases several children onto a giant tree stump. The stump rises from the earth and lifts the children out of harm's way. In one version, the bear falls off and dies, and the children make a rope with wildflowers and lower themselves down. In another, the children are borne into the heavens where they become the Seven Sisters constellation.

Today, the tower and its surrounding landscape combine aspects of three rich habitats—mountain, prairie, riparian—and bring into close proximity disparate plant and animal species. On the tower itself, prairie falcons nest among the ledges. Least chipmunks, pack rats, and woodrats also live at the top of the tower, nibbling at grasses, forbs, and shrubs. At the tower's base, ponderosa pines form a breezy canopy over a sun-dappled forest floor where white-tailed deer spend much of the day browsing among the shrubs. On the valley floor stretch large meadows teeming with rodents: mice, shrews, voles, gophers, and a very large colony of black-tailed prairie dogs. The rodents attract a

Devils Tower

wide variety of predators: coyotes, red foxes, badgers, long-tailed weasels, hawks, and owls.

Through the meadows flows the clear, swift water of the Belle Fourche River, which meanders beneath high bluffs of vermilion mud and red sandstone. Cottonwoods along its banks form prime nesting spots for wood ducks, great horned owls, and red-headed woodpeckers. Great blue herons wade along the banks on stilt legs, alert for frogs and small fish.

What to See and Do

Exhibits at the **visitor center** cover climbing history (admire Fritz Weissner's rope-soled climbing shoes) and provide a rundown on the monument's major life zones. During summer, rangers offer 15- to 20-minute interpretive talks on a variety of natural and cultural history topics. They also lead a one-hour interpretive walk around the base of Devils Tower and present 30-minute climbing demonstrations that explain the use of ropes and other climbing gear. Spotting scopes along the parking lot allow visitors to watch climbers inch their way up the soaring stump of striated stone.

The paved, 1.6-mile **Tower Trail** circles the base of the tower, threading among large boulders and winding in and out of the shade of ponderosa pines and junipers. The trail offers plenty of neck-craning perspectives of the tower and leads to several sweeping vistas of the **Black Hills** and the shallow valley carved across the land by the **Belle Fourche River.** Interpretive signs posted along the way trace climbing routes, describe animals living at the top and at the base, and explain how erosion occasionally peels off one of the tower's massive columns.

The 2.8-mile **South Side/Red Beds Trail** circles Devils Tower from a more distant perspective. From the visitor center it loops through pine groves and meadows, skirts the park's prairie dog colony, then winds past vivid, iron-stained bluffs known as the **Red Beds.**

Located in the park's northern section, the 1.5-mile **Joyner Ridge Trail** tours the various life zones found near Devils Tower. From the trailhead off the monument's West Road, it stretches through a ridgetop forest, drops past sandstone cliffs into a meadow (look for deer), and then loops back to the start through a grove of deciduous trees and a prairie. The trail offers tremendous sunset vistas of the tower's north face and includes interpretive plaques that describe the ecological checks and balances of the area.

Along the monument's entry road, you'll find a large **prairie dog town** that sprawls across a flat expanse of shortgrass between the foot of the tower and the river. Trails skirt the perimeter of the bustling colony, and an excellent brochure describes the rodents' burrow system and their strict territorial rules. It also explains how they use warning barks and body language for mutual defense against predators. ■

Pronghorn

Thunder Basin National Grassland

■ 562,000 acres ■ Northeast Wyoming; main unit is west of Newcastle off Wyo. 433 ■ Best months May-Sept. ■ Primitive camping, mountain biking, bird-watching, wildlife viewing ■ Contact Douglas Ranger District, Medicine Bow-Routt National Forest, 2250 East Richards, Douglas, WY 82633; 307-358-4690

A SPRAWLING PATCHWORK of private and public lands, Thunder Basin National Grassland lies in northeast Wyoming and takes in nearly 880 square miles of rolling, shortgrass plains punctuated by forested ridges, rocky knobs, high plateaus, and steep, eroded slopes. Vistas seem endless, humans are scarce, and the sky often fills with gleaming thunderheads that tower tens of thousands of feet above the darkened land and stab the prairies with lightning bolts like Jove on a rampage.

Grasses such as blue grama, needle-and-thread, and western wheat-grass carpet most of this semiarid landscape, but sagebrush and prickly pear cactus also dominate in certain areas. Ponderosa pines and juniper trees gather in small forests along the tops of some ridges, and narrow groves of cottonwoods follow the few shallow watercourses.

More pronghorn live here than anywhere else in Wyoming. They dash across the plains in large herds, graze casually along the fence lines, and add a dash of the Serengeti to the Great Plains. Though pronghorn are the most visible ungulate, they share the terrain with mule deer, white-tailed deer, and elk. Mountain lions stalk the grazers, and other predators such as coyotes, badgers, hawks, and eagles feast on a bountiful harvest of small rodents and rabbits.

The area's rivers, streams, and many small ponds attract an abundance of birds, both wetland and upland. Western grebes, American white pelicans, double-crested cormorants, great blue herons, and many types of ducks stick to the moister spots, while prairie falcons, hawks, sage grouse, and yellow warblers grace the plains.

Shortgrass prairies, like those of Thunder Basin, are the driest and most fragile of all grasslands. A small decline in precipitation can shift the balance from prairie to desert—especially when dry weather is coupled with the wrong sort of human interference. During the 1930s, a combination of unsound farming methods, overgrazing by livestock, and years of drought turned much of the region into a dust bowl. The federal government bought up hundreds of failed homesteads, reseeded the prairie, planted windbreaks, and built dams and ponds. Within a decade, the desert retreated and a new shortgrass prairie grew in its place.

White-tailed doe among big bluestem

For a taste of this grand and open landscape, follow Wyo. 59 between Gillette and Bill. Side roads wander for dozens of miles and make for rewarding mountain bike excursions, especially in the early morning or late evening, when wildlife is most active. Pronghorn will be up and about; so will deer. Birds of prey, which may pass much of the day on fenceposts, will glide through the sky in search of rodents, rabbits and snakes. Contact the Douglas Ranger District (see p. 223) for detailed maps. ■

Renewable Grasses

Perennial grasses protect themselves from grazing animals by retaining most of their biomass underground and through an unusual growth system in their leaves. By centering growth at the base of the grass, cows, bison elk, or deer can clip away without interfering with the plant's ability to renew itself.

Glacier-Panhandle

Grinnell Glacier Trail, Glacier National Park

STRETCHING WEST FROM THE VERY EDGE of the Great
Plains, this spectacular region of glaciated mountains, wild
rivers, and pristine lakes takes in the northwest corner of
Montana, the northern tip of Idaho's Panhandle and Waterton Lakes National Park in southern Alberta province. Its
eastern perimeter is formed by the great Rocky Mountain
Front, a vast mountain wall that extends southeast from
Canada nearly to Helena. Beyond that initial rampart lie
range after range of tightly packed mountains that grow

gentler, lower, and wetter the farther west you go. This procession of mountain crests is interrupted just twice by major valleys. The first, the Rocky Mountain Trench, starts near St. Ignatius, Montana, cradles Flathead Lake, and stretches northwest into Canada as far as the Yukon. The second, the Purcell Trench, separates the major mountain ranges of the panhandle and includes Lake Pend Oreille and Coeur d'Alene Lake.

Glacier National Park crowns the region's northeastern sector and adjoins Canada's Waterton Lakes National Park. Both preserve classic alpine terrain and harbor an abundance of wildlife. To the southeast sprawl the equally spectacular but remote wildlands of the Bob Marshall, Great Bear, and Scapegoat Wilderness areas. To the west and southwest, major mountain groups include the Swan, Mission, and Whitefish Ranges, which form the eastern wall of the Rocky Mountain Trench and face the Salish Mountains. Next come the Purcells, Cabinets, and Coeur d'Alenes, which form the east wall of the Purcell Trench and face the Selkirk Mountains.

The Continental Divide meanders along the region's eastern margin, splitting precipitation between the Atlantic and Pacific watersheds. Rivers spilling out of the mountains onto the plains include the Sun, Teton, and tributaries of the Marias, which flow into the Missouri. Major west-bound watercourses include the luscious forks of the Flathead River. The divide also marks an abrupt climatological boundary. To the east the weather is drier and colder and supports vegetation typical of the northern Rockies. West of the divide, warmer, wetter weather predominates.

Scattered along the divide's west side are several exceptionally large and beautiful lakes: Flathead, Pend Oreille, Coeur d'Alene, and Priest. Havens for bald eagles and ospreys, the lakes warm sufficiently during late summer to offer a tolerable swim.

The region's most dependable wildlife sites lie within Glacier and Waterton Lakes, which provide homes for grizzlies, black bears, gray wolves, mountain goats, bighorn sheep, elk, deer, moose, mountain lions, pronghorn, and a host of smaller animals. Many of these same animals roam throughout the region, and other sites add species that the Glacier area lacks. A herd of bison clips the grass at the National Bison Range, for instance, and woodland caribou tread the forests near Priest Lake.

At first glance, the region's eastern mountains seem to have little in common with those of the panhandle. Along the Rocky Mountain Front, the peaks jut far above tree line as jagged, knife-edged ridges or as great bulky masses of bare rock. Cirques, amphitheaters, and hanging valleys pockmark the high country, and vast cliff faces plunge thousands of feet into deep, glacially carved valleys. In contrast, the panhandle's mountains are smoother, rounder, and lower. They have broad backs and are usually covered over with moist evergreen forests.

Though scenically distinct, the two sets of mountains share an important geologic thread that binds them not just to one another but to virtually every rock that lies between them. With few exceptions, the region's mountains are composed of ancient sedimentary rock slabs that slid into place from the west. At first, the rocks moved on very deep thrust faults, shoved along by the

Flathead Lake, Montana

titanic collision between the Pacific and North American tectonic plates. The collision thickened and raised the continent's western margin and formed an unstable bulge that began shedding enormous slabs of rock 60 million to 70 million years ago. The huge slabs plowed eastward for almost 100 miles before grinding to a halt and eventually forming the mountains of Glacier, the Rocky Mountain Front, and the rest of the mountain ranges that pile up to the west as far as the Rocky Mountain Trench. Taken together, they are known as Montana's Overthrust Belt and appear to have slid off the rocks that now compose the Salish Mountains. Farther west stand the Cabinets and Purcells. They, too, are comprised mainly of sedimentary slabs that slid into place from the west. Unlike their eastern neighbors, however, they peeled away from a rising mass of granitic magma known as a batholith. The granites of that batholith now compose parts of the Selkirks.

All of this movement happened long before ice age glaciers completely revamped the surface of the land. Those giant glaciers explain in large part why the panhandle's mountains look so different from those along the Rocky Mountain Front. In the northern panhandle, glaciers 6,000 feet deep buried most of the peaks and plowed them smooth. In the east, many of the mountains were high enough to protrude from the ice. They retained many of their rough edges and were further cut apart by small alpine glaciers that formed among the heights.

The ice ages were also responsible for a series of cataclysmic floods that originated in this region, swept across eastern Washington, and blasted out to sea through the Columbia River Gorge. Known as the Spokane Floods, they were caused by a glacier that repeatedly dammed the Clark Fork River at the northeast corner of present Lake Pend Oreille. Each time it formed, the ice dam impounded a reservoir as large as Lake Ontario, then blew apart, unleashing all of the water in a matter of days. ■

Hiker in the Rockies, Glacier National Park

Glacier and Waterton National Parks

■ 1 million acres (Glacier), 129,920 acres (Waterton Lakes) ■ Northern Montana, north of Kalispell on US 2; southern Alberta Rte. 6 ■ Best months late June-Sept. Snow sometimes closes Going-to-the-Sun Road until late June, and fresh blizzards descend on it in late Oct. ■ Camping, hiking, boating, whitewater rafting, swimming, horseback riding, bird-watching, wildlife viewing ■ Adm. fee ■ Bear-country precautions pertain while hiking and camping ■ Contact Glacier NP, West Glacier, MT 59936; phone 406-888-7800, www.nps/gov/glac/. Waterton Lakes NP, Waterton Park, Alberta, Canada T0K 2M0; phone 403-859-2224, parkscanada.pch.gc.ca/waterton/

RANKING EASILY AMONG the most spectacular natural preserves in North America, Glacier and Waterton Lakes National Parks rise from the edge of the Great Plains in northwestern Montana and sprawl westward across the Continental Divide toward some of the wildest lands in the northern Rockies. They encompass a magnificent, powerfully glaciated landscape of brawny, bare-rock peaks, knife-edged ridges, and grand cliff faces that plunge thousands of feet into spacious, densely forested valleys. Snowfields and glaciers dot the high country, and hundreds of creeks and waterfalls stream into long, fjordlike lakes at the base of the mountains.

Established in 1910, Glacier is sometimes thought to have been named for the 30 to 40 small glaciers that nibble away at its highest summits. Instead, it stands as a testament to the overwhelming force of immense ice age glaciers, which began gnawing away at the park's mountains at least two million years ago and which have left their mark at nearly every turn. Cirques, amphitheaters, hanging valleys, humpbacked moraines, razor-sharp crests, and huge, U-shaped valleys all attest to the work of those ice monsters.

In addition to its splendid terrain, Glacier—along with the adjoining Canadian national park, Waterton Lakes—is a first-class wildlife preserve.

Mountain goats step nimbly among the crags. Grizzly bears hunt for berries and glacier lily bulbs, and dig up ground squirrels in high country meadows, and black bears roam the forests. Without much effort, you can also see bighorn sheep, deer, elk, moose, birds of prey, and a host of smaller animals. More elusive are the gray wolves that independently colonized Glacier's remote North Fork Valley during the mid-1980s.

Though it is vast, rugged, and wild, Glacier is an easy park to visit. Major highways hug its perimeter, and its east and west sides are connected by the Going-to-the-Sun Road, one of the nation's most spectacular mountain drives. Historic stone-and-timber lodges adorn some of the park's most popular vistas. And an excellent trail network opens up the backcountry, offering everything from casual strolls to rigorous, cross-country treks.

The geologic story of both parks began more than 1.5 billion years ago, when this part of the continent lay along the shifting coast of a primordial sea. Layers of sand, silt, and limy mud were deposited along the coast and across the seabed. Over the course of hundreds of millions of years, the sediments grew to a thickness of 3 to 5 miles, preserving within themselves ripple marks and mud cracks that can still be seen today. The accumulated weight caused the seabed to sag and also changed the deposits into limestone, dolomite, siltite, and argillite.

The bottom portion of those rock layers now compose Glacier's mountains, but they originally rested roughly 50 miles to the west. They began rising toward the earth's surface approximately 60 million years ago during the general mountain-building phase that created the Rockies. But instead of simply rising in place, the slab broke away in pieces and slid slowly eastward, perhaps across a lubricating layer of clay and silt. It finally ground to a halt in what is now Glacier (and Waterton Lakes) National Park.

The cliffs that rise so abruptly from the plains on Glacier's east side represent the leading edge of the slab, called the Lewis Overthrust

Mountain Goats

Superbly adapted to life among the Rockies' cliffs, mountain goats have strong forequarters to pull themselves up rock faces and two-toed hooves with spongy central pads that help grip any smooth surface. The rocky habitat protects them from predators but does not offer much grazing. As a result, the goats fiercely defend their food sources. They jab at intruders with their sharp horns, and sometimes even try to butt them off cliffs.

Mountain goat   Following pages: Moose and calf, Glacier National Park

West Side Forest

On Glacier's warmer, moister west side, a deep forest of hemlock, cedar, larch, white pine, and birch surrounds Lake McDonald and spreads over the lower slopes of the mountains. Like most forests, it divides into layers. At the top, a dense canopy of branches forms a protective roof over the forest community. Below it grows an understory of young trees, then a shrub layer of plants that grow to head height. Next comes the herb layer of wildflowers, grasses, and ferns. Finally, on the forest floor, you'll find mosses, fungi, and vines.

Fault. And the very line of the thrust fault itself can be seen clearly at Marias Pass, where rock more than one billion years old lies on top of rock just 60 to 70 million years old.

For tens of millions of years, erosion chipped away and carried off the upper layers of the thrust fault block. Eventually, the strata we see today was exposed, waiting only for the onset of the great ice ages to carve the peaks and ridges into their present form.

The results of all that uplift, overthrust, and glaciation are two parallel mountain ranges that extend across the heart of Glacier from northwest to southeast. They are the **Livingston Range,** the more westerly of the two, and the **Lewis Range,** which overlooks the Great Plains. Along the crest of the mountains runs the Continental Divide, which follows the spine of the Livingstons south out of Canada and then skips over to the Lewis Range.

The park's western waters collect in the Flathead River drainage and eventually flow to the Pacific by way of the Columbia River. On the east side, some of the water takes the Missouri River route to the Gulf of Mexico, while some heads northeast across the Canadian interior and eventually to Hudson Bay.

But the Continental Divide does more than split Glacier's precipitation. It also forms a climatological boundary. Warm, moist air moving in from the Pacific gets trapped behind the mountain barrier, which robs the clouds of their moisture and casts a long, dry rain shadow over the cooler eastern plains. The effect on plant growth is unmistakable. On the west side, in McDonald Valley, you'll find misty groves of cedar and hemlock that tower over a spongy floor of moss and decomposing vegetation. On the east side, drier forests of spruce, fir, and pine alternate with broad prairie meadows.

As elevation increases, differences between east and west diminish. Broad bands of evergreen forest cloak both sides of the divide. Lodgepole pine and Douglas-fir predominate along the middle slopes. Higher up, Englemann spruce, subalpine fir, and whitebark pine share an increasingly difficult foothold with thickets of berry bushes and meadows of wildflowers, sedges, and grasses. Eventually, the combined effects of cold, wind, poor soil, and intense sunlight stunt the trees to near shrub status and confine them in tiny, forlorn pockets surrounded by the exhilarating, open terrain of the high country.

Lake McDonald, Glacier National Park

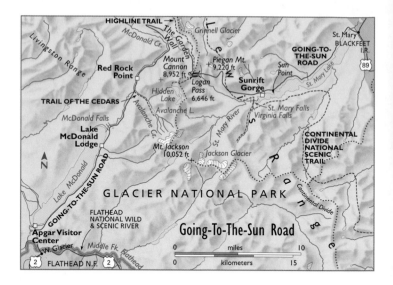

What to See and Do

Going-to-the-Sun Road

Most visits to Glacier begin with a trip across Logan Pass on this aptly named alpine highway, and no wonder. It climbs over some of the park's most spectacular mountains, offers many chances to see wildlife, and visits all of the park's most important habitats. It also takes in Glacier's major interpretive centers and leads to many of the park's most popular day hikes.

Though the road covers just 52 miles, it is so full of interesting stops that you can easily spend an entire day making the trip—and then decide to spend the next several days going back to linger at your favorite spots. (Check with park officials for oversize vehicle restrictions.)

It's best to start from the east side, early in the day, when the morning light favors the peaks looming over St. Mary Lake. A **visitor center** just inside the park

entrance offers an orientation film, exhibits, weather information, and advice from a battery of friendly park employees.

The road sets off along the shore of **St. Mary Lake,** which runs for 10 miles, occupies a deep, glacial trough, and penetrates far into the mountains. If you get started early enough, you may see deer, elk, and coyotes in the prairie meadows north of the road.

Toward the head end of the lake, stroll the **Sun Point Nature Trail,** which leads to a stunning panorama of the widely spaced, glaciated mountains that rise so gracefully from St. Mary Lake. From there, you can also see the distant top of the Continental Divide. A peaks-finder chart bolted to a rock helps to identify the summits.

Farther along, narrow **Sunrift Gorge** cuts through a cliff and funnels the waters of Baring Creek down to a 30-foot waterfall (take the quarter-mile trail below the road). Shortly beyond Sunrift Gorge, you'll find the 1-mile trail to **St. Mary Falls,** a fierce double-stranded cascade that boils through a tight chasm. Another half-mile's walk along the same trail leads to 100-foot **Virginia Falls.**

Beyond Sunrift Gorge, the road begins its long climb through the broad bands of evergreen forest that cloak the midriff of Glacier's mountains. This is deep forest, home to black bears, grizzly bears, deer, grouse, and red and ground squirrels. From the **Jackson Glacier Overlook,** gaze across the canopy to the distant slopes of **Mount Jackson** and see the remnant of **Jackson Glacier,** which has shrunk in recent years to a fraction of its 19th-century size.

Wild rose

At **Siyeh Bend,** the road makes a hairpin turn and passes from dense forest into the scrubby, subalpine vegetation typical of Glacier's high country. Bighorn sheep and mountain goats are often spotted on the cliffs above the bend, and grizzly bears roam high open valleys like the one just beyond the road.

As you approach 6,646-foot **Logan Pass,** the road traverses the sheer walls of Piegan Mountain, opening up nearly airborne vistas of the **St. Mary Valley.** The pass, an open saddle surrounded by vast wildflower meadows and the upper ramparts of some of Glacier's finest peaks, was scoured by two immense glaciers that formed about a million years ago on either side of an intervening ridge. One hollowed out the St. Mary Valley, while the other carved the **McDonald Valley,** which opens to the west. In time, the glaciers wore completely through the rock separating them and then merged. The last of the ice finally melted from the pass several thousand years ago.

The **Logan Pass Visitor Center** has exhibits that explain more about the glaciers and identify plants and animals that live in the glorious but harsh alpine tundra environment surrounding the pass.

Mountain goats frequent the pass, but your best chance for seeing them up close lies along the 1.5-mile, mostly boardwalk trail that climbs through the meadows behind the visitor center to **Hidden Lake Overlook** (see pp. 241-43). Even without goats, the walk is worth the time just for the wildflowers, ground squirrels, and the plunging vista of **Hidden Lake.**

From Logan Pass, the road descends along the flank of **The Garden Wall,** which is covered with pockets of dwarf subalpine fir and thickets of berry bushes where black bears and grizzlies fatten up

Grizzly bear

during autumn. Roadside exhibits identify hanging valleys and ribbony waterfalls, point out the effects of wildfire, and describe some of the fascinating adaptations plants and animals make to the high-country environment.

Soon you're down on the valley floor, following **McDonald Creek** through the moist, west side forest of cedar, larch, hemlock, and cottonwood. Duck through the trees at **Red Rock Point** to admire the vivid blue water of the creek zigzagging through tilted blocks and ledges of red mudstone. Mount Cannon juts 5,000 feet above the current.

Not far beyond, pull into the Avalanche Creek parking area and follow the 1-mile **Trail of the Cedars,** which loops through an ancient climax forest of colossal western redcedar, hemlock, and black cottonwood. At the trail's upper end, the sapphire waters of **Avalanche Creek** spill through a chasm of smooth red mudstone and emerald green moss. The trail to **Avalanche Lake,** which breaks off nearby, parallels the chasm for several hundred yards.

Continuing west on Going-to-the-Sun Road, look for the footbridge that spans McDonald Creek at **Sacred Dancing Cascade,** a quarter-mile series of rapids and falls. The trail here leads downstream a quarter mile to the lip of **McDonald Falls.**

Then, back on the road, it's on to **Lake McDonald,** that irresistible, late-summer oasis shaded by cedars and warm enough for swimming. You might drop by the historic **Lake McDonald Lodge** (602-207-6000), built in 1913, but the real draw here are the unmarked beaches of red

Glacier's Grizzlies

Despite their ferocious reputation, Glacier's roughly 200 grizzlies subsist on a mainly vegetarian diet. During spring and summer, they wander the high country, scarfing up leaves, roots, stems, and insects. In the autumn, they rove wherever they can find ripe berries. Some even follow berry-rich stream courses out onto the Montana plains. For meat, they dig through avalanche debris in the spring, looking for mountain goats and bighorn sheep that have been swept to their deaths. They also dig Columbian ground squirrels from their burrows—easy autumn prey once the rodents go into hibernation.

and green pebbles that you'll find beyond the forest fringe at almost every turnout along the road. The lake occupies yet another glacial trough, bounded on either side by high lateral moraines.

Hike to Hidden Lake Overlook
One of the most popular short hikes in Glacier, this easy, 3-mile, round-trip trail to Hidden Lake Overlook starts behind the Logan Pass Visitor Center and climbs 460 feet to a drop-away vista of Hidden Lake. Along the way, you're likely to see mountain goats, and there is always the chance you might spot a distant grizzly bear.

As you start out, you'll pass through an island of stunted subalpine fir. These are not saplings,

Hidden Lake Overlook

but old growth. Some trees just a few inches in diameter can be hundreds of years old. Their size reflects the harsh environment, with its short growing season, cold temperatures even in summer, bitter winds, intense sunlight, high evaporative rates, and gravelly soils.

Soon you step onto a boardwalk built to protect the fragile alpine meadows from foot traffic. Directly ahead is 8,760-foot **Clements Mountain.** The similar peak to the left is 9,125-foot **Reynolds Mountain.** Both are "horns," which form when three or more glaciers gnaw away at a mountain from different directions and hew the rock into a sharp point.

The tiny wildflowers, sedges, and grasses around you have adapted to the ferocious climate in remarkable ways. Their compact size conserves moisture and requires fewer nutrients. Many contain chemicals that turn sunlight into heat, and some can grow through a layer of snow.

Few animals live all year in Glacier's high country, but one of them, the Columbian ground squirrel, teems in these meadows during summer. True hibernators, the squirrels pass the winters in their burrows, where their body temperatures can drop to 37°F.

Once off the boardwalk, start looking for mountain goats among the tree islands and rocky outcroppings below Clements Mountain. Soon you reach the overlook, with **Hidden Lake** nestled 750 feet below in its glacially carved basin.

Many Glacier

A favorite visit among hikers, climbers, and bear-watchers, Many Glacier lies off the park road from Babb on the park's east side, where three glacial basins converge amid a glorious tangle of soaring peaks and ridges, gemlike lakes and waterfalls. Anchored by the historic **Many Glacier Hotel** *(602-207-6000),* a Swiss-style lodge built in 1914-15 by the Great Northern Railway, the area forms the hub of a large trail network that offers everything from an hour's stroll to week-long treks. It is also one of the most dependable sites in the park for seeing black bears and grizzlies, mountain goats and bighorn sheep.

Drop by the hotel's immense but rustic lobby to take in the boffo vista of **Swiftcurrent Lake.**

The U-shaped, glacial profile of the converging valleys is very clear from this spot, especially along the slopes of **Grinnell Point,** the massive peak straight across the lake.

The options for hiking from Many Glacier are virtually endless, but you might try the easy, 2.5-mile **Swiftcurrent Nature Trail,** which begins at the picnic ground across from the Many Glacier Hotel and circles the lake. A shorter but more strenuous hike climbs about 700 feet to **Apikuni Falls,** a 2-mile round-trip moderate trek; find the trailhead a mile east of the hotel. Another popular walk is along the easy, 3.6-mile (round-trip) **Swiftcurrent Pass Trail,** which leads from the end of the Many Glacier Road to **Redrock Falls,** a lovely cascade that tumbles and pools into the upper end of Redrock Lake.

Other classic day hikes include trails to **Cracker Lake** *(12.2 miles round-trip, moderate, starts from parking area behind Many Glacier Hotel);* **Grinnell Glacier** *(10.2*

Prince of Wales Hotel overlooking Upper Waterton Lake, Waterton Lakes NP

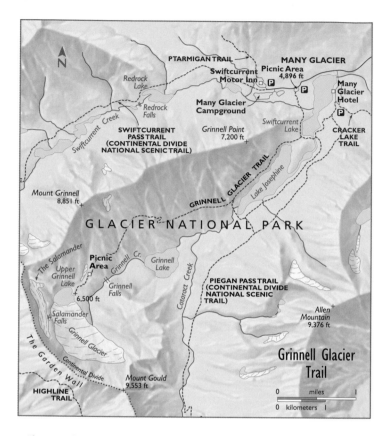

N

PTARMIGAN TRAIL

MANY GLACIER

Swiftcurrent Picnic Area
Motor Inn   4,896 ft

Redrock
Lake

Many
Glacier
Hotel

Many Glacier
Campground

Redrock
Falls

SWIFTCURRENT
PASS TRAIL
(CONTINENTAL DIVIDE
NATIONAL SCENIC TRAIL)

Swiftcurrent Creek

Grinnell Point
7,200 ft

Swiftcurrent
Lake

CRACKER
LAKE
TRAIL

Mount Grinnell
8,851 ft

GRINNELL GLACIER TRAIL

Lake Josephine

G L A C I E R   N A T I O N A L   P A R K

The Salamander

Picnic
Area

Grinnell Cr.

Grinnell
Lake

Cataract Creek

Upper
Grinnell
Lake

6,500 ft

Grinnell
Falls

PIEGAN PASS TRAIL
(CONTINENTAL DIVIDE
NATIONAL SCENIC
TRAIL)

Salamander
Falls

Grinnell Glacier

Allen
Mountain
9,376 ft

The Garden Wall

Continental Divide

Mount Gould
9,553 ft

**Grinnell Glacier
Trail**

HIGHLINE
TRAIL

0   miles   1
0   kilometers   1

miles round-trip, moderate, starts
from picnic area, see below); **Ice-
berg Lake** (9.4 miles round-trip,
moderate, starts on Ptarmigan
Trail); and **Swiftcurrent Lookout**
(16.2 miles round-trip, difficult,
begins on Swiftcurrent Pass Trail).

Some of these day hikes are
routinely led by park naturalists
during summer. You can pick up
a schedule at the ranger station,
located near the campground at
the end of the road.

Hike to Grinnell Glacier
This pleasant, 11-mile, round-trip
day hike to the foot of one of the
park's largest glaciers begins at the
Many Glacier picnic area and fol-

lows a chain of lakes through the
forest and up into a sensational
amphitheater of ice-laden rock
streaming with waterfalls. In
autumn, bears feast in berry thickets near the trail, and all summer
long you're likely to see bighorn
sheep and mountain goats among
the ledges and boulder fields.

The first 2 miles are easy, skirting the western shorelines of
Swiftcurrent Lake and **Lake
Josephine.** At Lake Josephine's
southwest end, bear right and
begin the steady climb up 8,851-
foot **Mount Grinnell.** As you pass
through the layer of vermilion
mudstone, look for ripple marks
and mud cracks that formed hun-

dreds of millions of years ago when the region lay beneath an ancient sea.

Soon, the trail passes above tiny **Grinnell Lake.** The water gets its turquoise color from rock powder milled by upstream glaciers. The powder, sometimes called glacial flour, remains in suspension and refracts blue light into this lovely shade of bluish green. Farther along, the trail starts switchbacking and two glaciers come into view on the great wall of rock straight ahead: **The Salamander,** the higher of the two, and **Grinnell,** which terminates in Upper Grinnell Lake.

Eventually you reach a small picnic area at the base of a steep, lateral moraine. The trail climbs over the moraine to a grandstand vista of the lake and its glaciers. Grinnell and The Salamander once formed a single body of ice, but they receded and separated in recent geologic time. You can make your way down to the edge of Grinnell Glacier (0.4 mile), but walking on its surface can be mighty dangerous and is not recommended.

Two Medicine Valley

Just a shade less dramatic than Many Glacier but much less crowded, Two Medicine Valley is located off Mont. 49 south of Kiowa. This lovely, high-country valley was plowed out by glaciers that carved the surrounding peaks into interesting shapes and left behind chains of lakes and waterfalls. It's a great spot for hiking and a likely one for seeing bighorn sheep, mountain goats, and bears.

Have a quick look at **Two Medicine Lake,** then double back on the entrance road to the trail for **Running Eagle Falls,** an easy, half-mile round-trip walk. This curious, double-channeled waterfall, formerly known as Trick Falls, spills both over the edge and through the face of a beautiful limestone cliff. Or, take the boat *(fare)* to the upper end of Two Medicine Lake and walk an easy mile to **Twin Falls,** where two strands of cascading water tumble from a shaded cliff and pool over a bed of red mudstone.

More ambitious day hikes include trails to **Upper Two Medicine Lake** *(10 miles round-trip, easy);* **Oldman Lake** at the foot of Pitamakan Pass *(11 miles round-trip, moderate);* and **Scenic Point** *(6.2 miles round-trip, difficult),* which offers a commanding view of the Two Medicine Valley.

A short drive south of Two Medicine Junction on Mont. 49 brings you to **East Glacier Park,** worth a stop just to see **Glacier Park Lodge** *(602-207-6000).* Another legacy of the Great Northern Railway, the hotel was built in 1912-13 on a post-and-beam frame made from massive, unpeeled logs. The biggest members—cut from trees 500 to 800 years old—stand as columns in the hotel's lobby.

North Fork Valley

Occupying Glacier's northwest sector, this broad valley embraces the **North Fork Flathead River** and accesses a handful of large mountain lakes gripped by densely forested ridges and sheer, glaciated cliffs. It's the park's quietest corner accessible by road, and is especially rewarding to those with hand-

Following pages: Lake McDonald

powered watercraft. Various entry points along the river offer scenic float trips spiced by Class II and III rapids. Still-water paddlers can penetrate far into the backcountry on **Bowman** or **Kintla Lakes,** both of which offer backcountry camping.

Deer, moose, elk, and bears live in the North Fork Valley, but the real stars are the gray wolves—rarely seen—that were reestablished here in the mid-1980s.

Two parallel roads on both sides of the river lead through the valley to Polebridge and beyond. Most people drive the western route, which begins at Apgar and follows the **Camas Road** through forest and meadow. At the park's western boundary with the Camas Road, consider a walk along the easy, 1-mile **Huckleberry Mountain Nature Trail,** a study in how forests recover from wildfire. Near Polebridge you'll pass through a more recent and more extensive burn (1988) now covered with wildflowers and young lodgepole pines.

Waterton Lakes National Park

Lying just across the Canadian border from Glacier, Waterton Lakes National Park offers much of the same scenery, wildlife, and geologic history as Glacier, but without the crowds.

The park's main valley encloses a chain of the three **Waterton Lakes,** beginning with **Upper Waterton Lake**—a long, narrow lake ringed by peaks that stretches south across the border into Glacier. With a maximum depth of 487 feet, Upper Waterton Lake is the deepest lake in the Canadian Rockies. Its frigid waters support trout, whitefish, sculpin, and suckers. Windswept, it is a popular, though chilly, board sailing destination. The middle and lower lakes run out to the prairie east of the park and clog every autumn with flocks of migratory waterfowl.

Drop by the visitor reception center for a map and a schedule of the park's guided hikes. One of the most popular departs from behind the building and climbs a steep three-quarters of a mile to **Bear's Hump,** which offers a grandstand vista of the upper lake. Nearby, stroll through the 1927 **Prince of Wales Hotel** *(403-236-3400),* an elegant, Swiss-style lodge that also overlooks the upper lake.

In the town of Waterton Park, a visit to the **Heritage Centre** *(Waterton Ave. 403-859-2224)* will catch you up on the park's natural history. Or consider a cruise *(Waterton Inter-Nation Shoreline Cruises 403-859-2362. Fare)* the length of Upper Waterton Lake to **Goat Haunt,** in Glacier, where an easy, 1-mile trail leads to **Rainbow Falls.** The cruise and stroll make for one of the nicest day trips in the area.

Elsewhere in Waterton, follow the Akamina Parkway to **Cameron Lake,** tucked into the subalpine forest beneath a cirque of high peaks. Or follow Blackiston Creek through a glaciated valley to **Red Rock Canyon,** a lovely chasm of pink rock and sapphire water where bighorn sheep congregate. On your way out of the park, take the loop road through the **bison paddock,** where 12 to 20 plains bison live in a large, grassy enclosure.

Sperry Glacier

More Activities

Guided Hikes

One of the ways to see and learn about Glacier or Waterton is to take one of the many guided hikes offered each week from such centers as Lake McDonald, Logan Pass, St. Mary Lake, Many Glacier, Two Medicine, Goat Haunt, the Waterton Park Information Centre, and Cameron Lake. These excellent interpretive hikes cover the geology, plants, and animals in all of the parks' major habitats and range in length from about an hour to an entire day. Some link up with excursion cruises on the major lakes.

Campfire Talks

If you're spending the night in either park, consider attending one of the informal lectures offered on the park's human or natural history, usually led by park rangers or interpreters at the campgrounds.

Boating

Excursion cruises *(fares)*, sometimes led by staff, are available on Lake McDonald (from Lake McDonald Lodge), St. Mary Lake (from Rising Sun), Two Medicine Lake, Swiftcurrent Lake (from Many Glacier), and Upper Waterton Lake. You can also rent canoes, rowboats, or lightly powered motorboats at Apgar, Lake McDonald Lodge, Many Glacier, Two Medicine, Waterton Park townsite, and Cameron Lake. You can also book white-water rafting trips on the forks of the Flathead through several private outfitters (*contact the parks for a list of outfitters*).

Horseback Riding

Guided trail rides *(fee)* are available in both parks, with stables near Apgar, Lake McDonald Lodge, Many Glacier, and the Waterton Park townsite.

Biking

Bicyclists are welcome in both parks, but roads are crowded and tend to be narrow with little or no shoulder. For this reason, sections of Going-to-the-Sun Road are closed to bicycles during some parts of the day in summer. One of Glacier's more secluded rides follows the Inside North Fork Road from the west end of Lake McDonald to Polebridge and on to Bowman and Kintla Lakes. ∎

Red Squirrels

The red squirrel—bold, irritably territorial, smart—is probably the most familiar creature of the deep forest. It eats mostly seeds, nuts, and cones but also dines on insects, birds' eggs, even nestlings. It also harvests fungi, hangs them on branches to dry, and then caches them.

Kid goat

Jewel Basin Hiking Area

■ 16,000 acres ■ Northwest Montana, east of Kalispell off Mont. 83 ■ Best months late June-Sept. ■ Hiking, fishing, wildlife viewing ■ Contact Flathead National Forest, 1935 3rd Ave., East Kalispell, MT 59901; phone 406-755-5401

SET ASIDE FOR FOOT travelers, this glaciated tract of subalpine forest, meadow, lake, and stream lies in the northern crest of the Swan Range. It's a small area, ideal for day hikes, with 35 miles of trails that link more than two dozen lakes and lead to panoramic vistas of the **Flathead Valley.**

Mountain goats, deer, elk, and bears—both black and grizzly—are abundant, as are mountain lions, bobcats, wolverines, coyotes, marmots, and many types of birds. Abrupt changes in elevation (more than 3,000 feet of variation) account for Jewel Basin's rich variety of habitats, which range from deep montane forests to scrubby patches of spruce and fir.

The **Swan Range,** which extends southeast from this point for nearly 100 miles, lies along the western margin of Montana's Overthrust Belt. Like the mountains of Glacier National Park, it is a vast, glaciated block of Precambrian sedimentary rock that slid eastward tens of millions of years ago.

You can reach trailheads for Jewel Basin from both sides of the range, but perhaps the closest access from Kalispell is along Forest Road 5392 *(take Mont. 83 E, turn N on the Echo Lake Rd., follow signs),* which switchbacks high into the west-facing slopes. Many hikes are possible, but one pleasant loop of 5 miles round-trip follows **Trail #8** north over the dividing crest, then drops to **Twin Lakes** before heading back south on **Trail #7,** with possible tangents into Jewel Basin proper, **Black Lake,** and **Picnic Lakes.** (An excellent topographic map is available at ranger stations in Hungry Horse or Bigfork.) ■

Classic Backcountry Trips

YOU CAN SPEND A contented lifetime skimming along the fringe of the northern Rockies' wildest lands by taking day trips along the region's trails and pristine rivers. But nothing can compare with spending some time safely out of reach of the nearest internal combustion engine. Here is a very brief list of classic hiking and boating trips that lead into the heart of the backcountry, where nothing will stand between you and the night sky but a scrim of ripstop nylon.

Teton Crest, Grand Teton NP and environs. Trails allow strong backpackers to traverse the entire length of the Teton Range from Teton Pass to the northern tip of Jackson Lake. But most opt for the shorter trek from Phillips Canyon to Leigh Lake, which winds through the craggy upper

Mount Moran, Grand Teton National Park

reaches of the range and descends to Jackson Hole through Paintbrush Canyon. 3-4 days. Contact Grand Teton NP 307-739-3300.

Highline Trail, Glacier NP. Starts at Logan Pass and crosses Glacier's high country for 43.6 miles to Waterton townsite, following the slopes of a razor-backed arête between McDonald Valley and the Many Glacier area. Connecting trails from Swiftcurrent Pass make a loop possible through Many

Glacier. Or continue north on the Highline to link with trails to Upper Waterton Lake. 4-6 days. Contact Glacier NP 406-888-7800.

Elkhart Park to Titcomb Valley, Wind River Range, Wyoming. The hike climbs from Elkhart Park trailhead at the end of Fremont Rd. northeast of Pinedale to expansive, boulder-strewn meadows and stunning lakes at the foot of Fremont Peak. Connecting trails go north to Green River Lakes and south to Cirque of the Towers. 5-14 days. Contact Pinedale Ranger District, Bridger-Teton NF, 307-367-4326.

East Rosebud Trail, Alpine to Cooke City, Beartooth Range, Montana. Hike along steep watercourses onto the glaciated back of the Beartooth Plateau, passing within sight of Granite Peak. Prime grizzly habitat. 3-4 days, one way. Contact Beartooth Ranger District, Custer NF, 406-446-2103.

Upper Missouri Wild and Scenic River. Located in north-central Montana, this 149-mile stretch of the Missouri extends from Fort Benton to US 191 and passes through a classic, high plains valley of badlands, prairie hills, and sandstone cliffs. 7-8 days; shorter floats are possible. Contact Lewiston Field Office, BLM, 406-538-7461.

Salmon River, central Idaho. One of the most sought-after stretches of wilderness white water, the Salmon booms westward through a deep gorge for 80 miles. Private permits are scarce but those willing to pay can easily book a commercial trip. 4-6 days. Contact North Fork Ranger District, Clearwater NF, 208-865-2383. ■

Flathead Lake State Park

■ 2,620 acres ■ Northwest Montana, south of Kalispell on US 93 ■ Closed Oct.-May; Wayfarers Unit open year-round ■ Camping, hiking, boating, swimming, wildlife viewing ■ Adm. fee ■ Contact park, 4901 N. Meridian St., Kalispell, MT 59901; phone 406-752-5501

DEEP, CLEAN, AND INVITING, Flathead Lake is the largest natural freshwater lake west of the Mississippi. It occupies a glacially formed basin south of Kalispell and stretches for 28 irresistible miles beneath the steep, densely wooded flank of the **Mission Range,** which looms nearly 3,500 feet above the eastern shore. Spilling off to the west are the **Salish Mountains,** with their more gently graded forests and open prairie foothills.

Among the bays, coves, points, and peninsulas that compose the lake's shoreline, the state park lies scattered in six small units that reflect the area's varying terrain, vistas, and wildlife. There are deep forests, pebble beaches, cliffs, open grasslands, and a large island. There are deer, elk, and even bighorn sheep, but you're more likely to spot bald eagles and ospreys roosting in the pines or plucking trout from the glimmering water.

Mule deer on Wild Horse Island, Flathead Lake

Located along the western fringe of Montana's Overthrust Belt, Flathead Lake was formed during the last ice age when glaciers carved much of the surrounding terrain. As the glaciers retreated, they stranded an enormous block of ice at the base of the Mission Range. Sand, mud, stones, and gravel washed down from the highlands and filled in around the block. When the ice melted, it left the basin now occupied by the lake.

What to See and Do

Most of the state park units lie along the west and east shores of Flathead Lake. Compact, shaded, always pleasant, they generally encompass just enough room for a campground, picnic area, boat ramp, beach, and perhaps some casual walking trails.

Along the west shore, look for **Big Arm,** with its canopy of pon- derosa pines, grassy meadows, and pebble beach. It makes a convenient launching point for Wild Horse Island (see p. 256), the largest but most difficult to reach of the state park units. Farther north, you can stroll through the larch and fir forest of **West Shore** and pause atop a set of glacially carved cliffs that face the Mission and Swan mountains. Down by the boat ramp, you'll find trails running along the park's narrow strip of rocky shoreline (good swimming if the waves aren't high).

Swimmers will want to linger in Flathead Lake, one of the Rockies' few large bodies of water to reach comfortable temperatures. Since the swimmer's itch parasite is common in shallow waters, it's important to towel off immediately or take a shower.

Three more units dot the eastern shore. The southernmost, **Finley Point,** lies on a narrow, curving peninsula and caters to RV owners with large boats. It offers good views of the lake and the string of islands that divide the lake like stepping-stones. Sweet cherry orchards abound near **Yellow Bay,** a tiny park unit with a big gravel beach. **Wayfarers,** the only park unit open year-round although difficult to access in winter, lies near the town of Bigfork and offers lovely vistas of the gently rolling Salish Mountains across the lake. It has a good beach, but many swimmers prefer the low cliffs and rocks that also line the shore.

By far the biggest and most appealing of the park's units, **Wild Horse Island** juts roughly 800 feet above the water and offers grandstand vistas of the lake and the surrounding mountain ranges. Its knobby upland prairies, cliffs, and mature Douglas-fir and ponderosa pine forests provide a home for bighorn sheep, deer, coyotes, and a few wild horses. Though a trip to the island takes some time and planning, the excursion combines some of the best experiences Flathead Lake has to offer: a nautical jaunt, a pleasant hike, good chances to spot wildlife, splendid vistas of mountain and lake, enticing swimming holes, peace and quiet.

The island is accessible only by private boat. If you don't have your own, you can rent one in the Polson area *(Chamber of Commerce 406-883-5969)*, or from one of the marinas on Big Arm Bay. You should also pick up the park's free pamphlet guide to the island, which includes a topographical map and logistical advice; it's available from any of the park branches, the park headquarters in Kalispell, or at any local state park.

Once afloat, head for **Little Skeeko Bay** on the island's northwest side, where a loop trail climbs into the highlands. You're free to roam virtually anywhere on the island as long as you keep clear of several dozen private cottages. ∎

Ponderosa Pines

Most of the evergreens overlooking Flathead Lake are ponderosa pines. These long-needled pines can grow as high as 150 feet with trunk diameters of 3 to 4 feet. They prefer a hot, dry climate and collect water through a taproot and a wide radius of lateral roots. A thick, platy bark protects them from grass fires. Creases in the bark of older trees often smell like vanilla, butterscotch, or pineapple.

Bison

National Bison Range

■ 18,564 acres ■ Northwest Montana, west of Ravalli via Mont. 200 ■ Best months mid-May–Sept. ■ Hiking, bird-watching, wildlife viewing, auto tour ■ Adm. fee ■ Contact the range, 132 Bison Range Rd., Moiese, MT 59824; phone 406-644-2211

ESTABLISHED IN 1908 to help save North America's largest land mammal from extinction, the National Bison Range lies among the rumpled Palouse prairie hills south of Flathead Lake and faces the crags and yawning glacial canyons of the Mission Range. Within this spectacular setting, some 350 to 500 bison roam in large groups—grazing, dozing, competing for mates, bearing their young, and tolerating carloads of people toting binoculars, spotting scopes, and cameras.

Though bison remain the principle attraction, the range also supports a surprising variety of other big game species and a host of smaller animals. Pronghorn, elk, mule deer, white-tailed deer, black bears, bighorn sheep, and even mountain goats live among the reserve's grasslands, verdant stream corridors, wetlands, and steep mountain forests.

Though bison no longer face

Bison Facts

Weighing up to a ton and standing as high as 6 feet, the bison is North America's heaviest land animal. Well-adapted to a plains environment where water sources are widely scattered, these giants can store huge amounts of water. Bison had a profound effect on the prairie ecosystem. By cropping, digesting, and excreting grasses, they played a major role in building up the very soil they thundered across.

extinction, their current population of a few hundred thousand represents just a slim remnant of their former glory. Scientists estimate that perhaps 30 million once grazed throughout much of North America. Their range extended from the Atlantic into the mountain valleys of the Rockies, and from the Gulf of Mexico far into Canada.

The seemingly infinite number of bison amazed early European visitors to the West. In 1806, Meriwether Lewis estimated he could see 10,000 within a 2-mile circle near Great Falls, Montana. And, of course, the tribes of the western plains, rivers, and mountains had hunted and struck a harmonious balance with the bison until horses arrived on the scene sometime around the 17th century.

But as European civilization encroached on western lands, suitable habitat for the bison shrank, and the species' population waned until the great slaughter of the 1870s and '80s. Driven by a hot market for high quality leather and linked to that market by transcontinental rail, thousands of buffalo hunters descended on the plains and decimated the herds. Within 30 years, the bison teetered on the brink of extinction, and so did the Native American way of life.

The National Bison Range attempted to rejuvenate the bison population starting with 37 animals bought from small, private herds. Efforts here and at other reserves soon led to the species' rebound. Population on the range has fluctuated through the years, but managers try to keep the herd at 350 by holding a public roundup and sale of surplus animals each October.

What to See and Do

Excellent exhibits at the **visitor center** tell the sad tale of the bison's near extinction and chronicle the range's efforts to save the species and then strengthen and diversify its bloodlines. You'll find a map showing the bison's greatly diminished range, historic photos of hunters and their carnage, as well as artifacts such as a buffalo rifle and skinning knives. Other displays outline seasonal events on the range, such as the bison's spectacular rut in late July and August—a time of much bellowing, wallowing, and occasional head-to-head shoving matches.

To see bison on the hoof, pick up a map at the visitor center and follow **Red Sleep Mountain Drive** (*allow at least two hours*). This 19-mile loop road climbs 2,000 feet over a rumpled mountain covered with grass and pockets of evergreen forest. It offers knockout vistas of the **Mission Range** and the **Flathead Valley** as well as the range's best chances for seeing not only bison, but also pronghorn, elk, deer, bighorn sheep, and mountain goats. Near the crest of the mountain, stretch your legs on two trails: the easy, half-mile **Bitterroot Trail** and the moderate, 1-mile **High Point Trail.**

Near the visitor center, a picnic area is tucked into the luscious riparian corridor of **Mission Creek.** Cool off in the shade, and consider a jaunt along the 1-mile **Nature Trail,** which explores stream and wetland habitats. ∎

Sunrise over the Mission Range and Flathead Lake

Mission Mountains Wilderness

■ 73,877 acres ■ Northwest Montana, southeast of Bigfork off Mont. 83
■ Best months June-Sept. ■ Primitive camping, hiking, boating, horseback riding
■ Bear-country precautions pertain ■ Contact Swan Lake Ranger District,
Flathead National Forest, Bigfork, MT 59911; 406-837-5081

THE SPECTACULAR MISSION RANGE stretches along the Mission Valley's eastern side as a steep, dark, and abrupt wall of evergreen forests topped by a sharp crest of bare rock summits. The mountains rocket skyward for more than 5,000 vertical feet and loom as a magnificent and riveting presence over the relatively flat, open floor of the valleys.

They form the westernmost rampart of Montana's Overthrust Belt, which includes Glacier National Park and the vast wilderness areas that surround it and extends eastward to the Great Plains. Like Glacier's mountains, the Missions slid into place from the west roughly 60 million years ago as great blocks of sedimentary rocks. Millions of years of erosion carried off the upper layers of rocks, and then ice age glaciers carved the glorious Missions landscape of today.

The range's serrated crest lies within the Mission Mountains Wilderness—73,877 acres of cirque, stream, and subalpine forest. It is rough, broken country, linked by 45 miles of narrow, steep, and difficult trails. Though the best views are from the west side, most of the major trailheads are along the **Swan River** (at Glacier Creek, Cold Lakes, Piper Creek, Fatty Creek, and Beaver Creek). Access from the west leads through the **Flathead Indian Reservation** and requires a tribal permit, available through most sporting goods stores or from the Confederated Salish and Kootenai Tribal Recreation Department in Pablo *(406-675-2700).* ■

Following pages: Flathead Valley near the Mission Range

Blackfoot River

■ 120 miles long ■ West-central Montana, off Mont. 200 between Helena and Missoula ■ Best months for boating and swimming June-Sept. ■ Camping, boating, bird-watching ■ Contact Lincoln Ranger District, Helena National Forest, 7269 Hwy. 200, Lincoln, MT 59639; phone 406-362-4265

SPILLING FROM THE CONTINENTAL DIVIDE northwest of Helena, the Blackfoot River flows west to the outskirts of Missoula, passing through rich marshlands, shortgrass prairies, and a series of mountainous canyons before draining into the Clark Fork River. The Blackfoot is not the region's biggest, wildest, or most spectacular river, but it strings together such a gratifying variety of landscapes in such a modest distance that it's well worth the visit.

East of Missoula, follow Mont. 200 past Bonner and into a steep, sparsely forested canyon. It's a terrific stretch of river, but the scenery improves if 11 miles from Bonner you take the left-hand turnoff for the **Blackfoot River Recreation Corridor.** There, a rough but passable gravel road hugs the river canyon for 10 miles before emerging onto a broad prairie and rejoining Mont. 200. Along the way, you'll find nine beautiful fishing access points where you can stretch your legs, picnic, camp, or shuttle a canoe. The abandoned railroad bed above and below **Whitaker Bridge** offers excellent mountain biking and walking.

Beyond the canyon, Mont. 200 glides over a broad prairie, with the dark mountains of the Bob Marshall Wilderness Complex (see opposite) rising to the north. Glaciers that formed in the Swan Range extended down into this valley and left a legacy of eroded moraines, old stream courses, and outwash plains. Numerous ponds and small lakes have formed, including **Browns Lake** (SE of Ovando), popular with bald eagles and ospreys and, in spring, sandhill cranes.

Near the Continental Divide, the river branches into several tributary creeks. One of them, **Alice Creek,** leads to the divide's crest at **Lewis and Clark Pass,** an open saddle of grass, stunted evergreens, and meadows overlooking the Great Plains. The scenery is magnificent, but equally compelling are the vivid travois ruts left in the meadows by generations of Indians traveling across the mountains. The hike to the pass begins at the end of the Alice Creek Road (10 miles E of Lincoln. Maps available at Lincoln Ranger District, Helena NF) and takes about 45 minutes. ■

Lewis Return Route

As Lewis and Clark headed home across the Rockies in 1806, they split their party near present day Missoula in order to explore areas they had not seen on their outbound journey. Lewis followed the Blackfoot River and its tributary streams east to the Continental Divide, then descended onto the plains and followed the Sun River to Great Falls. Had they known about the route in 1805, Lewis and Clark could have saved seven weeks and more than 400 miles of hard traveling.

Rafting the Middle Fork Flathead River

Bob Marshall Wilderness Complex

■ 1.5 million acres ■ Northwest Montana, northwest of Helena ■ Best months June-Sept. ■ Camping, hiking, boating, bird-watching, wildlife viewing ■ Prime grizzly habitat; take precautions ■ Contact Hungry Horse Ranger District, Flathead NF, Box 190340, Hungry Horse, MT 59919; phone 406-387-3800

EXTENDING SOUTHEAST FROM Glacier National Park for nearly 125 miles, this vast and precious tract of open land is comprised of three contiguous wilderness areas—the Bob Marshall, Great Bear, and Scapegoat. Taken together, they encompass roughly 1.5 million acres of high, glaciated peaks, plunging canyons, pristine rivers, deep evergreen forests, and boundless, high-country wildflower meadows. Toss in the million or so acres of national forest lands that surround them, and you're looking at an ecosystem larger than Delaware and Rhode Island combined.

It's an immense and amazing place, full of grizzly bears and bighorn sheep, mountain goats, wolverines, mountain lions, moose, elk, deer, even wolves. It contains two long wild and scenic river corridors (along the Middle Fork and South Fork of the Flathead) and preserves a range of habitats that run the gambit from wind-hammered prairie ridges and marshy lowlands to montane forests and the alpine tundra.

It is, in short, an irreplaceable national treasure.

Along its eastern margin stretch the imposing ramparts of the **Rocky Mountain Front,** which rises abruptly from the Great Plains as an almost continuous wall of rock jutting 5,000 feet above the prairies. Packed tightly behind it, crest after crest of equally impressive peaks extend for another 80 miles—clear to the Mission Range. All of these rocks slid into place from the west about 70 million years ago and form a significant portion of Montana's Overthrust Belt.

Flathead Range in the Great Bear Wilderness

Walkin' Bob

By the time Bob Marshall was 36, he had logged upward of 250 day hikes of 30 miles, 51 hikes of more than 40 miles, and several day hikes of up to 70 miles. He wrote that pushing oneself to such extremes develops "a body distinguished by a soundness, stamina and elan unknown amid normal surroundings." But some of his longer hikes took a heavy toll. At the end of one 50-miler, he was so tired that he repeatedly stumbled, fell, and then lay on the ground for a while before hiking onward.

The Continental Divide gerrymanders along the crests of the mountains, sending three important rivers off to the east—the Dearborn, Sun, and Teton. As they spill from the mountains, they carve deep canyons that offer spectacular routes to the interior. Three more rivers drain the lush forests and slopes west of the divide—the Swan and the Middle and South Forks Flathead.

The largest of the three wilderness areas was named for Bob Marshall, founder of the Wilderness Society, potent voice for the preservation of wildlands during the 1930s, the first recreation chief of the Forest Service who helped preserve 5.4 million acres, and a legendary long-distance hiker. The roughly one million acres that now bear his name suits his brand of exercise—a big, generous landscape with several mountain ranges and plenty of room to stretch the legs. Perhaps its best known landform is the **Chinese Wall,** a remarkable line of 1,000-foot limestone cliffs that runs for 12 miles down the center of the wilderness.

The **Great Bear Wilderness,** named for its dominant resident, the grizzly bear, fills the gap between "The Bob" and Glacier National Park. It takes in the wild and scenic section of the Flathead's Middle Fork and extends along the crest of the Flathead Range, which rises over the eastern shore of Hungry Horse Reservoir.

The **Scapegoat Wilderness** wraps around the southern edge of The Bob, encompassing an extension of the Chinese Wall and nearly 250,000 acres of prime wildlife country.

What to See and Do

Access to the heart of this magnificent landscape is by foot or horseback only, which is as it should be. Still, there are several areas along the east slope of the Rocky Mountain Front where, without much trouble, you can get a sense of what lies beyond.

A good place for a casual day hike, the **Blackleaf Wildlife Management Area** *(14 miles W of Bynum on Blackleaf Rd.)* lies tight against the base of the mountains and offers a lovely mix of rolling prairie grasslands, marsh, forest, and canyon. Grizzlies and black bears frequent it in the spring, elk winter here, and mountain goats live here all year. Start at **Antelope Butte** *(turn S at fork in Blackleaf Rd.)*, a prominent sandstone escarpment and the most promising spot on the preserve for wildlife viewing. Marshes and ponds at the butte's south end are especially rewarding for birdwatchers. Don't miss a walk up **Blackleaf Canyon** *(trail begins where Blackleaf Rd. dead-ends)*, which penetrates the dizzying, 1,000-foot cliffs of **Volcano Reef.** A stroll of less than a mile takes you to where various hawks, eagles, and falcons nest in the rocks and a herd of 75 mountain goats amble among the crags.

For a taste of the high country and a glimpse of The Bob, head for **Our Lake** *(trailhead 24 miles NW of Choteau via US 89 and Teton Canyon Rd.)*, a tiny gem of bone-chilling water. The moderate 3.5-mile (one way) hike climbs beyond tree line into vibrant wildflower meadows. Mountain goats are commonly seen among the cliffs, and from the saddle overlooking the lake you can gaze west into the mountainous heart of the wilderness area and see a portion of the Chinese Wall.

The road to the trailhead for Our Lake also passes **Pine Butte Swamp Preserve** *(entrance 15 miles NW of Choteau along Teton Canyon Rd.)*, another springtime haven for grizzly bears (rarely seen) where a vast swamp stretches along the base of a high, sandstone butte. A short trail leads from the parking area to an overlook.

For a good chance of seeing bighorn sheep, consider a trip to the **Sun River Canyon Wildlife Viewing Area** *(22 miles NW of Augusta via Willow Creek and Sun River Rds. 406-466-5341)*, home to one of the largest herds in North America. The road into the canyon is spectacular, following Sun River through a sheer limestone wall and then cutting through row upon row of high, steep-sided mountain ridges all the way to Gibson Reservoir. The mix of cliff, rushing water, forest, and broad fields of grass provides excellent habitat for elk,

Continental Divide Trail
Stretching from Canada to Mexico on the line that divides the Pacific watershed from the Atlantic watershed, this work in progress traverses some of America's best wildland. It's not a specially constructed path, but a designation of existing trails that stick as close to the divide as possible. In Bob Marshall country, it runs north from Rogers Pass on Mont. 200, parallels the spectacular Chinese Wall, and emerges at Marias Pass on the edge of Glacier NP—a splendid week-long trip for strong hikers.

deer, and bighorns. Some 800 to 1,000 sheep graze among the hillsides and talus fields of the canyon. In late autumn, you can watch the rams knock heads for mating rights with the ewes.

Far to the north, you can reach the Great Bear Wilderness after just a short walk from US 2. Trail 155, which begins several miles southeast of Essex, hugs the banks of the **Middle Fork Flathead River** through deep forest. You can also reach the **South Fork Flathead** without much bother by driving the length of the **Hungry Horse Reservoir.**

Serious backcountry routes through the wilderness are legion, but the classic traverse starts at **Holland Lake** *(E of Mont. 83 in the Swan River Valley),* makes its way to the South Fork Flathead, follows the **White River** (Trail 112) to Larch Hill Pass in the Chinese Wall, and then goes on to Sun River trailhead at Benchmark *(S of Gibson Reservoir).* ■

Fall ride in the Bob Marshall Wilderness Area

Great blue heron

Missouri River Recreation Road

■ 30 miles long ■ Western Montana, southwest of Great Falls between Wolf Creek and Cascade exits off I-15 ■ Best months June-Sept. ■ Primitive camping, hiking, boating, fishing, canoeing, bird-watching ■ Contact the Bureau of Reclamation, P.O. Box 1160, Lewistown, MT 59457; phone 406-538-7461

THIS TWO-LANE ROAD follows the Missouri River through a magnificent canyon in the Adele Mountains and offers many opportunities to wade the river, cast a fly line, or coast along in a canoe. It's an unusual canyon of grassy slopes, wooded glens, and bulbous outcroppings of volcanic rock that tower over the quick, clean current of the **Missouri River.**

Rich in aquatic vegetation, this section of the Missouri is a blue-ribbon stretch of trout water and an open-air market for various types of fishing birds. American white pelicans preen themselves on gravel bars; great blue herons stalk the lush banks. If you're lucky, you might see a bald eagle or osprey plunge from the sky and snatch a trout from the surface. Boaters will find eight excellent boat ramps between the tiny towns of Wolf Creek and Cascade, making day trips, and even trips of a couple of hours, possible.

Near Wolf Creek, a good, gravel spur road climbs along the river to **Holter Lake** *(Adm. fee; 406-494-5059)*, an attractive reservoir nestled among rolling foothills peppered with ponderosa pine. At the lake's upper end, the water narrows into a deep serpentine gorge that eventually leads to what Meriwether Lewis named in 1805 the Gates of the Rocky Mountains (see pp. 268-270). You can launch a boat at Gates of the Mountains Marina and follow the gorge's slack water to a takeout at Departure Point. It's a great trip of 11 water miles, where limestone cliffs rise 1,000 feet or more from the water.

If you'd rather stretch your legs, continue on the gravel road to the knob above Departure Point and amble over the expansive shortgrass hills of the **Beartooth Wildlife Management Area,** a first-rate birding area frequented by mountain bluebirds, mule deer, bighorn sheep, and elk. ■

Gates of the Rocky Mountains

■ 28,500 wilderness acres ■ Western Montana, 18 miles north of Helena off I-15 ■ Best months June-Sept. ■ Camping, hiking, boating, swimming, bird-watching, wildlife viewing, pictographs ■ Contact Helena Ranger District, Helena National Forest, 2001 Poplar St., Helena, MT 59601; phone 406-449-5490

NAMED BY MERIWETHER LEWIS in 1805 and easily visited today, this exceptionally narrow limestone chasm grips the Missouri River for roughly 6 miles, cutting between 1,000-foot cliffs and precipitous ridges black with evergreen forests. Eroded pinnacles, arches, and great brows of creamy white limestone rise directly from the water. Eagles and ospreys glide overhead, scanning for unwary fish, while bighorn sheep and mountain goats nibble at vegetation along the river banks.

    As Lewis and his men paddled upstream through this craggy gorge

Gates of the Rocky Mountains

on July 18-19, 1805, he remarked that there was just one patch of ground in the first 3 miles large enough for a man to "rest the soal of his foot." There are even fewer places now because Holter Dam raised the water level 15 feet.

The canyon formed as the Missouri carved its way down through layers of Paleozoic limestone that had been warped and in some places tightly folded during the general upheaval of the Rocky Mountains. These spectacular folds—silent records of titanic, mountain-building forces—are clearly seen today.

Audubon's bighorn sheep lived within the canyon until they were hunted out during the 1890s. The sheep you see today are Rocky Mountain bighorns that were introduced to the area in the 1970s. Besides the sheep and goats, look for mule deer, peregrine falcons, turkey vultures, red-tailed hawks, and American white pelicans. In spring or fall, you might even hear the strange whistling call of a migrating loon echo off the canyon walls.

What to See and Do

For a quick, informative excursion through the gorge, take the two-hour **Gates of the Mountains Boat Tour** *(18 miles N of Helena off I-15. 406-458-5241. Mem. Day–Labor Day; fare)*. Boat pilots are well-versed in the canyon's natural history as well as in Lewis and Clark lore. Bighorn sheep and mountain goats are often seen, and the pilots also point out Native American pictographs and recount the tragic story of the Mann Gulch fire, which killed 12 Forest Service smoke jumpers in 1949 (see sidebar below).

The boats make a stop at the **Meriwether Picnic Area**, upstream from where most

historians believe the Lewis and Clark expedition spent the night of July 19, 1805. There, you can jump off for a day of loafing, hiking, and swimming before catching the last boat home.

You can also arrange longer stays. It is an easy 1-mile hike from the boat drop-off at Meriwether Picnic Area to **Colter Campground,** a primitive Forest Service camp where you can spend the night or several days. From that base camp, you can explore steep side canyons that climb away from the river and offer high vantage points of the Missouri's narrow, winding course. Eagles, ospreys, hawks, and other birds of prey roost within the side canyons and are frequently seen circling high above the rocky walls.

If you have your own boat, you can also paddle or motor through the gates at your own pace, camping along the way and emerging at Holter Lake.

East of the gorge, the **Gates of the Mountains Wilderness** protects about 28,500 acres of limestone cliff, rugged forest, and wildflower meadow in the Big Belt Mountains. It's not a large wilderness area, but it's lightly traveled and makes for a pleasant backcountry overnight—especially when combined with a day along the Missouri. The easiest entry is by boat; road access is round-about and confusing. (For maps, contact the Helena Ranger District, Helena National Forest.) ∎

Mann Gulch Fire

On Aug. 5, 1949, 15 smoke jumpers parachuted into the head of Mann Gulch to fight what appeared to be a routine forest fire. After the men established a base camp, the fire suddenly accelerated. They tried to escape down the gulch toward the river, but the firestorm surrounded them. The foreman set fire to a small area, intending to create a haven by burning out the light fuel. He urged the others to join him within the protective fire ring, but the rest of the crew plus one firefighter on the ground set off for the ridge top. The foreman survived without even scorching his clothes. Two others outran the fire. The rest died.

Ross Creek in Kootenai National Forest

Cabinet Mountains Wilderness

■ 94,360 acres ■ Northwestern Montana; west of Libby via Mont. 56 or US 2
■ Best months June-Sept. ■ Camping, hiking, wildlife viewing ■ Contact Kootenai National Forest, 1101 US 2 W, Libby, MT 59923; phone 406-293-6211

THE LONG, JAGGED spine of the Cabinet Mountains seems a bit out of place in far northwestern Montana, where mountain ranges tend to present a gentler, smoother, rounder face to the world. The Cabinets, though, stab into the sky as a crest of sharp, naked rock points, even though they share much the same creation story as their amiable neighbors, the Purcells, which lie to the northwest of the Kootenai River.

The difference is that the crest of the Cabinets was high enough to have ridden above the vast ice age glaciers that completely enveloped most of the mountains here and in Idaho's panhandle. Instead, small alpine glaciers went to work among the heights of the Cabinets and left a splendid, footloose landscape of steep-sided cirques, knife-edged ridges, high cliffs, open meadows, and small but very deep alpine lakes.

Grouse

The west slope of the Cabinets lies within the wettest part of the Rockies, and here you'll find remnants of the

A moose family

forest primeval—misty groves of immense cedars and hemlocks towering over a spongy understory of moss, ferns, devil's club, fungus, and rotting tree trunks. Higher up, the forests dry out and look much the same as elsewhere in the northern Rockies.

The Cabinet Mountains Wilderness protects a narrow corridor of 94,360 acres that straddles the crest of the range for about 35 miles. Many trails suitable for day hikes penetrate from both sides of the range, climbing along streams and ridges from trailheads at the end of forest roads. The most popular is the steep climb to **Leigh Lake,** which is nestled beneath the cliffs of 8,738-foot **Snowshoe Peak.** The 5-mile round-trip hike is occasionally demanding; reach the trailhead via Bear Creek Road off US 2.

For a more casual stroll, head for the **Ross Creek Scenic Area of Ancient Cedars** *(12 miles S of US 2 via Mont. 56. 406-295-4693),* where a 1-mile loop trail wanders among colossal, moss-laden cedars that stand 175 feet high and have trunk diameters as great as 8 feet. The spongy forest floor consists of decomposed vegetation—twigs, needles, branches, entire tree trunks—overlain with a thick layer of iridescent moss and lichens.

And don't miss **Kootenai Falls** *(10 miles W of Libby on US 2),* one of the Rockies' largest and most spectacular waterfalls. Its crashes over a wide cliff band, then shatters into several white-water channels that race for hundreds of yards over stairstepping ledges and subsidiary cascades. As the river drops, high rock walls rise from the water's edge. A 1-mile trail leads through the forest and down a long stairway to the brink of the falls. Farther downstream, a suspension bridge spans the chasm and offers a comprehensive view of the falls, rapids, canyon, and surrounding mountains. ■

Kootenai National Wildlife Refuge

■ 2,774 acres ■ Northern Idaho, 5 miles west of Bonners Ferry on Riverside Rd.
■ Open year-round, but snow closes some roads ■ Hiking, bird-watching,
wildlife viewing, auto tour ■ Contact the refuge, HCR 60, Box 283, Westside
Rd., Bonners Ferry, ID 83805; phone 208-267-3888

LOCATED IN NORTHERN IDAHO along the Kootenai River's verdant flood-plain, this expansive wildlife refuge doubles as a great birding spot and showcase for classic panhandle terrain. It lies between the **Selkirk Mountains** (west) and the **Purcells,** (east), which are covered with deep ever-green forests and appear rather low, dark, broad-backed, and smooth.

The refuge also lies within the great **Purcell Trench,** a major geologic structure that runs the length of the panhandle and extends far into Canada as a deep, roomy trough. This portion of the trench formed when a burgeoning mass of magma pushed through the earth's surface to become the Selkirks. As the magma rose, the overlying rocks shifted eastward to become the Purcells. Ice age glaciers smoothed both ranges and flattened the floor of the trough by filling it with glacial debris.

Today, the refuge meadows, wetlands, forests, and grainfields attract at least 218 species of birds and 45 species of mammals. Tundra swans, Canada geese, and various ducks lay over during the migration seasons. Throughout the summer you can spot great blue herons, bald eagles, ospreys, owls, and ruffed grouse. Early in the day, or as dusk falls, you might also see deer and moose. Elk are occa-sionally present during the winter.

Drop by refuge headquarters for a map and a bird list. Nearby, a short footpath winds through a forest of ponderosa pine and Douglas-fir to **Myrtle Falls,** which plunges from a narrow chasm. Also at headquarters you'll find the start of a 4.5-mile self-guided auto tour that rings the bot-tomlands and passes a turnout for the **Myrtle Pond Observation Blind,** where you can watch or photograph nesting mallards and geese dabbling among the weeds. If you're looking for a long walk, head for the easy, 2.2-mile (one way) **Deep Creek Nature Trail,** which follows a meandering creek along the refuge's southeast border. ■

Preening Swans

In springtime, tundra swans are commonly seen gliding across small lakes and ponds on the Kootenai NWR. Like all birds, the swans often pause to preen. Preening is an essential activity that involves a careful cleaning, rearrange-ment, and oiling of the feath-ers. Oil is squeezed onto the bill from a preen gland on the swan's rump, then worked into the feathers. The oil helps keep the feathers flexible and waterproof. It may also inhibit the growth of fungi and bacteria.

Farragut State Park

■ 4,733 acres ■ Northern Idaho, 4 miles east of Athol on Idaho 54 ■ Hiking, biking, boating, swimming, wildlife viewing ■ Adm. fee ■ Contact the park, 13400 E. Ranger Rd., Athol, ID 83801; phone 208-683-2425

THIS LARGE AND INVITING state park lies at the southern tip of **Pend Oreille Lake,** an extraordinarily deep lake that extends for roughly 70 miles along the base of the Coeur d'Alene and Cabinet Mountains in northern Idaho.

Once a boot camp for World War II Navy recruits, the park encompasses deep evergreen forests, open fields, and miles of rocky shoreline. The lake (pronounced PON-der-ay) lies within the Purcell Trench and reaches depths greater than 1,200 feet, deep enough for the Navy to test scaled-down versions of its submarines. It formed at the end of the last ice age, when retreating glaciers left a huge block of ice stranded here. Rocks, sand, mud, and gravel filled in along the sides of the ice, which eventually melted and left the lake. Before the glaciers retreated, though, they also dammed the mouth of the Clark Fork River, which backed up to form Glacial Lake Missoula—that immense body of water responsible for the greatest floods known to the geologic record.

Within the park, **visitor center** exhibits recount Farragut's history and offer a quick rundown of the area's plants and animals. Here, too, you can pick up maps for the park's hiking and biking trails, which include a self-guided nature trail and a 3-mile jaunt along the lake. To get a glimpse of mountain goats, head for the **Willow Picnic Area** and train your binoculars on the cliffs across the lake. ■

Heyburn State Park

■ 7,838 acres ■ Northern Idaho, 35 miles south of Coeur d'Alene via US 95 ■ Best months May–mid-Oct. ■ Camping, hiking, mountain biking, horseback riding, boating, bird-watching, wildlife viewing ■ Adm. fee ■ Contact the park, 1291 Chatcolet Rd., Plummer, ID 83851; phone 208-686-1308

TUCKED INTO THE HIGH HILLS and deep forests that overlook Coeur d'Alene Lake's marshy southern end, this state park combines the tranquillity of the deep forest with the sometimes raucous clamor of wetland birdlife. Trails skirt the lakeshore, penetrate portions of **Plummer Creek Marsh,** and wind through lush cedar-and-hemlock forests to open stands of huge ponderosa pines overlooking the lake (try the 3-mile **Indian Cliffs Trail).**

The park is an especially appealing spot for paddlers who recognize the intimate rewards of a marsh—the sweep of the bullrushes past the gunwales, the secretive backwater sloughs, the splash of a diving otter, and the frogs and salamanders.

Exhibits at the **visitor center** offer an introduction to the culture of the Coeur d'Alene Indians and the area's history and wildlife. ■

Priest Lake

■ 19 miles long ■ Northern Idaho, northwest of Sandpoint via US 2 and Idaho 57
■ Best months June-Sept. ■ Camping, hiking, boating, mountain biking, bird-watching, wildlife viewing ■ Contact Sandpoint Ranger District, Idaho Panhandle NF, 1500 Hwy. 2, Ste. 110, Sandpoint, ID 83864; phone 208-263-5111

REMOTE, PRISTINE, SEDUCTIVE as a Caribbean lagoon, Priest Lake lies in the far northwestern corner of Idaho's panhandle amid lush forests of cedar and hemlock, larch, grand fir, and western white pine. Ringed with excellent sand beaches, it stretches for 19 miles beneath the **Selkirk Crest**—a serrated backbone of shattered gray rock that cuts an anomalous profile above the smooth, stairstepping ridges of the surrounding mountains.

To the north, the lake connects with crystalline **Upper Priest Lake.** To the south, it drains into the **Priest River,** which meanders for 44 miles through marshland, meadow, forest, and canyon before emptying into the Pend Oreille River. In the forested mountains around the lakes and river live moose, elk, deer, black bears, grizzlies, and mountain goats. Lucky visitors to the Upper Priest Lake area might even catch a glimpse of woodland caribou.

Start at the **Sandpoint District Ranger Station** *(Idaho 57 N of Kalispell Bay)* to pick up information on the area's trails, campgrounds, and paddling routes. Boating, of course, is the best way to see the lakes and the river. Day trips are a pleasure from almost any point you care to launch a canoe, but those wishing to avoid most of the powerboat traffic would do well to head for Priest Lake's north end. There, you can put in at the Beaver Creek Campground and paddle 2 miles up **The Thorofare** to Upper Priest Lake. Paddlers can also design multiday circuits, tenting along the way at any of the dozens of campgrounds and primitive sites that dot the shorelines of both Priest and Upper Priest Lakes. There are also campgrounds on **Kalispell Island** and **Bartoo Island** in Priest Lake.

Floating the Priest River from the outlet to the Pend Oreille River takes two full days, though the trip can be broken up into smaller sections ranging from 1.5 to 4 hours. All of it is suitable for canoes, kayaks, and rafts, though canoeists may want to portage both Binarch and Eight Mile rapids, which are Class III. Water levels drop after mid-July, however, sometimes forcing late season paddlers to drag their vessels over the riffles.

Hikers and mountain bikers will also find plenty to do. Most of the major routes are open to both foot travel and bikes. The **Lakeshore Trail** runs south from Beaver Creek Campground for 7.6 easy miles along Priest Lake's west shore, leading past secluded beaches and campsites. From Beaver Creek, you can also head north to Upper Priest Lake and beyond on the 10-mile **Navigation Trail**. Strong bikers can make a day of it by pedaling along Forest Service roads and the **Upper Priest River Trail** all the way to **Upper Priest Falls**. ■

Following pages: Priest Lake solitude

Resources

The following is a select list of resources. Contact state and local associations for additional outfitter and lodging options. For chain hotels and motels operating in the northern Rockies, see p. 282.

IDAHO

Federal and State Agencies

Bureau of Land Management
3380 American Terrace
Boise, ID 83706
208-373-4000
Maps and information about BLM-controlled lands; camping information.

Idaho Dept. of Commerce
700 W. State St.
P.O. Box 83720
Boise, ID 83720
208-334-2470
or 800-842-5858
www.idoc.state.id.us
www.visitid.org/accom/index.html
Information on travel in Idaho, including camping, hotels, and an RV guide.

Idaho Dept. of Fish and Game
P.O. Box 25
Boise, ID 83707-0025
208-334-3700
Fishing and hunting licenses.

Idaho Dept. of Parks and Recreation
P.O. Box 83720
Boise, ID 83720-0065
208-334-4199
General information on Idaho's parks, trails, and bodies of water.

Idaho Dept. of Tourism
P.O. Box 2018
Lewiston, ID 83501
800-473-3543
General tourism and recreation information, including camping and hotels.

Idaho Non-residence License Buyer Program
800-554-8685
Hunting and fishing licenses for non-residents.

Idaho State Travel Council
800-635-7820
Lodgings brochure.

Yellowstone/Teton Territory Travel Committee
P.O. Box 50498
Idaho Falls, ID 83402
208-523-1010
or 800-634-3246
Area travel information.

Outfitters and Activities

Hurricane Creek Llama Treks, Inc.
63366 Pine Tree Rd.
Enterprise, OR 97828
541-432-4455
or 800-528-9609
www.hcltrek.com
Week-long treks in Hells Canyon and Wallowa Mountains. June-Aug.

High Country Outfitters
P.O. Box 26
Joseph, OR 97846
541-432-9171
Combo float and horse-packing trips through Hells Canyon.

Idaho Afloat
P.O. Box 542
Grangeville, ID 83530
800-700-2414
White-water rafting and fishing trips on the Snake and Salmon Rivers.

Idaho Angling Services
P.O. Box 703
Picabo, ID 83348
208-788-9709
Arranges fishing trips throughout the state.

Idaho Outfitters and Guides Association
P.O. Box 95
Boise, ID 83701
208-342-1438 or
800-847-4843
www.ioga.org
Offers booklet of outfitters for the main Salmon River.

Northwest River Co.
P.O. Box 403
Boise, ID 83701
208-344-7119
Selway River outfitter.

Whitewater Adventures
P.O. Box 7071
Boise ID 83707
208-939-4324
www.selway.net/wwamain.htm
Outfitter for the Selway and Middle Fork Salmon Rivers.

Lodgings

See Idaho Dept. of Commerce, Idaho Dept. of Tourism, and Idaho State Travel Council above.

U.S.D.A. Forest Service
Northern Region Office
200 E. Broadway
Missoula, MT 59807
406-329-3511
Information on cabin and lookout rentals in northern Montana and northern Idaho.

Hells Canyon NRA

Gateway towns to Hells Canyon NRA offer a wide range of accommodations. Contact the Chambers of Commerce in Joseph, Oreg. (541-432-1015), and Lewiston, Idaho (208-743-3531).

Copper Creek Lodge
P.O. Box 1243
Lewiston, ID 83501
208-743-4800
or 800-522-6966
22 cabins overlooking the river. Closed Jan.-Feb. Accessible by river and trail only.

North-central Idaho

Three Rivers Rafting Resort
HC 75, Box 61
Kooskia at Lowell
ID 83539
208-926-4430
or 888-926-4430
www.threeriversrafting.com
Full-service resort with cabins and motel; outfitter for Selway, Lochsa, and lower Salmon Rivers. Closed Nov.-April.

Salmon River

Lodge at Riggins Hot Springs
P.O. Box 1247
Salmon River Rd.
Riggins, ID 83549
208-628-3785
www.rhslodge.com
Luxury wilderness lodge on the Salmon River.

Sawtooth NRA and vicinity

Gateway towns to the Sawtooth NRA offer a wide range of accommodations. Contact the Chambers of Commerce in Sun Valley/Ketchum (800-634-3347) or Stanley (208-774-3411).

Idaho Country Inn
134 Latigo Ln.
Sun Valley, ID 83353
Mailing address:
P.O. Box 2355
Sun Valley, ID 83353
208-726-9027 or
800-250-8341
(reservations)
10 themed rooms.

Idaho Rocky Mountain Ranch
Idaho 75
HC 64, Box 9934
Stanley, ID 83278
208-774-3544
www.ruralnetwork.net/
~idrocky
1930 lodge and cabins
on 1,000 acres in the
Sawtooths. Open mid-
June–mid-Sept. and
Thanksgiving–March.

Knob Hill Inn
P.O. Box 800
Ketchum, ID 83340
208-726-8010
or 800-526-8010
www.knobhillinn.com
24 lavish rooms in down-
town Ketchum.

Camping

The U.S.D.A. Forest Service
operates campgrounds
throughout the state's
national forestlands. Call specific national forests. Information on some campgrounds
can be found at the Great
Outdoors Recreation Page at
www.gorp.com.

Hells Canyon area

Contact Payette (208-634-
0700), Nez Perce (208-983-
1950), and Wallowa-Whitman
(541-523-1405. www.fs.fed.us/
r6/w-w) National Forests.

Sawtooth NRA area

Contact Boise (208-373-
4100), Sawtooth (208-737-
3200. www.northrim.net/
sawtoothnf/list_camping.html),
and Salmon-Challis (208-756-
5100) National Forests.

MONTANA

Federal and
State Agencies

Bureau of Land Management
P.O. Box 36800
Billings, MT 59107
406-896-5000
Maps and information on

BLM-controlled lands,
including camping.

Montana Dept. of Natural
Resources and Conservation
1625 11th Ave.
Helena, MT 59620
406-444-2074
Licenses and permits for
stream fishing; camping
information.

Montana Dept. of Transportation Bicycle Program
Box 201001
Helena, MT 59620
406-444-9273
Information on biking trails
and tours in Montana.

Montana Fish, Wildlife
and Parks
1420 E. 6th Ave.
Helena, MT 59620
406-444-2535
Hunting licenses and state
park information. For a list
of recreational activities,
call 900-225-5397.

Travel Montana
800-VISIT MT
General travel information,
including camping and
hotels.

Outdoor Education
and Resources

Audubon Society
P.O. Box 595
Helena, MT 59624
406-443-3949
Offers classes on the
environment and birdlife
in Montana.

Glacier Natural
History Association
Box 327
West Glacier, MT 59936
406-888-5756
Educational materials and
park programs.

Lewis and Clark Trail
Heritage Foundation
Box, 3434
Great Falls, MT 59403
406-454-1234
or 800-701-3434
www.lewisandclark.org
Maps and guidebooks for
hiking the trail.

Outfitters
and Activities

Adventure Cycling Assoc.
150 E. Pine St.

P.O. Box 8308
Missoula, MT 59807
406-721-1776
or 800-755-2453
www.adv-cycling.org
Information on tours, races,
and events for cyclists.

Federation of Fly Fishers
P.O. Box 1595
Bozeman, MT 59771
406-585-7592
Information on all aspects
of fly-fishing in Montana.

Glacier Raft Company
P.O. Box 210 C
West Glacier, MT 59936
406-888-5454
or 800-235-6781
www.glacierraftco.com
Rafting in Glacier area.
Open late May–late Sept.;
cabins available late
spring–mid-winter.

Glacier Wilderness Guides
and Montana Raft Company
P.O. Box 330
West Glacier, MT 59936
406-387-5555
or 800-521-RAFT
www.glacierguides.com
Variety of trips in and
around Glacier NP: white-
water rafting, backpacking,
fishing, etc. Season runs
late May–Sept.

Great Northern Whitewater
P.O. Box 270
West Glacier, MT 59936
800-735-7897
www.gnwhitewater.com
Rafting outfitter for Glacier
area. Open May-Oct.;
chalets available year-round.

Montana Rockies Daylight
800-519-7245
Scenic train rides through
southern Montana. Pro-
vides public transportation
to some of Montana's more
remote towns.

Wild River Adventures
P.O. Box 373
Lucille, ID 83542
800-826-2724
www.riverwild.com
River rides in both
Montana and Idaho. Season
runs Mem. Day–Labor Day.

Lodgings

See Travel Montana (p. 279).

Montana Bed and Breakfast
Association

406-582-8440
or 800-453-8870
www.mtbba.com
Information and maps for
B&Bs across Montana.

Montana Innkeepers
Association
P.O. Box 1272
Helena, MT 59624
406-449-8408
Information on hotels,
motels, resorts, and B&Bs.

U.S.D.A. Forest Service
Northern Region Office
200 E. Broadway
Missoula, MT 59807
406-329-3511
Information on cabin and
lookout rentals in northern
Montana and northern
Idaho.

**Glacier NP, Waterton
Lakes NP, and vicinity**

Two gateway towns offer a
wide range of accommoda-
tions. For listings as well as
information on activities and
recreation, contact the
Chambers of Commerce
in Kalispell (406-758-2800)
and Columbia Falls (406-892-
2072).

Glacier Park, Inc.
P.O. Box 147
East Glacier, MT 59434
602-207-6000
www.glacierparkinc.com
Park concessioner runs
Many Glacier Hotel, Lake
McDonald Lodge, Rising
Sun Motor Inn, Glacier
Park Lodge, Swiftcurrent
Motor Inn, The Village Inn
(all in Glacier NP); and the
Prince of Wales Hotel in
Waterton Lakes NP.

Averill's Flathead Lake Lodge
Flathead Lake Lodge Rd.
Bigfork, MT 59911
406-837-4391
www.averills.com
20 cabins and lodge on
2,200 acres near Jewel
Basin and Bob Marshall
Wilderness. Closed mid-
Sept.–May.

Apgar Village Lodge
P.O. Box 410
West Glacier, MT 59936
406-888-5484

Aspen Village Inn
P.O. Box 100
Waterton Lakes NP

Alberta T0K 2M0
403-859-2255
50 rustic rooms, many
with lake views. Closed
mid-Oct.–April.

Bayshore Inn
P.O. Box 38
Waterton Lakes NP
Alberta T0K 2M0
403-859-2211 (summer)
or 604-717-1911 (winter)
www.bayshoreinn.com
70-room lakefront inn.
Closed mid-Oct.–March.

Crandell Mountain Lodge
P.O. Box 114
Waterton Lakes NP
Alberta T0K 2M0
403-859-2288
www.crandellmountain
lodge.com
Country-themed lodge in
Waterton townsite.

Good Medicine Lodge
537 Wisconsin Ave.
Whitefish, MT 59937
406-862-5488
9 guest rooms in cedar
chalet and annex.

Isaak Walton Inn
P.O. Box 653
Essex, MT 59916
406-888-5700
Built by Great Northern
Railway; Amtrak still stops
at the door. Located 30
miles southeast of Glacier
NP. Popular with cross-
country skiers.

Yellowstone area

Gateway towns offer a wide
range of accommodations. For
listings as well as information
on activities and recreation,
contact the Chambers of
Commerce in Cody (307-587-
2297) in Wyoming; and Gardiner (406-848-7971), Red
Lodge (406-466-1718), and
West Yellowstone (406-646-
7701) in Montana.

Camping

See Travel Montana (p. 279).

The U.S.D.A. Forest Service
operates campgrounds
throughout the state's
national forestlands. Call
specific national forests.
Information on some camp-
grounds can be found at the
Great Outdoors Recreation
Page at www.gorp.com.

In and around Glacier NP

The National Park Service
oversees 13 campgrounds
within the park. All but two
operate on a first-come,
first-served basis; reservations can be made for Fish
Creek and St. Mary Camp-
grounds. Call the National
Park Reservation Service,
800-365-CAMP.

The Forest Service runs
campsites in the following
national forests surrounding
Glacier: Flathead (406-758-
5200) and Lewis & Clark
(406-791-7700).

KOA Campground
106 West Shore
St. Mary, MT 59417
406-732-4122
or 800-KOA-1504
www.koa.com

KOA Campground
P.O. Box 215
West Glacier, MT 59936
406-387-5341
or 800-KOA-3313
www.koa.com
Closed Oct.-April.

**In and around
Yellowstone NP**

The Forest Service operates
campsites in the following
national forests in Montana
adjacent to Yellowstone:
Custer (406-657-6200) and
Gallatin (406-587-6701).

WYOMING

**Federal and
State Agencies**

Bureau of Land Management
5353 Yellowstone Ave.
Cheyenne, WY 82009
307-775-6256
Maps and information
on BLM-managed land.
Recreational guide and
small pamphlet includes
camping information.

Wyoming Division of Tourism
I-25 at College Dr.
Cheyenne, WY 82002
307-777-7777
www.wyomingtourism.org
Travel information and
guidance, including camping
and hotel information.

Wyoming State Parks and
Historic Sites

122 W. 25th St.
Herschler Building 1-E
Cheyenne, WY 82002
307-777-6323
Visitor guidance, including
camping.

Wyoming Fish and
Game Dept.
5400 Bishop Blvd.
Cheyenne, WY 82006
307-777-4600
www.gf.state.wy.us
Fishing and hunting
licenses.

Wyoming Recreation
and Parks Assoc.
P.O. Box 953
Rawlins, WY 82301
307-328-4570
General information and
brochures on the state's
parks, trails, and lakes.

Outdoor Education
and Resources

Wyoming Audubon Society
101 Garden Creek Rd.
Casper, WY 82604
307-235-3485
The educational center
offers classes on the
environment and birdlife
in Wyoming.

Grand Teton Natural History
Association
P.O. Box 170
Moose, WY 83012
307-739-3606
www.grandteton.com/
gtnha/
Books and maps on
the Teton and greater
Yellowstone area;
educational materials
on park programs.

Teton Science School
P.O. Box 68
Kelly, WY 83011
307-733-4765
www.tetonscience.org
Hands-on natural science
education; including adult
seminars lasting 1-4 days.

Yellowstone Ecosystem
Studies
P.O. Box 6640
Bozeman, MT 59771
406-587-7758
www.yellowstone.org
Week-long research expe-
ditions on wildlife, water,
and surrounding environ-
ment of Yellowstone.

The Yellowstone Association
Institute
P.O. Box 117
Yellowstone NP
WY 82190
307-344-2294
www.yellowstoneassoc
iation.org/yellinst.htm
Offers 2- to 5-day environ-
mental studies classes.

Yellowstone Natural History
Association
Box 117
Yellowstone NP
WY 82190
307-344-7381
Educational materials on
park programs.

Outfitters
and Activities

Yellowstone Visitor
Services Office
307-344-2107
www.nps.gov/yell/home.
htm
Provides activity-based lists
of outfitters.

Exum Mountain Guides
P.O. Box 56
Moose, WY 83012
307-733-2297
www.exumguides.com
Mountaineering instruction
and guide services in the
Grand Teton area.

Jackson Hole
Mountain Guides
Teton Village, WY 83025
307-733-4979
or 800-239-7642
www.jhmg.com
Mountaineering instruction
and guide services in the
Grand Teton area.

Lodgings

Wyoming Directory of Bed
and Breakfasts
www.virtualcities.com/ons/
wy/wyonydex.htm

Wyoming Homestay
Outdoor Adventures
307-237-3526
Information on Wyoming's
B&Bs, inns, and ranches.

Grand Teton NP and vicinity

Grand Teton Lodge Company
P.O. Box 240
Moran, WY 83013
307-543-3100
or 800-628-9988
www.gtlc.com

Park concessioner operates
Jackson Lake Lodge, Jenny
Lake Lodge, and Colter Bay
Village (campground).

Jackson Hole Bed &
Breakfast Association
800-542-2632
www.jacksonholebnb.com
Information on B&Bs in and
around Jackson Hole.

Jackson Hole Chamber
of Commerce
Wyoming State
Information Center
532 N. Cache St.
Jackson, WY 83001
307-733-3316
Recommends local accom-
modations and recreation.

A Teton Tree House
P.O. Box 550
6175 Heck of a Hill Rd.
Wilson, WY 83014
307-733-3233
www.cruisingamerica.com/
tetontreehouse
Multi-story house with
6 guest rooms; located
south of Jackson.

Cowboy Village Resort
at Togwotee
P.O. Box 91
Moran, WY 83013
307-543-2847
or 800-543-2847
www.cowboyvillage.com
Secluded log cabins and
lodge; excellent snowmobiling. Closed April and Oct.

Nowlin Creek Inn
660 East Broadway
Jackson, WY 83001
307-733-0882
www.jacksonholenet.
com/JH/Lodging/
SBB/NCI.htm
4 elegant rooms and
1 cabin, bordering National
Elk Refuge. Open year-
round.

Signal Mountain Lodge
P.O. Box 50
Moran, WY 83013
307-543-2831
www.signalmtnlodge.com
On shore of Jackson Lake,
within the national park.

The Wildflower Inn
P.O. Box 11000
3725 Teton Village Rd.
Jackson, WY 83002
307-733-4710
www.jacksonholenet.com

/JH/Lodging/SBB/WI.htm
5 romantic rooms in a log
house.

Shoshone NF

Brooks Lake Lodge &
Guest Ranch
458 Brooks Lake Rd.
Dubois, WY 82513
307-455-2121
www.brookslake.com
Elegant 1922 lodge and
cabins, offering horseback
riding in summer and
cross-country skiing and
snowmobiling in winter.

Yellowstone NP and area

Gateway towns to Yellow-
stone offer a wide range of
accommodations. Contact
the Chambers of Com-
merce in Cody (307-587-
2297); and, in Montana,
Gardiner (406-848-7971),
Red Lodge (406-446-1718),
and West Yellowstone (406-
646-7701).

Amfac Parks & Resorts
P.O. Box 165
Yellowstone NP
WY 82190
307-344-7311
www.travelyellowstone.
com
This park concessioner
runs these lodges within
Yellowstone: Old Faithful
Inn, Old Faithful Lodge,
Canyon Lodge, Lake
Yellowstone Hotel and
Cabins, Mammoth Hot
Springs Hotel and Cabins,
Roosevelt Lodge, Grant
Village, Lake Lodge, and
Old Faithful Snow Lodge.

Camping

See the BLM, Wyoming
Division of Tourism, and
Wyoming State Parks
(p. 281).

The U.S.D.A. Forest Service
operates campgrounds
throughout the state's
national forestlands. Call
specific national forests.
Information on some camp-
grounds can be found at the
Great Outdoors Recreation
Page at www.gorp.com.

National forests in the
Yellowstone/Teton area
include Shoshone (307-527-
6241) and Bridger-Teton
(307-739-5500).

Grand Teton NP and area

The National Park Service
operates five campgrounds
within the park on a first-
come, first-served basis.
Concession-operated
campgrounds are available
by reservation at Flagg
Ranch (800-443-2311) and
Colter Bay (307-543-2811).

Teton Village KOA
Campground
P.O. Box 38
Teton Village, WY 83025
307-733-5354
or 800-KOA-9043
www.koa.com
Closed mid-Oct.–April.

Yellowstone NP

The National Park Service
operates seven camp-
grounds on a first-come,
first-served basis. Only
Mammoth is open year-
round; the rest are open
late spring/early
summer–early/mid-fall.
Contact the park (307-
344-7391) for more
information.

AmFac Parks & Resorts
operates five other camp-
grounds within the park
(Bridge Bay Campground,
Canyon Campground,
Grant Village Campground,
Madison Campground, and
Fishing Bridge RV Park)
and accepts reservations.
Call 307-344-7311 for
information.

KOA Campground
Yellowstone Park/West
Entrance
P.O. Box 348
West Yellowstone
MT 59758
406-646-7606
or 800-KOA-7591
www.koa.com
Closed Oct.–mid-May.

Hotel & Motel Chains in Idaho, Montana and Wyoming

Accommodations in
all three states unless
otherwise noted

Best Western International
800-528-1234

Budget Host
800-BUD HOST
Except Idaho

Choice Hotels
800-4-CHOICE

Clarion Hotels
800-CLARION
Except Wyo.

Comfort Inns
800-228-5150

Days Inn
800-325-2525

Doubletree Hotels and
Guest Suites
800-222-TREE
Idaho only

Econo Lodge
800-446-6900

Embassy Suites
800-362-2776
Except Mont.

Fairfield Inn by Marriott
800-228-2800

Friendship Inns Hotel
800-453-4511

Hampton Inn
800-HAMPTON

Hilton Hotels
800-HILTONS

Holiday Inns
800-HOLIDAY

Howard Johnson
800-654-2000

Independent Motels
of America
800-841-0255

La Quinta Motor Inns, Inc.
800-531-5900
Wyo. only

Utell Hotels
800-448-8355
Except Mont.

Motel 6
800-466-8356

Quality Inns-Hotels-Suite
800-228-5151

Radison Hotels Intl.
800-333-3333
Mont. only

Ramada Inns
800-2-Ramada

Red Lion
800-547-8010

Red Roof Inns
800-843-7663
Except Mont.

Sheraton Hotels & Inns
800-325-3535

Super 8 Motels
800-843-1991

Travelodge International,
Inc. 800-255-3050
Except Wyo.

Westin Hotels and Resorts
800-228-3000

About the Authors

Although he spends part of every year traveling the world on magazine assignments, **Jeremy Schmidt** feels truly at home only in the northern Rockies, where he has lived for more than 30 years. He and his brother Thomas have teamed up on three books before this one, including DK Publishing's *The Saga of Lewis and Clark*, based on the exploits of two of their favorite adventure travelers. He lives with his wife and daughter in Jackson Hole, Wyoming.

Thomas Schmidt is the author of five books and co-author of more than a dozen others. He wrote the *National Geographic's Driving Guide to America: The Rockies*, and the *National Geographic Guide to the Lewis and Clark Trail*. He lives in Victor, Idaho, with his wife and two children.

Illustrations Credits

Cover
Jack Dykinga. 1, Michael S. Quinton. 2-3, Paul Chesley. 4, Jim Gores/Wind River Photography. 9, Joel Sartore. 11, Dewitt Jones. 13, Ray Gehman. 14, Paul Chesley. 16-7, Ray Gehman.

Yellowstone Ecosystem
18-9, Ray Gehman. 22, Ray Gehman. 23, Paul Chesley. 24, Paul Chesley. 27, Paul Chesley. 28, Randy Olson. 32-3, Ray Gehman. 34, Ray Gehman. 37, Ray Gehman. 38, Ray Gehman. 40-1 (all) Ray Gehman. 42, Paul Chesley. 44, Ray Gehman. 46, Michael S. Quinton. 47, Daniel J. Cox. 49, Wendy Shattil/Bob Rozinski. 51, Paul Chesley. 52-3 (both) Ray Gehman. 54, Ray Gehman. 55, Paul Chesley. 57, Ray Gehman. 58-9, Ray Gehman. 61, Ray Gehman. 62, Ray Gehman. 64, Ray Gehman. 66, Ray Gehman. 69, Paul Chesley. 70, Paul Chesley. 71, Paul Chesley. 72-3, Paul Chesley.

Wyoming's Basins and Mountains
76-7, Jim Gores/Wind River Photography. 81, George Robbins Photo. 82, Robert E. Barber. 85, Paul Chesley. 86-7, Ed King. 89, Ray Gehman. 90, Ted Levin. 92, Jim Gores/Wind River Photography. 94-5, Paul Chesley/Photographers Aspen. 96 (both) Jim Gores/Wind River Photography. 98-9, Jim Gores/Wind River Photography. 101, Art Wolfe. 102, Scott T. Smith. 103, Paul Chesley. 104, Paul Chesley. 105, Phil Schermeister. 108-9, Scott T. Smith. 110-1 (both), Melissa Farlow.

Snake River Plain
112-3, David Hiser/Photographers Aspen. 117, George Wuerthner Photography. 118, Michael Lewis. 121, Randy Olson. 122, Randy Olson. 125, Michael Lewis. 127, William H. Mullins. 128-9, William H. Mullins. 130, George Wuerthner Photography. 132, Steve Bly. 134, William H. Mullins.

137, William H. Mullins. 139, Michael Lewis. 141, Robert Madden. 142, Kirkendall/ Spring. 144 (top), James P. Blair. 144 (bottom), Michael S. Quinton.

Central Idaho Rivers and Batholiths
146-7, Michael Lewis. 150, Paul Chesley. 151, Ray Gehman. 152, Paul Chesley. 154, Paul Chesley. 155, Ray Gehman. 156-7, Paul Chesley. 158, George Wuerthner. 160-1, George Wuerthner. 165, Michael S. Quinton. 167, Ray Gehman. 168-9, J. Schmidt. 171, Michael S. Quinton. 172, George F. Mobley. 174-5, William H. Mullins. 176, Jack Williams. 178, Ray Gehman. 181, Phil Schofield. 182-3, Ray Gehman. 185, David S. Boyer. 186, Michael Lewis. 187, Ray Gehman. 188, J. Schmidt. 189, Davis/Lynn Photography. 190-1, J. Schmidt.

Great Plains
192-3 Christian Heeb/Gnass Photo Images. 197, Steve Bly. 198, Christian Heeb/Gnass Photo Images. 200, Scott T. Smith. 202-3, Joel Sartore. 205, Scott T. Smith. 208-9, Christian Heeb/Gnass Photo Images. 210, Bates Littlehales. 213, Jean F. Stoick/ Peter Arnold Inc 214, ChristianHeeb/ Gnass Photo Images. 215, Paul Chesley. 217, George Wuerthner Photography. 218, Sam Abell. 221, Fred Hirschmann. 223, Michael Durham. 224-5, James Brandenburg.

Glacier-Panhandle
226-7, Ray Gehman. 231, Ray Gehman. 232-3 (both), Paul Chesley. 234-5, Paul Chesley. 237, Michael Lewis. 239, William H. Mullins. 240, Erwin & Peggy Bauer. 243, Paul Chesley. 246-7, Michael Lewis. 249, Paul Chesley. 251, William H. Mullins. 252-3, JC Leacock. 254-5, Ray Gehman. 257, Michael Lewis. 258, Ray Gehman. 260-1, Ray Gehman. 262, Michael Lewis. 264, Bruce Dale. 267, Dewitt Jones. 267, Michael S. Quinton. 268-9, Sam Abell. 271 (both), James P. Blair. 272, James P. Blair. 276-7 Michael Lewis.

Index

National Geographic Guide to America's Outdoors: Northern Rockies
by Jeremy Schmidt and Thomas Schmidt

Published by the National Geographic Society
John M. Fahey, Jr., *President and Chief Executive Officer*
Gilbert M. Grosvenor, *Chairman of the Board*
Nina D. Hoffman, *Senior Vice President*

Prepared by the Book Division
William R. Gray, *Vice President and Director*
Charles Kogod, *Assistant Director*
Barbara A. Payne, *Editorial Director and Managing Editor*
David Griffin, *Design Director*

Guides to America's Outdoors
Elizabeth L. Newhouse, *Director of Travel Books*
Cinda Rose, *Art Director*
Barbara A. Noe, *Associate Editor*
Caroline Hickey, *Senior Researcher*
Carl M. Mehler, *Director of Maps*

Staff for this Book
Barbara A. Noe, *Editor*
Cinda Rose, *Art Director*
Vickie Lewis, *Illustrations Editor*
Kimberly A. DeLashmit, Sean M. Groom,
  Rebecca Mills, Keith R. Moore, Jane Sunderland, *Researchers*
Lise Sajewski, *Editorial Consultant*
Thomas L. Gray, *Map Editor*
Thomas L. Gray, Mapping Specialists, Ltd., *Map Research*
Matt Chwastyk, Gregory Ugiansky, Martin S. Walz,
  Magellan Geographix, Mapping Specialists, Ltd., *Map Production*
R. Gary Colbert, *Production Director*
Gillian Carol Dean, *Assistant Designer*
Sharon Kocsis Berry, *Illustrations Assistant*
Julia Marshall, *Indexer*
DeShelle Downey, *Project Assistant*

Paul Schullery, Yellowstone National Park, *Consultant*

Manufacturing and Quality Control
George V. White, *Director;* John T. Dunn, *Associate Director;* Vincent P. Ryan, *Manager;*
Phillip L. Schlosser, *Financial Analyst*

Library of Congress Cataloging-in-Publication Data
Schmidt, Jeremy, 1949-
    Guide to America's great outdoors : Northern Rockies / Jeremy Schmidt and Thomas Schmidt.
    p. cm.
    ISBN 0-7922-7741-4
    1. Rocky Mountains—Guidebooks. 2. Parks—Rocky Mountains—Guidebooks. 3.
  Wilderness areas—Rocky Mountains—Guidebooks. I. Schmidt, Thomas, 1959- II.Title.
    F721 . S343 2000
    917.804'33—dc21   99-086035
                                                                        CIP